WHY THE LEFT LOSES

The decline of the centre-left in comparative perspective

Edited by Rob Manwaring and Paul Kennedy

P

First published in Great Britain in 2018 by

Policy Press
University of Bristol
1-9 Old Park Hill
Bristol
BS2 8BB
UK
t: +44 (0)117 954 5940
pp-info@bristol.ac.uk
www.policypress.co.uk

North America office:
Policy Press
c/o The University of Chicago Press
1427 East 60th Street
Chicago, IL 60637, USA
t: +1 773 702 7700
f: +1 773-702-9756
sales@press.uchicago.edu
www.press.uchicago.edu

© Policy Press 2018

British Library Cataloguing in Publication Data
A catalogue record for this book is available from the British Library

Library of Congress Cataloging-in-Publication Data
A catalog record for this book has been requested

ISBN 978-1-4473-3269-5 paperback
ISBN 978-1-4473-3266-4 hardcover
ISBN 978-1-4473-3270-1 ePub
ISBN 978-1-4473-3271-8 Mobi
ISBN 978-1-4473-3268-8 ePdf

Cover design by Hayes Design
Front cover image: istock

Contents

List of tables and figures

Tables

Figures

List of contributors

Editors

Rob Manwaring is Senior Lecturer at Flinders University, Adelaide, South Australia. His research interests include social democratic and labour politics, as well as wider democratic politics. In 2014, his book, *The search for democratic renewal*, was published with Manchester University Press.

Paul Kennedy is Lecturer in Spanish and European Studies at the University of Bath. He is author of *The Spanish Socialist Party and the modernisation of Spain* (Manchester University Press, 2013). His forthcoming publications include *Podemos and the art of the possible* (Manchester University Press, 2018), which he is co-authoring with David Cutts.

Contributors

Matt Beech is Senior Lecturer and Director of the Centre for British Politics at the University of Hull, UK. In 2017, he was a Visiting Scholar at the Institute of European Studies, University of California, Berkeley, USA, where he is researching his latest book, *The triumph of liberalism: British politics 1990-2016*.

Claes Belfrage is Senior Lecturer in Global Political Economy at the University of Liverpool Management School, UK. He researches the transformative processes of 'financialisation' through select European and emerging market economy case studies. He is also interested in critical research methodology.

Sheri Berman is Professor of Political Science at Barnard College, Columbia University, USA. She has written extensively on political development, democracy and democratisation; European politics; and fascism, populism and the history of the left. Her most recent book, *Democracy and dictatorship in Europe: From the ancient regime to the present day*, is forthcoming from Oxford University Press.

René Cuperus is Director for International Relations at the Wiardi Beckman Foundation, a think-tank for Dutch social democracy, Research Fellow at the Germany Institute of the University of Amsterdam, and political columnist for the Dutch daily *de Volkskrant*. In September 2017 he started working as Scholar in Residence at the Ministry of Foreign Affairs of the Netherlands.

Sophie Di Francesco-Mayot is Lecturer in European Politics at Deakin University, Melbourne, Australia. Her research interests include European integration, EU institutions, political parties and party systems, culture, religion and identity. She previously worked in the European External Action Service (EEAS) in Brussels, Belgium.

Grant Duncan is Associate Professor in Politics at Massey University, Albany Campus, Auckland, New Zealand. He teaches New Zealand politics and public policy as well as political theory. His recent publications in public policy have dealt with constitutional conventions and the Cabinet Manual, and with the 'new public management' in New Zealand. He is currently working on the nature of trust as a factor in political life.

Carol Johnson is Professor of Politics at the University of Adelaide, South Australia. Her main teaching and research interests are in Australian politics, the politics of gender and sexuality, the politics of emotion and analyses of ideology and discourse. She was elected to be a Fellow of the Academy of the Social Sciences in Australia in 2005.

Uwe Jun is Professor of Political Science at the University of Trier, Germany. Uwe has published extensively on a range of topics, including social democracy and political parties.

Mikko Kuisma is Research Fellow at the University of Tübingen, Germany. His current research interests lie in the politics of Nordic welfare reform, and in European populist parties, especially their programmatic discourses relating to welfare nationalism and welfare chauvinism. His book, *The social construction of welfare: Citizenship and Nordic welfare capitalism in an age of globalization*, is forthcoming from Edward Elgar.

David McGrane is an Associate Professor of Political Studies at St Thomas More College and the University of Saskatchewan in Canada. His research interests include Canadian political theory, political marketing and voter behaviour. He is the author of *Remaining loyal: Social democracy in Quebec and Saskatchewan* (McGill-Queen's University Press, 2014), and is currently writing a book about the New Democratic Party of Canada.

Chris Pierson is Professor of Politics at the University of Nottingham, UK, and author of *Hard choices* (Polity, 2001) and *Beyond the welfare state* (Polity, 2006). He is currently completing the third part of a three-volume history of the idea of property, *Just property* (Oxford University Press, 2013 and 2016).

Acknowledgements

This book would not have seen the light of day without the support, assistance and input from a number of people. We, as editors, set out our thanks and gratitude to some of those good people here. The genesis for the volume emerged on the back of the conference 'Is social democracy exhausted?' held at Flinders University, Adelaide, South Australia in 2012. A number of the papers, and wider discussion, helped fuel the impetus for this volume, and our thanks to all participants at the conference. It is perhaps worth noting that the joint editors of this volume first became acquainted at this event, via a video conference, which made short work of the 10,000-mile distance between Adelaide and Bath.

We thank all the contributors to this volume, and they have all responded with positive encouragement, and a general adherence to our editorial demands. In early 2016, we held a workshop attended by some of the contributors at King's College, London, and our thanks to Simon Sleight and colleagues at the Menzies Centre for his generosity in hosting us.

We offer our gratitude to all the colleagues at Policy Press for their support and positive engagement with the project. Emily Mew was instrumental at the outset of this journey, and we thank the very supportive Emily Watt and Jamie Askew for their work and efforts to help us complete this in a (relatively) timely fashion. Many thanks to Dawn Rushen for her editing work.

Rob wishes to thank a number of people for their involvement and support. Josh Holloway and Karen Austin, both PhD students at Flinders University, provided important research assistance for a number of the chapters, and some early editing work. Lionel Orchard gave crucial and much needed feedback on the final chapter. Rob also extends his thanks to colleagues at Flinders, not least George Crowder for sterling mentoring efforts, and Haydon Manning. He also adds his thanks to Carol Johnson for her ongoing support. Finally, his thanks to his partner, Sandy, for her unflagging support, and his two irrepressible children Matilda and Tess, for their love, nonsense, and inability to tidy their rooms.

Paul would once again like to thank his wife, Santina, who has been unstinting in her support despite academic concerns continually finding ways of stealing that most precious of things: time together. He's also grateful to his former colleague at Bath, David Cutts, whose encouragement was as timely as it was cherished.

Foreword

Sheri Berman

The decline of the centre-left over the past years is one of the most alarming trends in Western politics. During the latter part of the 20th century such parties either ran the government or led the loyal Opposition in virtually every Western democracy. Germany's Social Democratic Party (SPD), once the most powerful party of the left in continental Europe, currently polls in high 20s or 30s. The French Socialist Party was eviscerated in the 2017 elections, as was the Dutch Labour Party. Even the vaunted Scandinavian social democratic parties are struggling, reduced to vote shares in the 30 per cent range. The British Labour Party and the US Democrats have been protected from challengers by their country's first-past-the-post electoral systems, but the former has recently taken a sharp turn to the hard-left under Jeremy Corbyn, while the latter, although still competitive at the national level, is a minority party at the state and local levels, where a hard-right Republican Party dominates the scene.

The decline of the centre-left has hurt Western democracy. It has left voters free to be captured by extremist parties, particularly of the far-right populist variety, which threaten the liberal and perhaps even democratic nature of Western politics. In addition, centre-left parties played a crucial role in creating and maintaining the post-war order on which stable democracy was built following the Second World War. Without a revival of the centre-left, it is hard to see how this order and perhaps even well functioning democracy can be resuscitated. This book analyses the decline of the centre-left, and in so doing, may provide its supporters with the insights necessary to revitalise it.

Why the left loses focuses on three main issues the centre-left must confront: leadership, institutions/structural change and message/vision. The first is the most straightforward, but nonetheless crucial. Leaders represent and personify what parties stand for; in order to win, the centre-left needs leaders who can connect to a diverse and demanding electorate, and attractively, forcefully and effectively convey their party's messages. Attracting such leaders does not, of course, happen in a vacuum. Talented and ambitious individuals are drawn to parties they believe can deal with the challenges of the day. This brings us to issues of institutions/structural change and message/vision.

Institutional and structural changes over the last decades in domestic and international political economies have created major challenges for all traditional political parties, but particularly for those of the centre-left. After 1945 in Western Europe (and beginning with the New Deal in the US), the West began constructing a new type of political economy, one that could ensure economic growth while at the same time protecting societies from capitalism's destructive and destabilising consequences. This order represented a decisive break with the past: states would not be limited to ensuring that markets could grow and flourish, nor would economic interests be given the widest possible leeway. Instead, after 1945 the state was to become the guardian of society rather than the economy, and economic imperatives would sometimes have to take a back seat to social ones. This post-war order represented something historically unusual: capitalism remained, but it was capitalism of a very different type than had existed before the war – one tempered and limited by the power of the democratic state, and often made subservient to the goals of social stability and solidarity, rather than the other way round. This was a far cry from the revolutionary destruction of the capitalist order that orthodox Marxists, communists and others on the far left had demanded during the pre-war period, but it still varied significantly from what liberals had long favoured – namely, giving as much free rein to markets as possible. This was, in short, a social democratic order – and it worked remarkably well. Despite fears after the war that it would perhaps take decades for Europe to recover economically, by the early 1950s most of Europe had easily surpassed interwar economic figures, and the 30 years after 1945 were Europe's fastest period of growth ever. The restructured political economies of the post-war era seemed to offer something to everyone, and this, in turn, helped to eliminate the belief – long held by liberals, Marxists and others – that democratic states could not or would not protect particular groups' interests. Because the centre-left was most closely associated with this order and the most determined defender of it, it had the most to lose from its demise. And so the pressures put on this order since the 1970s by increasing globalisation, growing government deficits and the neoliberal and eventually austerity policies adopted by the European Union (EU) have left the centre-left scrambling to come up with new strategies for getting economies moving again, while also ensuring that democratic states continued to protect citizens from the changes brought by ever-evolving capitalism.

Alongside changes in domestic and international political economies, centre-left parties have also been challenged by social and cultural shifts that began in the 1960s and threatened traditional identities, communities and mores – a process further exacerbated, particularly in Europe, by growing immigration. Together these trends helped erode the social solidarity and sense of shared national purpose that had supported the social democratic post-war order and helped to stabilise European democracies in the decades following the Second World War. The US faced its own version of this with the growing political incorporation and mobilisation of minority groups since the civil rights era, and the increasing shift towards a non-majority white population destabilising traditional social and political patterns.

But economic, social and cultural institutional and structural changes have not doomed the centre-left to oblivion. They represent challenges, and how the centre-left (or any other party) responds to challenges determines how voters react and political systems evolve. The problem for the centre-left, in other words, is not merely the challenges it has faced over the past decades so much as its lack of convincing and coherent responses to them. Here is where *Why the left loses*' third issue comes in: message/vision. After the 2008 financial crisis many observers expected a significant swing to the left among Western electorates, since many blamed the economy's problems on the neoliberal policies that had proliferated during the end of the 20th and beginning of the 21st centuries. But the centre-left lacked a convincing message for dealing with the crisis, or a more general vision of how to promote growth while protecting citizens from the harsher aspects of free markets. Instead, it kept on trying to defend out-dated policies or proposed watered-down versions of neoliberalism that barely differentiated it from the centre-right. The centre-left also lacked a convincing message about how to deal with increasing diversity or a vision of social solidarity appropriate to changing demographic and cultural realities. Instead, the centre-left either ignored the challenge of diversity or especially among the intellectual left, put forward a message of 'multiculturalism' – neither of these responses was able to stem social conflict or electoral flight from the left, especially on the part of the working class.

It has now become fairly commonplace to note the support given by traditionally centre-left voters to the populist right. This connection was on obvious display in the Brexit referendum, where many traditional Labour strongholds and supporters voted to leave the EU, and it has been a prominent feature of elections in Europe as working-class voters have flocked to right-wing populist parties. And, of course, a version of this was present in the US, where Donald Trump garnered disproportionate support from less-educated and working-class voters. What is still worth stressing, however, is the causal connection between the failures or missteps of the centre-left and the rise of right-wing populist parties that offered simple, straightforward messages in response to citizens' economic and social fears. Economically, the populist right promises to promote prosperity, via increased government control of the economy and limits on globalisation. Socially, the populist right promises to restore social solidarity and a sense of shared national purpose, by expelling foreigners or severely limiting immigration, diminishing the influence of the EU and globalisation, and protecting traditional values, identities and mores.

For those who bemoan the decline of the centre-left and the rise of the populist right, the challenge is clear: you can't beat something with nothing, and if the centre-left can't come up with more viable and attractive messages about how to solve contemporary problems, and a more attractive vision of the future than those offered by its competitors, it can expect to continue its slide into the dust heap of history. The following chapters provide an excellent starting point for the debate about the centre-left's future.

ONE

Why the left loses: understanding the comparative decline of the centre-left

Rob Manwaring and Paul Kennedy

Introduction

Since the global financial crisis (GFC), if not before, there has been a general decline in the fortunes of social democratic and labour parties. Against these recent developments, there is a long-standing literature that appraises the electoral performance and impact of the left more broadly (Przeworski and Sprague, 1986; Kitschelt, 1994; Moschonas, 2002). Much of the literature on social democracy tends to be pessimistic, and there is a plethora of research that denotes recent developments as a 'crisis', on the 'back foot', 'in retreat', and perhaps most arrestingly, as 'dead' (Gray, 1996; Pierson, 2001; Keating and McCrone, 2013; Lavelle, 2013; Ludwigshafen et al, 2016). In a prescient address at the London School of Economics and Political Science (LSE) in 2011, David Miliband catalogued the general wreckage of the electoral fortunes of the centre-left across Western Europe. In his critical survey of European social democracy, he noted:

- The UK General Election in 2010 – the second worst result for Labour since 1918.
- Sweden, also in 2010 – the worst result since 1911.
- Germany in 2009 – the worst result since the founding of the Federal Republic, with a greater loss of support than any party in the history of the country.
- France in 2007 – the worst result since 1969.
- The Netherlands in 2009 – a traumatic transition from a junior coalition partner to Opposition.
- Italy – a yo-yo in and out of power, with personal and political divisions disabling opposition to Berlusconi.

More recent results generally confirm this overall trend, with British Labour losing both the 2015 and 2017 general elections. The Dutch general election in early 2017 saw the worst-ever result for the Dutch Labour Party (PvDA, Partij van de Arbeid). The PvDA lost 29 seats, only holding 9 in the 150-seat Parliament. The Dutch result is something of an outlier for the misfortunes of the centre-left. Later in this chapter we survey the state of the left more widely.

This collected volume investigates the electoral fortunes of the family of centre-left labour and social democratic political parties. In this chapter we set out the aims and scope of the volume, and its contribution to understanding the comparative political decline of the centre-left. After mapping the electoral fortunes of centre-left political parties, we then locate this volume in the current literature, and set out the distinctive approach offered here. From our perspective, one of the deficiencies of the current literature is that it focuses almost exclusively on the family of (mostly Western) European social democratic and labour parties. While much of this literature is incisive and important, we have a nagging concern that this narrow focus is missing a key part of the wider story. As we outline below, we need to expand the explanatory universe to better understand the current plight of the centre-left.

We have been a little mischievous in the title of this volume – *Why the left loses* – and it would be useful here to clarify the book's scope. The volume is not called 'Why the left *always* loses' or 'Why the left will never win again'. Rather, the focus is on examining the current electoral performance of a cohort of the family of social democratic and labour political parties *within a specific timeframe* (broadly, 2008-16). The title of the volume is deliberately provocative, in part, because we hope that it will reach a wider readership than just the academy. The term 'left' is deployed here as a proxy for these groups of political parties.[1] Our focus remains their fate of – often, but not always – the main carriers of wider social democratic values. The book does not seek to argue that the values and ideas associated with the 'left' are in decline – indeed, we argue that in a number of cases the opposite is true, that they have been readily co-opted by a number of parties on the centre-right, and other populist challengers. Nor are we suggesting that there are common or single causes for the current state of the full suite of centre-left political parties. And to be clear, by 'left' we mostly focus on the long-standing social democratic and labour parties rather than some of the alternative 'socialist' or 'left' parties such as Die Linke established in Germany in 2007. The social democratic parties remain important political actors, even if they are not in the best of electoral health.

The risk with the title *Why the left loses* is that by the time the volume is published, there will have been a turnaround in the electoral fortunes of the social democratic parties. Indeed, it was just at the point of Blair and Schröder declaring the hegemonic victory of the Third Way/Neue Mitte that the fortunes of the left began to decline. As Ralf Dahrendorf noted in a telling intervention, the highpoint in the late 1990s for the centre-left masked other key changes in the party systems of the advanced industrial democracies:

> The real trend – which is underlined by the European elections – is towards non-traditional parties, many of which did not exist 20 years ago. (Dahrendorf, 1999)

The key issue is that while the late 1990s may have signalled something like the 'magical return' of social democracy, we are more circumspect in predicting a 'second coming' by the time this volume is released. Moreover, if there were to be a revival of the centre-left, and clearly many of the writers in this volume would welcome a return to a more full-bloodied variant of social democratic politics, it would not necessarily undermine the central focus of the book. We look to explain why the left has been doing poorly in this period under review. Indeed, in one of our cases – state Labor in Australia – there has been something of a revival of the centre-left.

Overall, we focus predominately on the period from the mid-2000s to the mid-2010s. The crucial event here is the impact of the global financial crisis (GFC), and the response of the parties to this latest rupture in the global capitalist system. The response has not been overwhelming.

The state of the left

There have been a number of recent surveys of the family of social democratic parties (Keating and McCrone, 2013; Bailey et al, 2014, p 8), with the focus predominately on the European parties. Here we offer a related, but broader, survey.

While there is no clear, uniform trend, the overall picture is rather dismal for centre-left parties (see Table 1.1).

In France, the 2012 presidential election win proved a temporary highpoint for the Parti socialiste (PS) under François Hollande. Indeed, the seven-year term of the presidency arguably overstates the

Table 1.1: Centre-left parties in Office and Opposition (2008-16)

Country	2008	2009	2010	2011	2012	2013	2014	2015	2016
France					■	■	■	■	■
Germany	▒					▒	▒	▒	▒
Italy	■	■	■	■	■	▒	▒	▒	▒
Netherlands	▒	▒				▒	▒	▒	▒
Spain	■	■	■	■					
Sweden							▒	▒	▒
UK	■	■	■						
Canada								■	■
New Zealand									
Australia	■	■	▒	▒	▒				

Key

In Office	■
In Office (junior partner)	■
In Office (major partner)	▒
In Opposition	

Note: In Canada Justin Trudeau took the Liberal Party into office. There is a dispute as to whether to categorise the Liberals as centrist or social democratic, given the New Democratic Party espouses the clearest social democratic programme in Canada.

Source: European data drawn in part from Bailey et al (2014, p 9)

dominance of the PS. As outlined by Sophie Di Francesco-Mayot (see Chapter 10), there is a strong case that while the left was in office, it was 'losing the battle of ideas'. It was striking, and perhaps not that surprising, when Hollande announced that he would not be contesting the 2017 presidential elections – the first post-war president not to seek office. Strikingly, PS did not make the second round run-off in the 2017 presidential election, much like the dismal 2002 election. Indeed, the Macron phenomenon would suggest a further decline and fragmentation of the centre-left.

In Germany, the centre-left SPD (Sozialdemokratische Partei Deutschlands, or Social Democratic Party of Germany) has been unable for quite some time to puncture the dominance of Angela Merkel's CDU (Christian Democratic Union). Since 2005, Merkel has been unassailable in German politics, with the SPD first as a junior coalition partner, then back in Opposition. At the 2013 election, Merkel reluctantly turned to the SPD as junior partner once again. In

Uwe Jun's account (see Chapter 7), the factors for the SPD's electoral health are examined. What is striking about the SPD is that like other cases considered here, its troubles pre-date the GFC. To a large extent, the SPD, like the SAP (Swedish Social Democratic Party) and the UK Labour Party, is experiencing a prolonged hangover from its turn to the Third Way.

In Spain, the picture is arguably more pessimistic for the PSOE (Spanish Socialist Workers' Party). Since losing office in 2011, the party has lost consecutive general elections in 2015 and 2016, and, as Paul Kennedy outlines in his overview (see Chapter 9), it faces a range of pressures, not least the emergence of the left-populist Podemos party in 2014. Over this time, the PSOE has been haemorrhaging votes. As Kennedy notes, while the PSOE has not yet faced its own version of 'Pasokification' (the ultimate destruction of the once dominant Greek social democrats), its future is far from assured.

In Sweden, often claimed as having the purest form of social democracy, the SAP finds itself in turbulent times. It was in office from 1994 to 2002; it then lost both the 2006 and 2010 elections, and narrowly won the 2014 election, governing in coalition with the Green Party. The 2014 results obscure the thinness of SAP's victory with only a minor improvement of its vote, at 31 per cent. Here, we see a clear example of arguably a structural trend facing centre-left parties – a narrowing of its voter base. Whereas the PSOE faces a left-populist challenge, the striking characteristic of the Swedish party system has been the emergence of the nationalist right-populist Swedish Democrats. As Claes Belfrage and Mikko Kuisma argue (see Chapter 8), the SAP is confronted by long-standing economic constraints imposed by the capitalist system and is playing something of a 'losing game'. It remains unclear how far the 2014 result signifies a meaningful revival of the centre-left.

While this volume confines its European focus to these countries, the outlook for the centre-left across Europe is mixed, at best. In Italy, the fortunes of the centre-left have been – in David Miliband's words – something of a 'yo-yo'. The centre-right was dominant from 2001 to 2006. Under Romano Prodi, the centre-left briefly resumed office (2006-08), before losing again to the centre-right in 2008. It is telling that after the GFC, the Italian electorate placed its faith in the 'technocratic' government of Mario Monti, until the centre-left bloc took over in 2013. This recent development, however, can hardly be considered stable government, and the development of Beppe Grillo's Five Star Movement presents another populist challenge to both left and right.

In The Netherlands, the 2017 election was catastrophic for the PvDA. Prior to this calamity, it was in Opposition between 2002 and 2006, and again between 2010 and 2012. At the 2012 elections it entered as a junior partner in coalition with the centre-right VVD (People's Party for Freedom and Democracy). In the multi-party Dutch system, the PvDA has been unable to secure a firmer electoral base, and again, a xenophobic populist party – in this case, led by the ubiquitous Geert Wilders – poses both a strategic and ideational dilemma for both left and right.

It appears that the left not only loses elections; it can't win them outright either. In Austria, while the SPÖ (Social Democratic Party of Austria) has been the largest partner (just) in a grand coalition, Austrian politics has seen the emergence of the far-right, and both major parties recorded their worst ever results at the 2008 legislative elections.

In Norway, Jens Stoltenberg's Labour party (AAP) was a dominant force from 2005-13, but lost power to the centre-right bloc.

While these cases are not considered here, they remain emblematic of a range of problems and dilemmas facing social democratic and labour parties, especially in the context of a shifting party system, with new populist challengers.

We also include and survey the fortunes of the centre-left in the Anglosphere, and here we focus our attention on Australia, New Zealand, Canada and the UK. Controversially for some, we locate the UK Labour Party outside the core European family of social democratic parties (although the Brexit result provides further support for this case). As a range of writers and indeed, Labour figures, have pointed out, the UK Labour Party often has more in common with its Antipodean Labour sisters than its European social democratic counterparts. As Rob Manwaring and Matt Beech outline in Chapter 2, the picture here is fairly dismal for the centre-left. Labour has experienced 'Pasokification' in Scotland, and since the fall of New Labour in 2010 has been unable to claw its way back into power. While the 2010 result was widely anticipated, Labour's loss to the Conservatives in 2015 was not. While Corbyn-led Labour secured a better-than-expected result at the 2017 general election, Labour has now lost three elections in a row since Tony Blair stepped down as leader.

Elsewhere, there is a catalogue of defeat for the left. In two different contexts, Canada and New Zealand, there has been a dominance of the centre-right. From 2008-15, Stephen Harper's Conservative party has dominated Canadian politics, and it is only with the recent win of Justin Trudeau that there has been some shifting back to a more left-leaning position. Yet, as David McGrane outlines in Chapter 3, the fate of the NDP (New Democratic Party) illustrates the difficulty of seeking to impose a social democratic settlement at a time of Liberal Party resurgence. Strikingly, at the 2011 election, the NDP seemingly made a key breakthrough under the leadership of Jack Layton, but the fortunes of the NDP have since declined.

Likewise, in New Zealand, the NZ Labour Party has been unsuccessful in dislodging the centre-right National Party under the dominant leadership of John Key. Labour lost three straight elections, and despite the unexpected resignation of Key at the end of 2016, its chances of winning at the 2017 general election look marginal at best. Grant Duncan surveys the wreckage of the NZ Labour Party (in Chapter 4), and what is striking here is the flexibility of the centre-right, and, most notably, a shift away from a strident form of neoliberal politics.

Finally, in Australia, after 11 years in the wilderness, the ALP (Australian Labor Party) took office under the, initially, strong leadership of Kevin Rudd. Yet, within the space of a few years, the ALP turned in on itself, and Julia Gillard (just) secured a minority government in 2010. And in another rancorous turn, the ALP ditched Gillard weeks before the 2013 election. Since then, despite a promising election campaign in 2016, the ALP remains in Opposition. As Carol Johnson examines in her chapter on the ALP (see Chapter 5), Labor was beset by a range of both institutional and ideational problems. Most critically, Johnson examines the central dilemma facing centre-left parties in the capitalist system. We also include in this volume a chapter on a much neglected story of the centre-left – the Australian *state* Labor parties (see Chapter 6). During the mid-2000s, a rather intriguing phenomenon occurred when Labor held office in every single state and territory. Since then state Labor has been on the back foot. The chapter therefore offers the reader a clear comparative case study of sub-national social democracy to illuminate why the left loses elections.

If time and space permitted, we might also look beyond our cases and see the, at best, mixed picture for the centre-left. Critically, the 2016 presidential election victory by Donald Trump in the US seems to encapsulate many of the current dynamics of the modern party system, with a populist backlash against both major political parties. In Latin America, left-ist parties have also suffered setbacks (Aidi, 2015), although the extent to which we locate them in the 'social democratic' tradition is contested. The key issue from this brief survey is that the left is currently losing, or not winning well, and also recording some record losses in the period from the GFC to 2016. The aim of this volume is to explore and examine, comparatively, the reasons for this current state of play.

It is worth making a few caveats to this overall survey. First, most liberal democracies in advanced industrial settings operate on some turnover of governments. We are circumspect in over-emphasising any 'trend' of the 'left losing'. Second, in many cases, the left losing is, indeed, a noted part of their histories. To take the UK Labour Party as a prominent example, until New Labour, its electoral record was patchy at best (between 1945 and 1997 it held office for just 17 of those 52 years). Third, while we make comparative judgements, and see some common themes, such as populism, Third Way hangovers, out-dated political economic models, changing class patterns, and so on, there are specific conditions playing out. The left loses, but not always for the same reasons.

That said, the 'transformation' of social democracy has been well documented (Kitschelt, 1994; Moschonas 2002). Yet, since the heyday of the neoliberal turn in the 1980s, the social democratic project seems to have been significantly weakened. Ultimately, we are asking why the left has been losing in the modern era.

The cases

The focus of our study is on two broad cohorts of social democratic parties. First, the group we are loosely calling the left in the 'Anglosphere' focuses on the electoral performance of relevant parties in Australia, New Zealand, Canada and the UK. The second cohort are the cluster of parties that have formed part of the heart of the social democratic project in Europe – Sweden, Germany, Spain and France. We focus on these eight countries for the following reasons.

This volume builds on a well-established formula in political science by comparing broadly similar cohorts of (social democratic) parties (Paterson and Thomas, 1986; Kitschelt, 1994; Bonoli and Powell, 2004; Merkel et al, 2008; Callaghan et al, 2009; Lavelle, 2013). There are striking omissions (and odd inclusions) in any edited volume, and this collection is arguably no different. Austria, Finland, Norway and the Netherlands, for example, are all worthy cases for inclusion. The Australian states might seem anachronistic, but we defend that choice here (although see Chapter 6 for a fuller defence). The main reason for including a sub-national case is that it is both a neglected part of the centre-left story, and a sub-national comparator also offers some key variables to examine any overall trends or patterns for left losses. Given that the sub-national governments have much more limited policy levers, our attention is drawn to the different ways that 'labour' or social democratic ideas and institutions can be reinvigorated (or indeed, not) in a different political setting. In effect, the sub-national case invites us to ask if sub-national left governments lose for the same reasons as national left governments.

Our European cases are all prominent and core examples of social democracy, both nominally and in practice. We limit ourselves to eight countries for comparative purposes, and, truth be told, for brevity. *The Palgrave handbook of European social democracy in the European Union* (de Waele et al, 2013) features all 27 member states. While it is a fine achievement, we wager that even the most devout scholars of social democracy are unlikely to have read all cases. It is our aim that the cases included here are to be 'read across' with each other, and indeed, to be read. The key issue is that the chapters are not stand-alone; rather, they are part of a broader dynamic picture of institutional and ideational decline on the left. The cases selected here are emblematic of different parts of the wider story of the weakening of the left.

Unlike the fine Keating and McCrone, and Bailey et al collections, and indeed much of the social democracy literature (see, for example, Sassoon, 2013), we also deliberately include some cases from the 'Anglosphere'. As Chris Pierson (2001) notes, the diversity of social democracy is often ignored, and the temptation is to impose a Crosland-ite or Swedish set of inclusion criteria on all cases. A key contribution of this volume, and a corrective to some of the wider social democratic literature, is to broaden the scope of focus.

In addition, the recent collections on European social democracy, while important, do have some limitations. First, the Keating and McCrone volume only really has one dedicated case study, which is the Swedish one. Its thematic chapters are important, but for comparative purposes the challenge is to ensure that this collection has a clear underpinning integrity and reasonably sound architecture. As noted above, the focus on social democracy as a (Western) European phenomenon has a limiting effect. For example, one of the overarching factors widely cited for the problems of the European centre-left is the difficulties posed by membership to (and/or relationship with) the European Union (EU). A number of writers see the 'Faustian pact' as being at the heart of the problems of the centre-left (Escalona and Vieira, 2014). While no doubt a pressing dilemma, this focus has the net effect of over-playing certain variables over others. There are clear common problems for a cluster of centre-left parties – especially those that took a Third Way 'turn'. We argue that a stronger factor for the weakening of the centre-left in the UK, Sweden and other parts of Europe is the difficulty in reconciling with the Third Way agenda rather than a strategic position in relation to the EU. Here, the inclusion of the New Zealand and Australian Labo(u)r Parties is particularly instructive, because while many of the issues are similar to their European counterparts, the EU is clearly not central to the difficulties faced by the Antipodean sister parties. It might be that the European 'Faustian pact' is a localised metaphor for a wider political problem – the wider reconfiguration of the Keynesian welfare state political economy in the neoliberal era – but if that is the case, it ought to be more clearly circumscribed. The central issue is that the lens of the telescope has to be widened to enable a clearer picture.[2]

This is a comparative study, and falls within the comparative case study approach (see Yin, 2013). Indeed, one of the contributions this volume makes is to provide a stronger comparative focus for the political phenomena in question, which links in with some of the limits of several of the other collections, such as Bailey et al (2014). Often, the cases are too 'stand-alone' and don't enable meaningful comparison. Writers focus on their specific cases, and usually detail them well, with perceptive insights. Yet the scope for wider comparison is limited. Arguably, the volume that has the most sustained approach in adopting a comparative framework is by Bonoli and Powell (2004), with its policy regime emphasis. Their focus is slightly different from ours, as the ideological and policy contours of their cases are examined. In this volume, we focus on explanatory factors for electoral performance.

Understanding change and continuity in the left

To understand why the left is losing, we use what Randall (2003) calls a 'synthetic' approach. Randall helpfully outlines the main range of strategies that have been taken to understand change and continuity in the centre-left: (1) materialist, (2) ideational, (3) institutional, (4) electoral and (5) synthetic.

Without rehearsing all of Randall's arguments, each approach applies a specific lens to the issue at hand. *Materialist strategies* examine changes in the capitalist system; *ideational approaches* focus on the changing currents in social democratic traditions; *institutional approaches* focus on intra-party and related issues; and *electoral strategies* examine socioeconomic changes in the demos. Finally, *'synthetic' approaches* are probably best understood as hybrid strategies, adopting elements of them all.

The synthetic approach taken here is drawn from two sets of complementary literature – first, following Randall (2003), the well-established work on the left more broadly, and second, what might be termed the 'opposition' literature – the body of research that focuses on analysing the performance of parties out of office. We adopt the framework developed by Ball (2005) and Bale (2010). In Bale's excellent work on the UK Conservative Party, he asks, why did it take the party so long to regain office? Bale's crucial insight is that political parties are not purely 'rational' or 'vote-maximising' machines. A striking characteristic of the Conservative Party in Opposition was a long-standing refusal to adopt a quicker route back into power.

Bale's book is a single case of a party in Opposition, and his analysis focuses on three key dimensions: institutions, individuals and ideas.[3] This is the broad framework we apply in this volume. Each writer analyses his or her specific case through these three lenses. Each chapter examines the institutional and structural factors that explain lack of electoral success; the role of key individuals, especially party leaders; and finally, the role of ideas in explaining why the centre-left is currently in retreat. The strength of this approach is that it enables an analysis of the *structural* and *agency* conditions that might explain the state of the centre-left party in each case, but also attend to the *ideational* battleground where parties have sought to find a new or revised form of social democratic politics. The framework is both rigorous and focused, and crucially, enables flexibility for authors to identify key local and specific factors at play. Perhaps more importantly, for our purposes, it means that our chapters can 'wear their theory lightly', so the general reader is not subjected to some of the tedium that can sometimes engulf theoretical and conceptual debates in the academy. It is worth outlining in a little more detail these three broad thematic areas.

Institutions

Institutional factors relate to the structural conditions that shape (and can hinder) the centre-left. Broadly we might sub-divide these into endogenous and exogenous factors. An institutional and structural focus draws our attention to crucial political components of the electoral system, and elements such as the changing sociology of the left vote. The internal institutional factors include those such as the influence of the trade unions and dimensions like the factional divisions within the party. An institutional focus has long been a mainstay within the centre-left scholarly tradition, such as Minkin's 2014 opus on the UK Labour Party. Indeed, a focus on some of the constituent parts of the relevant party seems crucial, as Di Francesco-Mayot notes in her analysis of the PS, or the rise of Jeremy Corbyn as British Labour leader.

Individuals

A focus on *individuals* then shifts attention to the explanatory power of the role of agency. Here, the contributors focus on the role of key leaders and other figures who have been instrumental in shaping the fortunes of the party. Indeed, one of the strongest accounts of the UK Labour Party – David Marquand's (1992) *The progressive dilemma* – adopts this approach, plotting Labour's history through the influence of key individuals on the party. Leadership is often a neglected dimension of understanding the fortunes of the centre-left. For example, two of the most rigorous analyses of social democracy both note this is an element missing in their research. Kitschelt's (1994) path-breaking work offers perhaps the most conceptually rigorous account of social democracy. Yet, as Kitschelt acknowledges, in his structural/institutional account:

> … by and large leaves out the impact of the charisma of unique political personalities on the success of left parties. (Kitschelt, 1994, p 284)

Kitschelt notes the importance of leaders, but rightly also notes the difficultly in measuring their impact. We can't claim to solve this issue, but by giving this clearer prominence in our analysis, we give more attention to this dimension. Similarly, Moschonas (2002) notes that the issue of leadership is becoming increasingly important in understanding recent developments in what was originally a mass movement (although this approach admittedly risks caricaturing the history). Moschonas notes that party leaders are becoming more 'autonomous' of the party, which, for the leader '… secures extraordinary power, which is isolated and isolating. And fragile' (2002, p 315). If the parties are broadly shifting into new entities, and the liberal democracies are becoming more 'leader-centric' and personalised, then a focus on individuals and leadership is arguably becoming a stronger factor in understanding social democratic performance.

Ideas

Finally, the analysis looks briefly at *ideational* questions, and the ability of the parties to build a coherent narrative and ideological message in the face of these wider changes. The power of ideas is often difficult to capture, but, as Keynes noted, the 'world is ruled by little else', even if 'practical men' often assume they are exempt from them. Ideational questions are a long-standing prism to view the trajectories of political parties, and arguably the most significant ideational innovation has been the 'Third Way' debates of the 1990s (Giddens, 1998). Here, the debate has focused on the potential great betrayal of the much-vaunted 'labour tradition'. In many countries, including the UK, Australia, Sweden and elsewhere, the ideational debate has focused on the continuity/discontinuity thesis – the extent to which a neoliberal embrace of (mostly) economic policy settings has meant that the parties can no longer be considered social democratic or labour (see Lavelle, 2013). There have been several single case studies that have examined the Third Way legacy, and Goes' (2016) excellent book on the UK post-New Labour Party is an exemplar. Here, Goes tracks the ideational legacy of the Third Way, and the dilemmas facing Ed Miliband and the wider party in dealing with the ideational shift in the party. At the time of writing, the Corbyn phenomenon seems like a radical ideational and institutional reaction against the New Labour legacy.

For the purposes of this study, we invited the contributors to consider the ideational questions that continue to vex the parties. Broadly speaking, as Bramston (2011) notes in his study of the ALP in Australia, the party is often a site for the ideational struggle between different traditions. As most of the mainstream social democratic parties no longer draw heavily on the Socialist tradition, there seems a narrowing of ideas from the social liberal and social democratic traditions and, in some cases, the 'Labourist' tradition.[4] The extent to which the Third Way can be considered a 'new' tradition is open to interpretation (Manwaring, 2014). Nonetheless, in many cases, a key issue for the centre-left is its response to ideational re-positioning in neoliberal times (Glyn, 2001).

A poor diagnosis for the left

This chapter has set the scene for the book, and has laid out the comparative framework for the analysis of the state of the centre-left. The key themes of individuals, institutions and ideas are interdependent and dialectic. By this, we suggest that they are mutually reinforcing, and non-reducible. Ideational change requires both the force of agency, and the contextual conditioning of structure. For the academic reader, we locate this approach in the 'critical realist' tradition, yet we also recognise that not all the contributors might subscribe to this epistemological approach. Regardless, it allows for a meaningful comparative analysis, while allowing sufficient flexibility for case-specific variables. In this sense, we very much follow Marsh and Smith's (2001) view that there is more than one way to practice political science (see Marsh and Smith, 2001; Furlong and Marsh, 2010).

While we recognise that some chapters might give some prominence to some dimensions over others, we mitigate against this in at least two ways. First, a different emphasis – for example, more prominence on institutional problems – à la French Socialists – arguably reflects an empirical reality, whereas in other cases, perhaps the Swedish case, its deeper problems are ideational. Even if we accept that our different contributors have different epistemological approaches, our concluding chapters, where the wider comparative judgements are made, are a useful way to redress any imbalances in our case chapters. In sum, no edited volume can fully avoid some unevenness, but our claim is that unlike some other recent contributions, we tell a much more meaningful comparative story.

In our volume we are offering a distinctive approach to understanding the state of the centre-left. Our cases are more recent than other volumes, and our focus is wider than just Europe. Each of our chapters offers insights into wider theoretical and ideational approaches aimed at understanding the phenomena of the centre-left, although our approach, like most of the significant contributions on the left (see, for example, Sassoon, 2013), offers a contribution that is incremental, rather than path-breaking. Our cases mostly draw on secondary, rather than primary, sources. We are not claiming significant methodological innovation, but we are offering a distinctive contribution to the wider field of understanding political parties. The synthetic approach outlined and adopted here has not been used in a comparative context anywhere else.

Overall, at the time of our analysis, the 'health' of the left is hardly robust. The left is losing, and in many cases, at record levels. Without wishing to overplay the medical analogy, the aim of this volume is to gather some critical insights into the wider diagnosis of the condition of the family of centre-left political parties. Whether their condition is 'terminal' might well be a question that persists for some time yet.

Notes

1   There is a long-standing literature that notes the complexity of defining 'social democracy' and its variants (Bonoli and Powell, 2004, p 2, offers a useful synopsis). There are numerous disagreements about what constitutes its 'purest' form. In this volume we focus on the main social democratic and labour parties, but it is not the aim to wade into these wider definitional debates. While the parties we focus

on are often the main conduits for a 'social democratic' form of politics, we note that this is not always consistent in their histories, and indeed, their histories are complex and varied.

2 Gumbrell-McCormick and Hyndman (2013) usefully employ the motif of the telescope and the microscope to examine political phenomena – in their case, the plight of trade unions in Western Europe.

3 While Bale employs the three main dimensions, arguably, he gives greatest prominence to institutional factors. This can be a weakness in any 'synthetic' approach. In our volume, all contributors were asked to scrutinise their cases through the three dimensions, yet, invariably, some give greater attention to some over others. The *strength* of this approach is that the over-arching framework allows both methodological and case flexibility. A perceived weakness might be that it blunts the comparative explanatory power, and leads to some thematic incoherence.

4 Bramston focuses on the ALP (Australian Labor Party), and clearly there will be different ideological traditions across the wider family of social democratic parties. However, this schema is a useful snapshot to capture some of the main ideological differences on the centre-left.

References

Aidi, H. (2015) 'What's left of the Latin American Left?', *Al Jazeera*, 21 December, www.aljazeera.com/indepth/opinion/2015/12/left-latin-american-left-151220073320683.html

Bailey, D., de Waele, J.-M., Escalona, F. and Vieira, M. (2014) *European social democracy during the global economic crisis: Renovation or resignation?*, Manchester: Manchester University Press.

Bale, T. (2011) *The Conservative Party: From Thatcher to Cameron*, Cambridge: Polity Press.

Ball, S. (2005) 'Factors in opposition performance: The Conservative experience since 1867', in A. Seldon (ed) *Recovering power*, Basingstoke: Palgrave Macmillan, pp 1-27.

Bonoli, G. and Powell, M. (2004) *Social democratic party policies in contemporary Europe*, London: Routledge.

Bramston, T. (2011) *Looking for the light on the hill: Modern Labor's challenges*, Brunswick, NJ: Scribe.

Callaghan, J., Fishman, N., Jackson, B. and McIvor, M. (2009) *In search of social democracy: Responses to crisis and modernization*, Manchester; Manchester University Press.

Dahrendorf, R. (1999) 'What ever happened to liberty?', *New Statesman*, 6 September, www.newstatesman.com/node/149762

de Waele, J.-M., Escalona, F. and Vieira, M. (eds) (2013) *The Palgrave handbook of social democracy in the European Union*, Basingstoke: Palgrave Macmillan.

Escalona, F. and Vieira, M. (2014) 'It does not happen here either: Why social democrats fail in the context of the great financial crisis', in D. Bailey, J.-M. de Waele, F. Escalona and M. Vieira (eds) *European social democracy during the global economic crisis: Renovation or resignation?*, Manchester: Manchester University Press, Chapter 1.

Furlong, P. and Marsh, D. (2010) 'A skin is not a sweater: Ontology and epistemology in political science', in D. Marsh and G. Stoker (eds) *Theory and methods in political science* (3rd edn), Basingstoke: Palgrave Macmillan, Chapter 9.

Giddens, A. (1998) *The Third Way: The renewal of social democracy*, Cambridge: Polity Press.

Glyn, A. (ed) (2001) *Social democracy in neoliberal times: The Left and economic policy since 1980*, Oxford: Oxford University Press.

Goes, E. (2016) *The Labour Party under Ed Miliband: Trying but failing to renew social democracy*, Manchester: Manchester University Press.

Gray, J. (1996) *After social democracy*, London: Demos.

Gumbrell-McCormick, R. and Hyman, R. (2013) *Trade unions in Western Europe: Hard times, hard choices*, Oxford: Oxford University Press.

Keating, M. and McCrone, D. (eds) (2013) *The crisis of social democracy in Europe*, Edinburgh: Edinburgh University Press.

Kitschelt, H. (1994) *The transformation of European social democracy*, Cambridge: Cambridge University Press.

Lavelle, A. (2013) *The death of social democracy: Political consequences in the 21st century*, Aldershot: Ashgate Publishing.

Ludwigshafen, Piraeous and Valletta (2016) 'Rose thou art sick: The centre left is in sharp decline across Europe', *The Economist*, 2 April, www.economist.com/news/briefing/21695887-centre-left-sharp-decline-across-europe-rose-thou-art-sick

Manwaring, R. (2014) *The search for democratic renewal: The politics of consultation in Britain and Australia*, Manchester: Manchester University Press.

Marquand, D. (1992) *The progressive dilemma*, Portsmouth: Heinemann.

Marsh, D. and Smith, M.J. (2001) 'There is more than one way to do political science: On different ways to study policy networks', *Political Studies*, vol 49, no 3, pp 528-41.

Merkel, W., Petring, A., Henkes, C. and Egle, C. (2008) *Social democracy in power: The capacity to reform*, London: Routledge.

Miliband, D. (2011) 'Speech on the European left', *New Statesman*, 8 March, London: London School of Economics and Political Science, www.newstatesman.com/uk-politics/2011/03/centre-parties-social

Minkin, L. (2014) *The Blair supremacy: A study in the politics of Labour's Party management*, Manchester: Manchester University Press.

Moschonas, G. (2002) *In the name of social democracy: The great transformation, 1945 to the present*, New York: Verso.

Paterson, W. and Thomas, A. (1986) *The future of social democracy: Problems and prospects of social democratic parties in Western Europe*, Oxford: Clarendon Press.

Pierson, C. (2001) *Hard choices: Social democracy in the 21st century*, Cambridge: Polity Press.

Przeworski, A. and Sprague, J. (1986) *Paper stones: A history of electoral socialism*, Chicago, IL: University of Chicago Press.

Randall, N. (2003) 'Understanding Labour's ideological trajectory', in J. Callaghan, S. Fielding and S. Ludlam (eds) *Interpreting the Labour Party: Approaches to Labour politics and history*, Manchester: Manchester University Press, Chapter 1.

Sassoon, D. (2013) *One hundred years of socialism: The West European left in the twenty-first century* (2nd edn), London: I.B. Taurus.

Yin, R. (2013) *Case study research: Design and methods*, London: Sage Publications.

Part 1
The centre-left in the Anglosphere

TWO

The British Labour Party: back to the wilderness

Rob Manwaring and Matt Beech

Introduction

For a brief period of time in the late 1990s and early 2000s, New Labour seemed to offer a distinctive model for the renewal (or, according to some critics, a betrayal) of social democracy. For 13 years New Labour had seemingly found an electorally successful model that also offered clues for a recalibration of the centre-left in the 21st century. Yet, at the 2010 general election Labour was ingloriously ejected from office, under the unfortunate leadership of Gordon Brown. Brown's tired and exhausted government, battered by the MPs' expenses scandal, secured just 29 per cent of the vote, paving the way for David Cameron for the Conservative Party to secure office in coalition with the Liberal Democrats.

If the 2010 result was lacklustre for Labour, the 2015 general election, under the leadership of Ed Miliband, was far more damaging, in part, because it was unexpected. While Labour did increase its vote share to 30.4 per cent, Cameron secured a 12-seat majority. Since 2015, Labour has suddenly found itself in quite extraordinary territory, with the unexpected election of Jeremy Corbyn as party leader. In 2017, the Conservative Party was surging ahead in the polls, and Prime Minister Theresa May took a gamble and called a snap election for 8 June. Corbyn-led Labour performed better than was widely expected, and won an additional 30 seats, forcing a hung Parliament. Labour won 40 per cent of the vote, and the Tories clung to power with the support of the Democratic Unionist Party (DUP). Paradoxically, the mood in Labour was upbeat following the election, despite losing its third general election on the trot.

This chapter focuses on the period from 2010 to the 2017 general election to examine why the Labour Party is losing, and on its current trajectory, well may face a prolonged period of exile in the electoral wilderness. As Randall (2003) notes, there are multiple ways of examining centre-left political parties, including materialist, institutional, ideational and electoral strategies. Here, we adopt what Randall calls the *synthetic approach*, which integrates structural, institutional, ideational and agency factors. This is a comparative study, and this chapter is organised around the three core themes of institutions, ideas and individuals. By focusing on the interaction and symbiotic relationship between these three core elements, we can offer a view as to why the Labour Party is losing, and indeed, may well continue to do so.

In this chapter, we examine the institutional factors that are stymieing a renewal of the party. What is clear is that despite the influx of new members to Labour, both under Miliband and particularly under Corbyn, the core nexus between leader, unions, PLP (the Parliamentary Labour Party) and rank-and-file appears to be at a critical breaking point. The focus on individuals draws attention to the leadership styles of Miliband and Corbyn, and again, are key explanatory factors for Labour's current woes. Finally, the focus on individual factors then examines the extent to which Labour under Brown, Miliband and Corbyn has failed to find a coherent and electorally appealing renewal of the social democratic tradition.

It is also worth setting out here what this chapter adds to the existing literature on the travails of Labour in the post-New Labour era. First, it should be read in conjunction with the other cases in this volume, and is structured to enable comparative insights. (Much of the literature on the Labour Party tends to solely focus on the UK context.) Second, this chapter complements some existing literature, but also includes a distinctive analysis of the failures of the British left. For example, the two key statements of the Miliband period are offered by Goes (2016) and Bale (2015) – both important works. Goes focuses on ideational issues, and Bale has a stronger focus on institutional and electoral factors. Here, we seek to integrate such approaches into our analysis. In addition, while there is much journalistic critique of Labour's plight – much of it interesting – there is less academic material. Further, while the Beckett Report (2016) offers a candid, and no doubt painful, account of the 2015 election loss, it has shortcomings – not least in arguably over-playing structural factors such as the Fixed-term Parliaments Act (2011), and, to some extent, down-playing Miliband's muddled leadership. Finally, using a wider critical lens, and taking in the period that includes Brown, Miliband and Corbyn, we argue that Labour's woes require a deeper analysis than insightful, but one-off, electoral accounts (see, for example, Ross, 2015). The chapter proceeds by examining Labour through the prism of these key themes, and concludes with further reflections of Corbyn's current leadership of the party.

Institutions

When seeking to understand the failure of the British left in general, and the Labour Party in particular since 2010, a sensible place to start is by examining the institutional relationship between the Labour Party and the wider labour movement. The Labour Party is the political wing of the labour movement, and has responsibility for representing the labour movement in the UK Parliament. The elite of the labour movement comprise the first tier of the Labour Party – the Party Leader and Deputy Leader, both of whom are directly elected by party members. When in Opposition, as Labour have been since 2010, the Shadow Cabinet, with its junior Shadow Ministers and parliamentary Private Secretaries, make up the second tier of the elite. The backbenchers of the PLP can then be classed as the third tier. In the 2017 Parliament, Labour has 262 MPs.

As the UK is an asymmetric polity with devolved institutions, the labour movement has political representation through Scottish Labour in the Scottish Parliament. In the 2016 Scottish Parliament, Scottish Labour has 23 MSPs (Members of the Scottish Parliament). Welsh Labour represents Labour interests in the National Assembly for Wales, and in the 2017 Welsh Assembly Welsh Labour has 29 AMs (Assembly Members). The London Labour Party represents Labour in the London Assembly, and in the 2017 Assembly it has 12 seats. Labour does not contest elections in Northern Ireland, but the Social Democratic and Labour Party (SDLP) is a sister. In the House of Commons, the SDLP has 3 MPs, all of whom take the Labour whip voluntarily, and sit with Labour members. Finally, at the sub-national level, local representatives of the Labour Party are elected as councillors to town, borough, district, city and county councils, many of which are unitary authorities. In England and Wales since 2015 Labour controls 110 local authorities (Local Government Association, 2015). In Scotland since 2012 Labour has run 8 councils and is in a coalition in a further 8 (Curtice, 2012, p 24).

The wider Labour movement comprises affiliated trade unions, socialist societies, registered supporters and party members. In recent years Labour has been successful at engaging young people through social media, and in 2015 they offered younger supporters the reduced fee of just £3 to join. The number of young people who joined and, in particular, the number of young people who joined Labour to vote for Corbyn as leader in the summer of 2015 is evidence of this. Similarly, in July 2016, membership of the Labour Party was estimated to be nearly 600,000, as over 100,000 people had swiftly joined to participate in the leadership election after Angela Eagle initially challenged Jeremy Corbyn (Bush, 2016). In numerical terms, although Labour Party membership is currently at its highest for decades, many new registered supporters have not become regular activists within constituency Labour parties. The phenomenon of the sudden expansion of Labour membership appears to be one where people – especially younger people – have bought in to the leadership election process with the goal of voting for their preferred candidate. While to an extent the institutions of the labour movement are growing in numbers and reaching younger citizens, at the same time, the PLP is riven with bitter divisions. On 28 June 2016 Labour MPs voted by 172 to 40 for a motion of 'no confidence' in Corbyn's leadership (BBC News, 2016). During the 2017 election campaign and shortly after the unexpectedly positive result, there was an uneasy truce within the party. Yet flash points still remain. Corbyn, freshly emboldened from the election, sacked three Shadow Ministers, and there were internal struggles over the internal parliamentary committee.

The referendum on the UK's membership of the European Union (EU) is the most revealing example of the institutional challenges facing the Labour Party. The referendum was won on the issue of immigration (Jonas, 2016). The argument that carried the day was that uncontrolled, mass, low-skill immigration has had a deleterious effect on working-class communities. Brexit revealed a divided UK, with especially deep fissures in the English left over the type of country Labour-inclined voters want to see (Beech, 2016, p 128). This can be understood as the progressive left versus conservative Labour. According to YouGov, 65 per cent of people who voted Labour in the 2015 general election opted for 'Remain' while 35 per cent chose 'Leave' (YouGov, 2016). In a YouGov poll of Labour Party members, 90 per cent responded that they voted 'Remain' and 9 per cent responded that they voted 'Leave' (Curtis, 2016). Brexiteers were more likely to be older, modestly educated and to live in the provinces of England and Wales (Moore, 2016). Brexit has stirred a more conservative vision of the English left in the hearts and minds of many instinctive Labour voters.

The Brexit result demonstrates that there is no shared vision for the good society on the British left. The political identity and values of the vast majority of the PLP, party members and registered supporters is at variance with millions of Labour-inclined voters, especially those from working-class communities. The part that the institutions of the

British left has played in its malaise pertains to what can be explained as the *values gap*, the gap in social values between those voters who have historically been Labour-inclined, and the activists and politicians within the Labour Party. The Labour Party and labour movement has ceased to be a broad church in terms of social values, and is more accurately described as a handful of disputatious political sects. On issues such as membership of the EU, mass immigration from Eastern and South Eastern Europe, the culture of human rights, feminism, gay marriage and patriotism, Labour politicians and activists are firmly progressive (Edwards and Beech, 2016, p 494). But this is not the vision of Labour politics recognised by older voters, non-metropolitan voters and many working-class voters in Labour's heartlands. The *values gap* argument relates not to economic perspectives where the breadth of opinion within the labour movement is plain for all to see. The socialism of the hard left Corbynites is different from the soft left social democracy of Ed Miliband and his inner circle, which, in turn, was different from the centrism of the Brownite and Blairite centre-left. Labour-inclined voters do not clearly coalesce around one variant of Labour political economy.

The other factor in the *values gap* argument is that the more conservative vision of the left is alien to Londoners. London Labour is the epitome of cosmopolitanism, and is necessarily progressive. This leads us to the second point – geography matters. A further difficulty for the Labour Party comes, in part, from London's dominance. The nation's capital is a bedrock of the Labour Party, with 45 out of 73 MPs. Its voter base is disproportionally young, wealthier than average, socially liberal and represented (some might say, over-represented) in the mass media. Its voice is therefore loud and it receives multiple platforms in the broadcast and print media to press its case for progressive Labour values. When this progressive left voice reverberates outside of the metropolis, and is received in the Labour heartlands, it is as hard to comprehend as an unknown tongue.

Ideas

At the heart of Labour's current plight lies an ideational paradox. The spectre that continues to haunt the party is the legacy of New Labour. British Labour has not yet decisively, and in a unified way, answered the question of what the post-New Labour Party stands for. This is not an uncommon phenomenon. As Bale (2010) deftly points out, it took the Conservative Party four leaders and 13 years to reconcile itself to the Thatcherite legacy. The paradox for Labour is that 'New

Labour' was built on a broad consensus of ideas and principles, and yet remained quite contradictory (see Gamble, 2010; Manwaring, 2014). Thematically, New Labour was conceived around a new political economy largely accommodating the Thatcherite legacy; a focus on social inclusion (and not inequality); an enabling state; a focus on community; and a shift to equality of opportunity (not outcome) (Driver and Martell, 2000). Of course, these were synthesised most coherently by Anthony Giddens and his extensive writings on the Third Way, and Blair's own Third Way pamphlet. The key issue is that even if some normatively challenged the New Labour consensus, the range of ideas was relatively coherent, and it clearly found electoral support. The fragility and internal contradictions were exposed most fatally by the 2008 global financial crisis (GFC).

Ideationally, neither Brown, Miliband nor Corbyn have yet found a similar winning formula. As Beech (2009) argues, a striking feature of Gordon Brown's time as party leader was a refusal to build an ideological narrative for his government. Indeed, the party's manifesto at the 2010 election, while rich in policy detail, and with a strong focus on rebuilding the British economy, lacked a clear ideational identity. Of all the leaders post-Blair, Brown was most acutely caught between the Scylla and Charybdis of New Labour's ideational legacy and the response to the GFC. Perhaps the strongest point of ideational difference was Brown's, albeit limited, attempt to develop an agenda on democratic renewal (Labour Party, 2010). It remains unclear, however, if Brown had won in 2010 how far this push for devolution and the elusive 'new politics' would have been delivered.

Ideationally, of all three leaders, Ed Miliband remains the most intriguing in his quest to reformulate social democracy. As Goes (2016) critically outlines, Miliband flirted with and was restless with a wide range of ideas and principles during his tenure. Despite his claims, Miliband never quite fully broke with New Labour, yet in his ideational fluctuations we see an attempt to rethink some core principles, including:

- equality (via predistribution)
- the state (via Blue Labour)
- capitalism (via 'producers vs predators')
- class and social cohesion (via 'One Nation').

Brevity forbids a detailed examination of Miliband's ideas here, but the rough contours can be outlined. A defining, and clear, ideational break from New Labour was Miliband's interest in notions of inequality (see Miliband, 2016). Miliband tried to recalibrate policy around tackling structural forms of inequality, and his advisers flirted with Jacob Hacker's notions of predistribution. Simply, this refers to state interventions in the market before traditional redistribution/ tax transfers take place, childcare funding being commonly cited as an example. Tactically, this potentially meant a rediscovery of earlier social democratic traditions, but without recourse to a traditional 'tax and spend' approach. Predistribution remains a contested concept, and Miliband both struggled to articulate what it meant and to give it coherent policy expression. Second, Miliband attempted to offer a more sustained critique of capitalism with his focus on 'predators', not producers. The difficulty for Miliband was an ongoing tendency to raise ideas that either lacked coherence or clear policy expression.

Moreover, Miliband's ideational journey had then moved on. Early on he was influenced by the 'Blue Labour' notions most closely associated with Maurice Glasman (Davis, 2011). The insight here was Glasman's critique of the statist tradition in Labour thinking, and its abandonment of community and other sources of collectivist power. Miliband was influenced to some extent by this thinking, and found expression in his adoption of community organising and campaigns such as the 'Living Wage' (the latter co-opted by former Conservative Chancellor George Osborne). Yet, his views on the role of the state were not as clear as New Labour's 'enabling state' motif. As is well documented, Miliband backed away from Blue Labour following Glasman's controversial comments about immigration and engaging with supporters of the English Defence League (EDL). Again, a core ideational problem for Miliband and Labour has been to articulate a clear policy agenda on immigration that appeases working-class people and multiculturalists in London, while respecting the principle of the free movement of people. The vexed issue of Labour's stance on immigration was given full airing with Gordon Brown's ill-fated meeting with Labour voter Gillian Duffy in the run-up to the 2010 election.

The next 'big idea' was to re-claim Disraeli's 'One Nation' label to re-assert a more consensual form of governance, to some extent, more like a German social market model. Yet, as outlined elsewhere, despite much interest in the idea by Jon Cruddas during the policy review, Miliband's own personal commitment to the idea was lukewarm at best. Moreover, as an ideational principle it actually gave few clues for a clear re-formulation of social democracy. In sum, Miliband's ideational journey reflected both a determined effort to engage in new ideas and to break from New Labour orthodoxy, but was beset by inconsistent messages, poor policy proposals and ambivalence from Miliband himself on some of these agendas.

Ideationally, Corbyn is the clearest 'circuit-breaker' from the New Labour ideational model. His politics are much contested, and arguably, the 'radicalism' of his thinking is probably over-stated. Indeed, some commentators noted some policy continuity from Ed Miliband's period as leader. Corbyn's ideational agenda is organised around the following themes (Corbyn, 2016):

- a 'new politics' fostering particular forms of 'grassroots democracy'
- a 'new economics' linked to his strident anti-austerity agenda
- a focus on internationalism in foreign affairs.

Arguably, Corbyn's foreign policy agenda is the starkest break from the New Labour era. Ideationally, Corbyn's use of the term 'socialism' is not always clear, but it has its roots in traditions from the Bennite New left faction of the party in the 1980s. To date, it remains far from apparent how either Corbyn or John McDonnell (Shadow Chancellor) can forge a distinctive new political economy. It seems to hark back to a pre-1990s Swedish form of Scandinavian social democracy with an unashamed use of tax measures to defend core welfare state institutions. Nor is it obvious the extent to which Corbyn and McDonnell have engaged with the sustainability of a welfare state model that was best suited to the heyday of Keynesian demand management (for a more nuanced critique of this dilemma, see Andersson, 2014). For the 2017 election campaign, Corbyn placed nationalisation front and centre, although polling data suggested misgivings from the wider public about how this might all be funded.

Ideationally, Labour has shifted from its New Labour moorings quite considerably since the fall of the Brown government. While Miliband's efforts have been the most intellectually fresh, there was a failure to make them cohere. The existential crisis for British Labour continues, and it is unlikely that Corbyn can offer an ideational package that electorally succeeds where both Brown and Miliband failed. Labour is losing, largely because it has not shifted beyond the paradox of New Labour's ideational legacy.

Individuals

The leadership styles of Brown, Miliband and Corbyn are contrasting in tone and approach but similar in an important way, namely, their slow footedness and natural unease on multiple media platforms.

Brown struggled to display empathy while Prime Minister. Meeting members of the public did not sit comfortably with him, and the 'smiling Brown' appeared contrived (Saul, 2014). This was not the baron of HM Treasury that the public had seen bestriding Whitehall for the previous 10 years. Brown was better at the Despatch Box arguing data points and policy.

Miliband was even less convincing than Brown in the House of Commons. This view must be tempered, however, by the fact that as Leader of the Opposition, he did not control the political narrative of the day. Nor did he have the apparatus of the state surrounding him, which adds gravity to a political leader. Miliband was nonetheless a competent and calm interviewee, and appeared relaxed when interacting with the public. Criticisms of his leadership style came in the form of the politics of perception, that he was a 'policy-wonk' displaying occasional signs of social maladjustment. This was largely created and fuelled by the Conservative-supporting tabloid press. Miliband's shortcomings lay in the fact that he was considered, quite correctly, to be a left intellectual (Pickard, 2015), and despite representing Doncaster North, he came across as very much part of the Westminster establishment. When one recalls that Miliband (like many of his generation) never had a professional career outside of politics, coupled with the fact he was a long-time Treasury adviser to Brown, and that his brother is a former Labour Foreign Secretary, the view that he occupies the Whitehall-Westminster bubble is difficult to refute.

Corbyn is unique in the modern era – a Labour leader who appears uncomfortable when interviewed and unconvincing at the Despatch Box. His preferred environment is that of the extra-parliamentary protest where he is skilful in making speeches to like-minded supporters. A case in point is Corbyn's post-election performance at Glastonbury in June 2017. Corbyn is much less disposed to engage with those who sharply disagree with him or, in the media's case, appear to ask him critical questions. This is possibly due to the fact that throughout a long parliamentary career, Corbyn has been a backbench rebel. From 1997 to 2010 he was the most rebellious Labour MP in Parliament (Cowley, 2016). Corbyn's leadership style is reinforced due to the strength of his mandate from the overwhelming victory in the leadership contest of 2015 where he won in each of the three sections (BBC News, 2015). With invaluable assistance from Momentum – a dedicated group of supporters who have successfully targeted young voters through social media, and deployed groups of activists in many constituency Labour parties (especially in London) – the Corbyn brand has become a highly effective recruiting sergeant for Labour. This has reinforced Corbyn's control of the wider party, but highlighted the internecine struggle within the PLP, which is in constant discussion of how to remove him.

Brown, Miliband and Corbyn display quite significant weaknesses in leadership style, but arguably a more significant issue is the *values gap* mentioned above. As Prime Minister, Brown frequently spoke of 'Britishness' – understandably so, as a Scot, and MP for Kirkcaldy and Cowdenbeath, who believed in the Union of Great Britain and Northern Ireland. But England – barring London – was overlooked. This would prove costly for Labour in the long run. Miliband tried to connect his ideas of the 'squeezed middle' to the struggles of the employed strivers outside of the wealthy classes (BBC News, 2010). Yet he could not adapt his metropolitanism; grasping the depth of concern from Labour-inclined voters towards mass immigration from Eastern and South Eastern Europe, and gay marriage, was a cultural bridge too far for him to cross (Edwards and Beech, 2016). Corbyn, like Miliband, is London Labour. Their economic preferences, approach to foreign policy and the defence of the realm are very different. One is an acolyte of Tony Benn, the other a one-time Brownite. But what unites them, and the mainstay of Labour politicians and activists, is progressivism. Or, put another way, a worldview of ardent social liberalism. The problem of the *values gap* is both an institutional and a leadership problem for the Labour Party.

Conclusion

British democracy is in a state of unprecedented flux, buffeted by a fragmenting union, a political class still recovering from the MPs' expenses scandal, and, of course, divisions and uncertainty following the Brexit vote. Structurally, the biases in the electoral system are both masking and exacerbating deeper divisions. What was once a relatively stable two-party system is shifting to a new multi-party ecology. As many commentators have pointed out, at the 2015 election, UKIP attracted 3.88 million votes and won one seat. In contrast, with Labour annihilated in Scotland, the SNP (Scottish National Party), with 1.45 million votes, won 56 seats. Labour's loss has to be located in the wider public detachment from the major parties, which is masked by the surge in party members since Corbyn became leader. While we might attribute much of the loss in 2010 to tiredness and a backlash against the GFC, these wider structural factors are more important.

More widely, as Gamble (2010, p 641) notes, one way of understanding the trajectories of Labour is through a series of 'cycles'.

Arguably, the 2008 GFC marks a new cycle for Labour's identity. It is worth reflecting that while Labour is currently losing, until the advent of New Labour, this is not a particularly new phenomenon. British Labour's post-war electoral record is patchy at best. One interpretation might be to understand Labour's electoral appeal by borrowing a concept from public policy – 'punctuated equilibrium' (see Cairney, 2012). Broadly speaking, political systems are both stable and dynamic, and in between periods of incremental change there can be periods of intense activity. It could well be that even if there is support for wider social democratic ideals in the UK, voters have not historically always chosen Labour to deliver them. Labour's appeal might be to establish crucial public institutions and goods (for example, the NHS, British Rail, the National Parks and the Open University), and then be ejected from office. On this reading, it may well be several elections before it has a new political imagination to deliver the next set of critical public goods in the 21st century.

Relatedly, a key factor in explaining why Labour is losing, and might continue to lose, is the conservative impulse of the party. As David Marquand (1991, p 37) reminds us, for much of the post-war period, Labour was essentially 'conservative', partly because it was an instrument of a 19th-century economic model unable to meet the challenges of the 20th century. Marquand suggests that when Labour won office, British voters were asking it to restore a previous political order. Oddly, under Corbyn, there is a conservative impulse – ultimately to re-assert a form of social democracy from the 1980s. Indeed, writers like the late Tony Judt (2009) see a key impulse of a revitalised social democracy to 'conserve', by defending the achievements of the past undone by neoliberalism. Corbyn's agenda – probably what we might unhelpfully call 'old Labour' – might meet this criterion in its conservative mission to defend the NHS. However, this might not be enough in the complexity of modern politics, not least as there is a much clearer value placed on the role of leaders.

UK politics is now a multi-party system, the electorate is far more fragmented – especially with the shift to identity, not class politics in Scotland. More crucially, this is an era of 'valence' politics (Johnston and Pattie, 2010), with government shifting away from ideology and rather focusing on 'sound economic management'.

References

Andersson, J. (2014) 'Losing social democracy: Reflections on the erosion of a paradigmatic case of social democracy', in D. Bailey, J.-M. de Waele, F. Escalona and M. Vieira (eds) *European social democracy during the global economic crisis: Renovation or resignation?*, Manchester: Manchester University Press.

Bale. T. (2010) *The Conservative Party: From Thatcher to Cameron*, Cambridge: Polity Press.

Bale, T. (2015) *Five year mission: The Labour Party under Ed Miliband*, Oxford: Oxford University Press.

BBC News (2010) 'Miliband comes to defence of "squeezed middle"', 26 November, www.bbc.co.uk/news/uk-politics-11848303

BBC News (2015) 'Labour leadership results in full', 12 September, www.bbc.co.uk/news/uk-politics-34221155

BBC News (2016) 'Labour MPs pass no-confidence motion in Jeremy Corbyn', 28 June, www.bbc.co.uk/news/uk-politics-36647458

Beckett, M. (2016) *Learning the lessons from defeat: Taskforce report* (Beckett Report), London: Labour Party.

Beech, M. (2009) 'A puzzle of ideas and policy: Gordon Brown as prime minister', *Policy Studies*, vol 30, no 1, pp 5-16.

Beech, M. (2016) 'Internationalism', in K. Hickson (ed) *Reclaiming social democracy: Core principles for the centre left*, Bristol: Policy Press, pp 127-40.

Bush, S. (2016) 'Labour membership to hit 600,000', *New Statesmen*, 6 July, www.newstatesman.com/politics/staggers/2016/07/labour-membership-hit-600000

Cairney, P. (2012) 'Punctuated equilibrium', in P. Cairney, *Understanding public policy: Theories and issues*, Basingstoke: Palgrave Macmillan, pp 175-99.

Corbyn, J. (2016) 'Decision time: New politics, new economy, new Britain', Speech to the British Chamber of Commerce, London, 3 March.

Cowley, P. (2016) 'Jeremy Corbyn and the Labour Whip', *Revolts*, 16 May, http://revolts.co.uk/?p=932

Curtice, J. (2012) *Scottish Local Government elections: Report and analysis*, Electoral Reform Society, 3 May.

Curtis, C. (2016) 'Corbyn loses support among Labour Party membership', YouGov/Times poll of Labour Party members, 30 June, https://yougov.co.uk/news/2016/06/30/labour-members-corbyn-post-brexit/

Davis, R. (2011) *Tangled up in blue: Blue Labour and the struggle for Labour's soul*, London: Ruskin Publishing.

Driver, S, and Martell, L. (2000) 'Left, Right and Third Way', *Policy & Politics*, vol 28, no 2, pp 147-61.

Edwards, B.M. and Beech, M. (2016) 'Labour parties, ideas transfer and ideological positioning: Australia and Britain compared', *Policy Studies*, vol 37, no 5, pp 486-98.

Gamble, A. (2010) 'New Labour and political change', *Parliamentary Affairs*, vol 63, no 4, pp 639-52.

Goes, E. (2016) *The Labour Party under Ed Miliband: Trying but failing to renew social democracy*, Manchester: Manchester University Press.

Johnston, R. and Pattie, C. (2011) 'Where did Labour's votes go? Valence politics and campaign effects at the 2010 British General Election', *British Journal of Politics and International Relations*, vol 13, no 3, pp 283-303.

Jonas, M. (2016) 'Brexit: Why so surprised?', NatCen, 11 July, http://natcen.ac.uk/blog/brexit-why-so-surprised?gclid=CITVpOD98s0CFW8o0wodaP4IgQ

Judt, T. (2009) 'What is living and what is dead in social democracy', *The New York Review of Books*, 17 December, www.nybooks.com/articles/2009/12/17/what-is-living-and-what-is-dead-in-social-democrac/

Labour Party (2010) *A future fair for all*, London: Labour Party.

Local Government Association (2015) 'Local Government elections: Majority party for all councils at 07 May 2015', www.local.gov.uk/local-government-elections-2015-majority-party-all-councils-07-may-2015

Manwaring, R. (2014) *The search for democratic renewal: The politics of consultation in Britain and Australia*, Manchester: Manchester University Press.

Marquand, D. (1991) *The progressive dilemma*, London: Heinemann.

Miliband, E. (2016) 'The inequality problem', *London Review of Books*, vol 38, no 3, pp 19-20.

Moore, P. (2016) 'How Britain voted: Over-65s were more than twice as likely as under-25s to have voted to leave the European Union', YouGov, 27 June, https://yougov.co.uk/news/2016/06/27/how-britain-voted/

Pickard, J. (2015) 'Ed Miliband's move to the left lost Labour the election', *Financial Times*, 8 May, www.ft.com/content/734f0578-f34a-11e4-8141-00144feab7de

Randall, N. (2003) 'Understanding Labour's ideological trajectory', in J. Callaghan, S. Fielding and S. Ludlam (eds) *Interpreting the Labour Party: Approaches to Labour politics and history*, Manchester: Manchester University Press, pp 23-56.

Ross, T. (2015) *Why the Tories won: The inside story of the 2015 election*, London: Biteback Publishing.

Saul, H. (2014) 'Gordon Brown: Six moments the former PM would rather forget', *The Independent*, 1 December, www.independent. co.uk/news/uk/politics/gordon-brown-six-moments-the-former-pm-would-rather-forget-9895831.html

YouGov (2016) 'YouGov survey results: EU referendum', 23-24 June, https://d25d2506sfb94s.cloudfront.net/cumulus_uploads/document/oxmidrr5wh/EUFinalCall_Reweighted.pdf

THREE

Electoral competition in Canada among centre-left parties: liberals versus social democracts

David McGrane

In their introduction of *What's left of the left*, Cronin, Ross and Shoch (2011: 3) discuss how many electable parties in Western democracies could be categorised as centre-lefts. However, these parties are so diverse that it is more apt to talk of 'centre-lefts' that include 'social liberals, social democrats, democratic socialists, progressives, greens, and human rights campaigners' (Cronin et al, 2011, p 3). Despite the disagreements of these 'centre-lefts' on a variety of issues, Cronin et al hold that they share a common commitment to state intervention in the economy, wealth redistribution, environmental protection and individual cultural liberties while recognising the multiple constraints of economic internationalisation.

In Canada, the concept of 'centre-lefts' has been particularly pertinent over the last decade. Roughly two-thirds of Canadian voters have values and policy positions that could be broadly defined as 'left-of-centre' or 'progressive' in Canadian parlance (McGrane, 2015). During the decade of rule by a decidedly right-wing Conservative government under Stephen Harper's prime ministership, no less than four parties emerged as Canada's 'centre-lefts' to court this clientele of left-of-centre voters. Unlike other Western countries, where there is a more distinct left/right polarisation in party systems, Canada has two relatively large centre-left parties: the centrist Liberals, that has won successive majority governments during the 20th century, and the fledgling New Democratic Party (NDP), that often comes third in Canadian federal elections.

Scholarly explanations for the Liberals' dominance of Canadian federal politics abound. The most common explanations point to Canada's lack of an industrial base and lack of strong unions that would accompany that, the effectiveness of the Liberals in brokering a compromise between French and English linguistic groups, and the Liberals' efficient internal organisation (Carty, 2015; Johnston, 2017).

The other two centre-left parties are the social democratic Bloc
Québécois, who advocate for the separation of Québec from Canada,
and run candidates only in that province, and the Canadian Greens,
who run candidates in all constituencies but routinely struggle to elect
even one MP and win more than 5 per cent of the national vote.

Table 3.1, depicting the results of Canadian federal elections from
2006 to 2015, can be found below. Under Prime Minister Harper,
the Conservatives formed minority governments in 2006 and 2008 as
well as forming a majority government in 2011. In the 2011 election,
the NDP became the Official Opposition in the Canadian House of
Commons for the first time in its 80-year history, while the Liberals
were relegated to third party status. At the outset of the 2015 election
it appeared that it would be a two-way fight between the NDP and
Conservatives, but the Liberals came from third place in the publicly
available polling to win a resounding victory. The Liberals then formed
a majority government in 2015, and Justin Trudeau became Prime
Minister.

Table 3.1: Canadian federal election results (2006, 2008, 2011 and 2015)

	Conservatives		New Democratic Party (NDP)		Liberals		Bloc Québécois		Greens	
	Seats	Vote (%)	Seats	Vote (%)	Seats	Vote (%)	Seats	Vote (%)	Seats	Vote (%)
2006	124	36	29	17	103	30	51	11	0	5
2008	143	38	37	18	77	26	49	10	0	7
2011	166	40	103	31	34	19	4	6	1	4
2015	99	32	44	20	184	40	10	5	1	3

Source: Elections Canada

In these elections, the strategy of the Liberals and NDP was predicated
on stealing each other's voters and ignoring the right-wing voters who
made up the core of support of the Conservatives. The key institutional
variable that explains the strategies of the NDP and Liberals is the single
member plurality (SMP) electoral system that requires left-of-centre
voters to coalesce behind a sole alternative to the Conservatives to
avoid the election of a right-wing federal government. When it came
to leadership, both the Liberals and the NDP did better at stealing
voters from the other party when their leaders were hopeful, exciting
and charming as opposed to being seen as serious, experienced and

intellectual. In terms of ideas, the competition over left-of-centre voters forced the NDP to move to the right and the Liberals to move to the left while bold policies that differentiated the two parties from each other became pivotal. For social democrats, the key lessons to be drawn from the Canadian case are that electoral systems always shape party competition, the style of a leader can be as important as their ideology, and policies need to be audacious and memorable if they are to really inspire voters.

Institutions: The obsession with strategic voting

Like the UK, Canada uses an SMP electoral system to elect its House of Commons (the appointed Canadian Senate is quite powerless). A prominent feature of SMP is the problem of 'wasted votes' where voters are encouraged to support one of the two parties that have the best chance of winning their local constituency. Voting for a party that has little chance of winning one's local constituency is considered to be 'wasted' in the sense that it has very little impact on which party actually forms government. During the 1990s, the right-of-centre vote in Canadian federal elections was split between Progressive Conservatives and the Reform Party, resulting in a string of Liberal majority governments as left-of-centre voters flocked behind the Liberals, leaving the NDP with very few seats in the House of Commons. The Progressive Conservatives and Reform Party merged in 2003 to form the Conservative Party, resulting in a minority government for the Liberals in the 2004 federal election. Under the leadership of Stephen Harper, the Conservatives then won successive minority governments in 2006 and 2008, followed by a majority government in 2011, while the rest of the vote in those elections was split among the four centre-left parties: the Liberals, NDP, Bloc Québécois and the Greens. As many political observers pointed out, there was a left-of-centre majority of voters in Canada, but the right-wing Conservatives kept winning government because of vote splitting among Canada's centre-left parties (Adams, 2012).

Given this institutional setting, there was chatter about the Liberals and the NDP merging to defeat the Conservatives. However, because of the different histories of the parties and the fact that both saw themselves as having the potential to form a majority government without the other's help, the idea of a merger never got very far. Another option was post-election cooperation aimed at toppling the minority Conservative governments. In 2008, a Liberal-NDP coalition almost took place, as these two parties were displeased with what they perceived to be inadequate economic stimulus in the federal budget, and were opposed to a government proposal to phase out the per-vote public subsidies that parties received on an annual basis between elections. However, cooperation between the NDP and the Liberals eventually fell apart due to mutual distrust between the two, a decision to give the government more time before facing a non-confidence vote made by the Governor-General (appointed by Queen Elizabeth II on the advice of the Canadian Prime Minister) that allowed the Liberals to backtrack, and the unpopularity in English Canada of the coalition needing to be propped up by the separatist Bloc Québécois (Topp, 2010). In any case, the Conservatives won a majority in the 2011 election, and the possibility of the Liberals and NDP forming a governing coalition disappeared.

The Conservatives' strategy to attain its majority is important in understanding the tactics of centre-left parties in Canada. Given the SMP electoral system, the Conservatives realised that they could effectively win 100 per cent of the power with only 40 per cent of the popular vote. As such, the Conservatives decided to govern in a decisively right-wing manner to motivate their base of supporters to turn out to vote. They relied on 'political relationship marketing' (Ormrod et al, 2013, pp 113-32), targeting their policy offerings and advertising to specific groups of voters holding right-wing values in order to build long-term relationships of loyalty. As long as the Conservatives' base was highly motivated to vote and the left-of-centre vote split four ways, the Conservatives could win majority governments. By the time of the 2011 and 2015 federal elections, the Conservatives' prowess at political relationship marketing essentially closed off these right-wing voters to the Liberals and the NDP. The net result was an intensification of competition between the non-Conservative Opposition parties for the 60 per cent of citizens displeased with Harper's government. There was less of an effort made by the Liberals and the NDP to peel away soft Conservative voters. Rather, both parties concentrated on stealing each other's supporters in an effort to coalesce all of the anti-government voters behind themselves as the sole alternative to another Conservative government.

Ultimately, the operation of the SMP electoral system ended up having a very important implication for electoral competition in the 2011 and 2015 Canadian federal elections – it created an obsession by centre-left parties with what is called 'strategic voting'. This refers to a citizen deciding not to vote for the party that they actually prefer the most, but voting against the party they like the least to ensure that that party does not form a government. For instance, a voter who actually prefers the NDP may vote for the Liberals to prevent the Conservatives from coming into power, particularly if they feel that the NDP has no chance of winning in their constituency.

It is evident that appeals based on strategic voting have become an important part of the discourse of centre-left parties in Canada. On the first day of the 2011 election, the Liberal leader at the time argued that since his party was in second place in both publicly available polls and the House of Commons, his party was the only option for voters who disliked Prime Minister Harper and the Conservative government. He made it clear that voting for the NDP or any other party would be the same as voting for the Conservatives, since it would only split the anti-government vote and end up electing Conservative candidates across the country. The Bloc Québécois made a similar argument – but for Québec only. Based on past election results and polling reported in the media at the outset of the campaign, the Bloc Québécois contended that it had the ability to win any of the 60 Québec constituencies that had predominantly Francophone populations. As such, voting for the Bloc Québécois in those constituencies would deny the Conservatives the Québec seats that they needed to form a majority government. Having never won a seat in a federal election and with very low polling numbers, the Greens decided to publicly state that they were trying a new strategy in 2011, focusing all of their efforts on their leader's seat and giving only cursory resources to the other 307 seats where they were running candidates.

Since the NDP started the 2011 campaign well behind the Liberals in both House of Commons seats and publicly reported polling, it was very cognizant that its voters were susceptible to the Liberals' strategic voting appeals. With the media speculating about a minority government, the NDP stressed that it was open to working together with other parties to get results for voters, and claimed that it would be in a position to direct the policies of the next government as the potential kingmaker in the House of Commons. This message was meant to undercut the strategic voting argument that held that change could only come through voting for the Liberals, and to point out that voting for the NDP offered more influence for Québec voters since the Bloc Québécois separatist stance made it very difficult for it to cooperate with the other parties in the House of Commons. The NDP's arguments for strategic voting were the most persuasive as the party made a major breakthrough, winning 59 seats in Québec, where it had almost never won before, and a record high of 44 seats in English Canada. While the Greens did win their leader's seat, they won no others, and saw their total vote cut in half to only 4 per cent.

The Bloc Québécois fell from 49 to 4 seats, and the Liberals dropped from 77 to 34 seats.

The context concerning strategic voting was very different at the beginning of the 2015 campaign. In public domain polling, the Liberals had surged ahead of the NDP during most of 2014, and seemed to be on track to become the consensus choice of left-of-centre voters to replace the Conservative government. In the early part of 2015, the situation was reversed with the polls showing the NDP with approximately 30-35 per cent support and the Liberals falling back to support levels somewhere between 20 and 25 per cent. The NDP's response to this context was to completely ignore their main competitors on the centre-left: the Liberals in English Canada and the Bloc Québécois in Québec. The party focused all of its energies on attacking the governing Conservatives because attacking the Liberals or the Bloc Québécois would only give those parties credibility and undermine the sentiment among voters that the election was a two-way NDP/Conservative race. For their part, the Liberals and the Bloc Québécois had to do everything in their power to prevent such a situation from happening. The Liberals spent the early part of the campaign critiquing the NDP and spending large amounts of money on advertising to generate excitement. The Bloc Québécois focused its entire campaign on arguing that the NDP was not a true defender of Québec's interests and values. The Greens hoped to combat the strategic voting appeals of the larger parties by concentrating on their leader's seat and a handful of other seats, where they argued that internal polling showed that they had the potential to win.

On election day, it was obvious that the Liberal and Bloc Québécois plans around strategic voting had worked well and that the NDP's plans had failed. By the mid-point of the campaign the Liberals had pulled closer to the NDP in publicly reported polling, and their creative advertising had created a buzz around their campaign. The Liberals' momentum in the final stretch of the campaign bolstered their leader's arguments that voting for his party was the only chance that left-of-centre voters had to get rid of the right-wing Conservative government that had been in power for almost a decade. As it became apparent that the two-way Conservative/NDP race was not emerging in the final weeks of the campaign, the NDP was unprepared and put on the defensive. The NDP's commercials claiming that it had a better chance to defeat the Conservatives than the Liberals because it had won more seats than the Liberals in the previous election rang hollow in the face of daily polls and stories in the media about the surging Liberals. The Bloc Québécois' focus on criticising the NDP as a weak defender of

Québec also started to pay off as the campaign closed. As the potential for the NDP to form a government faded the Bloc Québécois made successful appeals to soft Québécois nationalist voters to come back to the Bloc Québécois to ensure a Québec-centric opposition to a Liberal government within the House of Commons. Due to the distortions of the SMP electoral system, the Bloc Québécois saw its popular vote go down compared to 2011, but more than doubled its seat total from 4 to 10. The Greens, on the other hand, were unable to overcome their perennial difficulties with strategic voting, and succeeded only in re-electing their leader as their popular vote fell even lower, to 3 per cent. As in 2011, the institutional variable of the SMP electoral system was again driving the strategies of centre-left parties as they all attempted to put forth the most convincing arguments around strategic voting to voters who had grown tired of the Conservative government.

Individuals: 'Sunny ways'

Electoral competition among centre-left parties in Canada in the 2011 and 2015 elections comes down to the stories of the four individuals who were the leaders of the NDP and Liberals during these two elections. Interestingly, it is not really the ideologies of these leaders that distinguish them from each other. Neither the NDP nor the Liberals went through ideological soul-searching from 2011 to 2015. Rather, it was the leadership styles of these four leaders that defined them and the role that they ultimately came to play in Canadian politics.

While he was born and raised in Canada, Michael Ignatieff spent most of his adult career as a journalist in London, England, and as a professor at Harvard University, USA. He had been enticed back to Canada to run for the leadership of the Liberals in 2006, and won the leadership of the party in his second attempt in 2009. The Liberals portrayed him as a serious politician with the global experience and intellectual capacity to tackle the problems facing Canada. For instance, he hosted a much publicised 'Thinkers Conference' in late 2009 from which the Liberals determined what Canada should look like in 2017, and created a map of how to get there. Ignatieff announced that the guiding principle of his government would be 'equality of opportunity' (a hallmark concept of liberal political theory), and he laid out detailed plans of targeted investments in health, education and pension reform to achieve this abstract goal.

Perhaps unfairly, Ignatieff was criticised through a series of Conservative attack ads that played off his absence from Canada with slogans like 'Michael Ignatieff – just visiting' and 'He didn't come back for you.' Through such ads, the Conservatives successfully implanted the notion in voters' heads that Ignatieff was a self-centred academic who did not really understand their daily lives. The 2011 Canadian Election Study found that 44 per cent of voters felt that the phrase 'really cares about people' did not at all describe Ignatieff compared to 49 per cent who believed that it described him fairly well and only 7 per cent who thought that it described him very well. He lost his seat in the 2011 election and returned to teaching at Harvard.

The biggest story of the 2011 campaign was how Ignatieff was upstaged by Jack Layton, the leader of the NDP, whose party had only about 10 per cent of the seats in the House of Commons before the campaign began. The 2011 campaign was Layton's fourth campaign as NDP leader, and the party had consistently tried to build up his brand as an honest broker in the House of Commons that would fight for results for average Canadians. They stressed his attributes such as trustworthiness, empathy and determination as well as being relentlessly optimistic and bursting with positive energy. In contrast to Ignatieff, the 2011 Canadian Election Study found that only 9 per cent of voters felt that 'really cares about people' did not at all describe Layton compared to 38 per cent who thought that it described him very well and 53 per cent who believed that it described him fairly well.

In 2011, NDP strategists aimed at voters they called 'Layton Liberals' – they had the Liberals as their first choice with the NDP as their second choice, and were unsure of Ignatieff but trusted Layton (McGrane, 2011). The NDP's advertising humorously criticised the Liberals and Conservatives, and its main focus was generating excitement around Layton's inspirational leadership and publicising the party's slogan of 'Working together'. Party strategists purposefully kept the slogan vague to allow it take on different meanings for different voters (McGrane, 2011). For some, it meant cooperation between parties within a minority Parliament, while for other voters it meant Québec and English Canada working together, new NDP voters and traditional NDP voters working together, average Canadians working together to defeat Harper, and Layton working with voters.

As the Liberals' campaign begin to falter, Layton Liberals gradually started to shift into the NDP's column. Even more surprising, since Québec voters had traditionally ignored the NDP, Bloc Québécois voters started to become excited by Layton's leadership, and polls showed them shifting towards the NDP. The NDP entered the final phase of the campaign with upwards momentum and scored a historic victory, with Layton becoming the first NDP Leader of the Official Opposition in Canadian history. Tragically, Layton died suddenly of cancer very soon after the campaign, and was replaced by Thomas Mulcair, his top MP in Québec.

However, Mulcair was a very different type of politician. He was known for his abilities as a public administrator in areas like environmental and economic policy, his aggressive critiques of his opponents, and his temper. In 2015, the NDP focused on voters who were displeased with the Conservative government and trying to decide between the Liberals and the NDP as an alternative – so-called 'Liberal/ NDP switchers'. The NDP portrayed Mulcair as a serious politician who was reassuring and capable in contrast to the new Liberal leader, Justin Trudeau, who was a political neophyte, despite being the son of a former Prime Minister. As such, the Mulcair brand was a simple one: experienced leadership. The election was framed as risky change (Trudeau) versus safe change (Mulcair). At the same time, the NDP campaign ran harsh and ominous negative advertising attacking the Conservatives, particularly for their ethical lapses and their failure to engineer economic growth.

Despite a barrage of negative Conservative commercials that branded Trudeau as 'just not ready' to be Prime Minister, the Liberals did not hesitate to put their leader at the forefront of their campaign. They portrayed Trudeau as new, fresh and exciting. They heralded him as the kind of leader that would be bold and bring '#realchange'. Framing Trudeau in this manner was meant to contrast him with the more serious and older Mulcair to attract NDP supporters. To reinforce the notion that Trudeau would do politics differently, the Liberals did not run any negative advertising. In fact, they attempted to turn the Conservatives' attacks on their head by showing images of Trudeau making inspirational speeches in front of excited crowds and ending the commercials with a black screen and one word of text – 'Ready'.

The Liberals' strategy appeared to work. Polling done by the Canadian Social Democracy Study found that between the beginning and end of the 2015 campaign, voters' sentiment that the Liberals were 'exciting' and Trudeau was 'inspiring' rose, while feelings that the NDP was 'exciting' and Mulcair was 'inspiring' decreased. The optimism and hopefulness of the Trudeau brand was on full display in his first speech as Canada's newly elected Prime Minister when he shouted over a crowd of cheering supporters: "Sunny ways, my friends, sunny ways. This is what positive politics can do." Mulcair attempted to stay on as NDP leader, but delegates to the 2016 NDP convention voted in favour of having a leadership race, thereby forcing his resignation. After almost a decade of being Prime Minister, it was clear that Canadians had grown weary of Harper, and he resigned on election night. Both of the Liberals' primary opponents are currently in the midst of leadership races.

Ideas: Centrism versus social democracy

Historically, the Liberal Party of Canada has not been a party with a solid ideological anchor as it has bounced back and forth between left and right as public opinion and circumstances dictated. Due to its official affiliation with the Canadian labour unions, the NDP has traditionally been uncompromisingly social democratic. By the time that the Liberals lost power in 2006, noticeable differences between the two parties were evident, with the NDP pushing for more public ownership and government intervention in the economy, and opposing the Liberals' agenda of promoting tax cuts and favouring new free trade agreements that would limit government regulation.

However, almost a decade of right-wing Conservative government changed the ideological framework of Canadian politics. The Conservatives moved federal government policy decisively to the right, leaving the four other parties to compete for left-of-centre voters among themselves. Further, all four Opposition parties in the House of Commons criticised the Conservative government daily from a centre-left perspective, and frequently ended up agreeing with each other in their opposition to many of the Conservatives' more hard-edged right-wing policies. The result was four parties offering only slightly different centre-left alternatives to the governing Conservatives.

In the 2011 election, the competition over left-of-centre voters forced the NDP to move to the right and the Liberals to move to the left, leading to a higher degree of ideological similarity between the two parties than had been the case in past elections. To attract so-called Layton Liberals, the NDP engaged in a strategy of copying the Liberals' policy offerings with just enough differentiation to make its brand distinctive. Both parties were in favour of an overall package of centre-left policies: a cap and trade system of greenhouse gas emission credits, keeping personal taxes stable as opposed to tax cuts, spending more on childcare spaces, reducing the cost of post-secondary education, rehabilitative criminal justice, a higher guaranteed income supplement for seniors, and increasing federal funding for affordable housing. Nonetheless, the NDP positioned themselves slightly to the left of the Liberals by proposing to increase corporate tax rates, double the benefits of federal pensions, and to cap credit card fees. Unlike past platforms, the 2011 NDP platform was silent on the expansion of public ownership in the economy, and did not advocate the creation of any new universal social programmes.

In 2015, the Liberals and the NDP once again agreed on a general set of proposals that differentiated themselves from the Harper Conservatives in the areas of social, environmental and economic policy. However, in an attempt to more clearly delineate its policy offerings from the Liberals, the NDP's 2015 platform did move to the left of its 2011 platform by proposing a universal childcare programme at $15 a day and a universal prescription drug insurance scheme. Both of these proposals were much more aggressive than anything that the Liberals were proposing in terms of new spending on social policy. Further, while the 2011 NDP platform had not mentioned labour or trade policy, the 2015 version came out strongly against the Trans-Pacific Partnership Agreement, and pledged to introduce legislation to ban the use of replacement workers during strikes and to increase the minimum wage in federally regulated sectors. For their part, the Liberals supported the Trans-Pacific Partnership Agreement and promised no more in the area of labour policy than the repealing of two very anti-union pieces of legislation that the Conservatives had passed (this was also being promised by the NDP). The NDP insisted that it could simultaneously pay for its new social spending and maintain a balanced budget through increasing the corporate tax rate and maintaining personal taxes at their present rates. The Liberals were against higher corporate taxes and proposed to cut personal income tax rates for the middle class. They promised to pay for their tax cuts and moderately increased social spending through a combination of running four years of deficits and raising the personal income tax rate for the top 1 per cent of the wealthiest Canadians. Since Canada's major political parties have always promised balanced budgets during federal elections since the early 1990s, the Liberals' deficit promise generated extensive media attention and was used by the party to portray Trudeau as a new and bold leader who was willing to break with political orthodoxy.

The details of the 2015 NDP and Liberal platforms illustrate how one party adhered to a moderate form of social democracy while the other party hugged the centre of the Canadian political spectrum. However, it was clear that such subtle details were lost on the general public and the media. Ignoring the parts of the NDP platform dealing with universal social programmes, trade liberalisation and labour policy, many in the media proclaimed that the Liberals were more 'left-wing' or 'progressive' than the NDP because they were promising to go into deficit. For their part, voters appeared unaware of the differences between the centrist Liberals and the social democratic NDP. Polling for the Canadian Social Democracy Study illustrated that 52 per cent of English Canadian voters and 64 per cent of Francophone Québecers found that there were only minor differences between the NDP and the Liberals.

Conclusion: Lessons for social democrats

There are three lessons emanating from the Canadian case for social democrats around the world. When it comes to institutions, electoral systems play an important role in structuring electoral competition and shaping party strategies. In Canada, the social democratic NDP is painfully aware of the ability of the centrist Liberals to 'steal' their voters by exploiting fears of a 'wasted vote' in the SMP system. In 2011, the NDP was successful in devising a plan to overcome strategic voting, but much less successful in 2015 in the face of surging Liberal popularity at the end of the campaign. Since the outcomes of both the 2011 and 2015 elections were uncertain, opinion polls and perceived momentum had a disproportionate impact.

In terms of individuals, style can be as important as ideology. The electoral battle between the two main centre-left parties in Canada came to be defined in terms of leader brands. As the cases of Layton and Trudeau illustrate, left-of-centre voters in Canada appeared to be more attracted to leaders who are branded as dynamic, inspiring and optimistic as opposed to leaders who are branded as experienced and competent. Social democrats must remember that elections are battles for *both the heads and the hearts* of voters – good policy ideas coupled with sharp critiques of their right-wing opponents are not enough. A leader who can emote, generate excitement and arouse hope is just as important. Indeed, since becoming Prime Minister, Trudeau has become defined as much by the photographs of him that have gone 'viral' on social media as he is by his government's policies.

Finally, high-risk policy ideas can bring large rewards. Voters live in an information-rich world, and politics can seem like a lot of white noise. Part of the media's fascination with the Liberals' deficit financing pledge in the 2015 campaign was because it was seen as a daring move that went against conventional wisdom in Canadian politics. Indeed, no Canadian political party had promised deficit financing of its programme for almost three decades. The Liberals' deficit financing pledge also put the NDP in the awkward position of agreeing with the Conservatives – a party vehemently disliked by left-of-centre voters – who were also promising to maintain a balanced budget. In this instance, the Liberals' promise cut through the white noise of politics and was very memorable. While the NDP in 2015 may have had reasonable policy offerings that fitted well within the tradition of social democracy, their policy was not memorable and was not communicated well. It was not bold enough to be seen as constituting a striking difference between the NDP and the Liberals. Polling from the Canadian Social Democracy Study showed that voters' levels of agreements with NDP policies and Liberal policies were quite similar. However, voters were much more likely to be able to correctly assign the Liberals to their promises than they were to correctly assign the NDP to its promises.

Institutions, leaders and ideas – the themes of this book – will continue to be pivotal for the future of Canadian social democracy. Publicly available polling following the 2015 Canadian federal election has shown left-of-centre Canadians coalescing behind the Liberals while the leaderless NDP's numbers have slumped. The NDP's new leader will have to find a set of ideas and a leadership style that inspires Canadian left-of-centre voters and convinces them to turn away from a young and popular Prime Minister who is growing in stature on the global stage. Initially, it appeared that a major institutional change was in store for Canadian politics that had the potential to undermine the Liberals' inevitable arguments around strategic voting in the next election. Trudeau had promised to change the electoral system away from the current SMP model during the heat of the 2015 election. As Canadians debated electoral system reform during the first year of the Trudeau government, it became clear that the Liberals' preferred electoral system would be the alterative vote, the NDP favoured a mixed-member proportional representation system, and the Conservatives wanted SMP to continue. Trudeau eventually declared that there was no consensus and that no change in the electoral system would take place. As such, social democrats in Canada are searching for a new leader and new ideas, but the same old electoral system, and the challenges that it brings for the NDP in terms of strategic voting, remain in place.

References

Adams, P. (2012) *Power trap: How fear and loathing between New Democrats and Liberals keep Stephen Harper in power – And what can be done about it*, Toronto, ON: Lormier Publishers.

Carty, K. (2017) *Big tent politics: The Liberal Party's long mastery of Canada's public life*, Vancouver, BC: University of British Columbia Press.

Cronin, J., Ross, G. and Shoch, J. (eds) (2011) *What's left of the Left: Democrats and Social Democrats in challenging times*, Durham, NC: Duke University Press.

Johnston, R. (2017) 'Polarized pluralism in the Canadian party system', in A. Gagnon and B. Tanguay (eds) *Canadian parties in transition* (4th edn), Toronto, ON: University of Toronto Press, pp 64-83.

McGrane, D. (2011) 'Political marketing and the NDP's historic breakthrough', in J. Pammett and C. Doran (eds) *The Canadian Federal Election of 2011*, Toronto, ON: Dundurn Publishing, pp 77-110.

McGrane, D. (2015) *Could a progressive platform capture Canada's youth vote?*, Ottawa, ON: Broadbent Institute.

Ormrod, R., Henneberg, S. and O'Shaughnessy, N. (eds) (2013) *Political marketing: Theory and concepts*, London: Sage Publications.

Topp, B. (2010) *How we almost gave the Tories the boot: The inside story behind the coalition*, Toronto, ON: Lormier Publishers.

FOUR

The 'soft target' of Labour in New Zealand

Grant Duncan

At the 2014 general election, the New Zealand Labour Party suffered what was arguably its worst election defeat ever, gaining 25 per cent of the party vote. One has to go back to 1922 to observe a lower level of electoral support. But in those days, Labour was a new party (formed in 1916) and was rising towards its historic victory of 1935, so the two results are hardly worth comparing. To make matters worse, 2014 was the third electoral defeat in a row to the centre-right National Party that had been in office since 2008. So why was Labour losing?

  This chapter covers the period from 2008 to 2015, but some background is called for. Prior to the 2008 election, a three-term Labour-led government under Prime Minister Helen Clark followed a Blairite 'Third Way' model. It moderated some of the policies of the more radical neoliberal years (1984-96), but the fundamentals of neoliberal reform, such as financial openness, central bank independence and fiscal responsibility, were kept in place. Some critics saw the Clark government as embedding neoliberalism (Kelsey, 2002); others observe that some of their policies ignored or even reversed the 'radical' neoliberal model set out by the Treasury in 1987, especially in public management (Chapman and Duncan, 2007). Clark's Labour-led government did not satisfy all social democratic aspirations, but its dominance in the 2000s showed that it was the first to master the art of political management under the mixed-member proportional representation system in place since 1996. So Labour took office in 1999 through a formal coalition with the (now defunct) left-wing Alliance Party, and it survived the two subsequent elections as a minority government with confidence-and-supply agreements with minor parties.[1] Nine years in office was a good run for Labour, exceeded only by the first Labour government (1935-49). Defeat came in 2008, however, in an election held shortly after the global financial crisis (GFC), and John Key's National Party-led government took over the reins. The recession that New Zealand experienced at that time could not be blamed on either the Labour-led or National Party-led government, but it did effect the latter's revenues and fiscal options. Nonetheless, Key promised 'no radical reforms', and so voters could aim for a change of government without jeopardising the achievements of the Clark years (Franks and McAloon, 2016).

A significant slump in support for Labour occurred between the 2005 and 2008 elections. Their party vote fell from 41 to 34 per cent. Meanwhile, support for the National Party had been steadily rising since its humiliating result of only 21 per cent in 2002. There are normally electoral 'pendulum swings' around the centre as disillusionment with an incumbent government sets in, but, following its win in 2008, the National Party appeared to 'defy gravity'. Its three successive electoral victories saw an increase in its party vote from 44.9 per cent in 2008 to 47.3 per cent in 2011 and then declining only slightly to 47 per cent in 2014. So, any analysis of Labour's poor electoral performance (and of the left in general) needs to take into account the prolonged high levels of support for Prime Minister John Key and his administration. The National Party's success can be attributed in part to its pragmatic adoption of elements of Keynesian or centre-left policies. This makes it a difficult target for the left-wing Opposition, as it was not a purely neoliberal government. Even when the National Party-led government adopted a measure that could be described as 'neoliberal' – signing up to the Trans-Pacific Partnership Agreement on trade in 2015 – Labour found itself internally divided over how to react. Ideological confusion, disunity and unconvincing leadership have dogged Labour since 2008.

To understand the social democratic left in New Zealand, we also need to consider the role and influence of the Green Party. A progressive social democratic government is most probably a Labour–Green coalition. In 2014, the Greens won 10.7 per cent of the party vote, and, thanks to proportional representation, they have secured a position as Parliament's third largest party. A combined Labour–Green vote of just under 36 per cent, however, was well short of the National Party's 47 per cent. Helen Clark had shut the Greens out of office for the entire nine years of her prime ministership, knowing that the Greens could not be seen to let the National Party gain office instead. In 2016, however, Labour and the Greens signed a pre-electoral agreement to coordinate their activities with the aim of changing the government. For the left to win in New Zealand, Labour and the Greens would need to work together and to demonstrate an ability to form a government. But the 2016 agreement did not commit the two parties to any form of collaboration *after* the election, let alone in government. It did clear the path, however, towards a formal coalition with shared seats in Cabinet.

Institutions

New Zealand has a unicameral legislature and follows Westminster conventions of government formation: a ministry is formed from among the elected representatives and governs so long as it enjoys the confidence of a majority in the House of Representatives. In the past, this placed a lot of power in the hands of the Executive. But, countervailing this (since 1996) is the mixed-member proportional electoral system (MMP), which makes it unlikely that a single party will hold the majority. Critical to understanding New Zealand politics, therefore, is the MMP system, which is based on the German model. MMP gives electors two votes: one for a local constituency member (on a first-past-the-post basis) and the other for the preferred political party. The latter results determine the final numbers in the House on a proportional basis. A party is allocated its proportion of seats if either it gains at least 5 per cent of the party vote, or it wins one or more electoral constituencies. Hence, regardless of whether a party is left, centre or right, to be a credible contender for office requires the ability to form a stable coalition or support an agreement that adds up to a majority, at least on confidence votes. And this normally requires indicating to the electorate *before* they cast their ballots that a credible coalition could be formed after the election. For example, well before the 2014 election, John Key indicated which other parties the National Party would be prepared to work with. That election gave National 60 seats out of 121, just shy of a majority. To form a government, it signed up the same three minor parties (comprising four seats) that had supported it on a confidence-and-supply basis in the previous two terms. National lost one electorate seat in a by-election in early 2015, but still had the numbers to govern.

Since 2008, National followed Helen Clark's example, forming minority governments supported by confidence-and-supply agreements with minor parties. For the subsequent two elections (2011 and 2014), Labour lacked a credible case for a stable alternative coalition. For instance, in the 2014 campaign, it was suggested that a Labour–Green–NZ First grouping might have mustered the numbers to govern. But because Labour refused to accept an olive branch from the Greens prior to the election, and the centrist NZ First refused to say which major party it would prefer to support in government, there was no such pre-electoral deal. NZ First, as its name implies, is a centrist economic–nationalist and protectionist party that sometimes resorts to anti–immigration rhetoric; its leader, Winston Peters, is a political veteran with a mercurial and populist style. NZ First has a record of refusing to be a partner to a government that includes the Greens in office. Such a tri-partisan arrangement could have been ideologically fraught, if not divisive, given their diverse leadership styles and values. So the centre-left lacked a credible coalition 'story' to tell to the electorate about a stable government-in-waiting. National's 2014 election campaign was based on statements about their 'track record' in office for the previous six years, and a promise of 'strong and stable government' – compared with the spectre of a supposedly unstable left-wing multi-party alliance. Potential swing voters were likely then to stay with 'the devil they knew'. And once the votes were counted, the incumbent National Party had the numbers to continue in office with support from three minor parties (Johansson and Levine, 2015).

On top of the centre-left's problem of credible government formation prospects comes a decline in voter turnout. In the 1984 election, when the fourth Labour government swept into power, 93.7 per cent of enrolled voters participated. This fell to a low of 74.2 per cent in 2011. Turnout tends to be lower among the very demographic groups that are normally more left-leaning: the young, and minority ethnic groups, including Māori. There is also a positive correlation (although a relatively weak one) between electorates' median household incomes and voter turnouts. In December 2015, 93.1 per cent of the estimated eligible population was enrolled, but the age group with the lowest enrolment was aged 18-24, at only 72.4 per cent, in spite of enrolment being compulsory. The seven Māori electorates generally get the lowest turnouts of all. This can partly be attributed to the fact that they also have the lowest median ages, but the Electoral Commission published figures from 2014 that show Māori voter turnouts were consistently lower than non-Māori in all age groups. Moreover, 'electorates with high populations of Pasifika and Asian New Zealanders have low participation' (Electoral Commission, 2015, p ii). Pasifika communities have relatively young median ages, high unemployment and low incomes. Many are loyal Labour supporters, but many also have conservative religious views at variance with some liberal policies, such as marriage equality.

In principle, there are numerous material concerns that could motivate young people, especially those from minority ethnic groups and low-income families, to vote Labour or Green. Many young people now see future homeownership as unlikely if not impossible; many acquire significant student debt; they are particularly prone to precarious employment; and they have a longer-term stake in sustainability and climate change. And some Labour politicians have speculated about winning an election by re-engaging those who had protested or passively withdrawn by not voting, or who had never voted before at all, especially the young (the so-called 'missing million'). In spite of a small increase in the turnout figure in 2014, there was no major 'return to the polls', however.

So one needs to take into account Labour's changing support bases. Its heritage is in the union movement, especially the radical anti-capitalist 'Red Feds' who led the general strikes of 1912-13 (Shor, 2002). The first Labour government's Cabinet included veterans of those strikes, and also moderate Christian Socialists. Union affiliation remains central to the party organisation, but militant industrial politics have since all but disappeared. Nowadays Labour is not funded primarily by, let alone acting at the behest of, trade unions (Franks and McAloon, 2016). The social and political influence of trade unions in general has been in decline. Union membership density in the workforce was virtually halved due to employment laws (since 1991) that are based on voluntary association, give little encouragement to collective bargaining and restrict the right to strike (Feinberg-Danieli and Lafferty, 2007).

Labour forged an historic accord with the politically active Rātana Church, and in 1935 two Rātana MPs joined the Labour caucus (Franks and McAloon, 2016, p 84). Labour subsequently held the Māori seats for most of the time until the 1990s. Since then, however, Māori voting has shifted, showing that this loyalty cannot be taken for granted. In 1996, all (then five) Māori seats were won by the NZ First Party. But many of these Māori voters felt betrayed when NZ First unexpectedly went into a coalition government with the National Party. In 2004, the Māori Party was formed due to disaffection with Labour's foreshore and seabed policy. It later won four out of seven Māori seats in 2005, but in 2008 supported John Key's government with confidence-and-supply agreements. So, recent elections have seen Māori voters return to the Labour fold. In 2014, Labour won six of the seven Māori seats, leaving the Māori Party with only one electorate and one list seat.[2]

A core project for any left-wing party is to combat discrimination. Hence, identity politics play a vital part in policy and in party organisations. For example, the Green Party orders its party list to ensure that the gender ratio of its MPs does not exceed 60:40 in favour of either gender. It has two co-leaders, one of each gender. The Labour Party, however, aroused public controversy for trying to equalise the genders in its caucus through candidate selection, and it still has no official quota. In 2015, Labour had 12 female MPs out of 32. Both

Green and Labour make commitments to uphold the principles of the 1840 Treaty of Waitangi, and both put forward candidates who reflect the diversity of the communities they serve. The Greens, however, have less internal conflict than Labour when putting identity politics into practice.

NZ Labour defines itself as 'democratic socialist'. The first Labour government made big strides towards a universalist welfare state, and hence towards the classic social democratic goals of reducing class stratification and de-commodifying labour (Esping-Andersen, 1990). At heart, it was a *working-class* party, and 'the dignity of labour' was a core value. Over time, New Zealand fell well behind the Scandinavians in pursuing a social democratic model, and it now fits better into the 'liberal' welfare type. Indeed, the Clark government actively pursued work testing and conditionality of welfare benefits, and saw employment as the route to 'participation'. A modern Labour Party also has to address the effects of institutional racism. The Clark government shifted the emphasis towards ethnicity and away from traditional class-based analyses, to the extent of even banning the use of the word 'poverty' – there were only 'low incomes'. Ironically, it is under the Key government that official use of 'poverty' has returned. Labour's internal conflict between traditional class-based material concerns and identity politics has affected its support. The three election defeats from 2008 to 2014 may partly be attributed to a perception that Labour was too 'politically correct'. Many elderly and low-income voters were thus attracted to NZ First. In contrast, liberal middle-class voters were attracted by National's economic pragmatism and its relative openness to socially liberal causes.[3]

In spite of MMP, the traditional party duopoly of the 1935-93 era remained in place. In the four elections from 2005 to 2014, the two major parties' combined share of the party vote ranged from 72 to 80 per cent. Be it National or Labour, to win office, one of the two was expected to dominate the centre – or to win the vote of a hypothetical median voter. Each aimed to be 'a broad church' seeking to appeal to a range of communities, values and doctrines. Labour leader Andrew Little openly challenged the very idea of a political 'centre', however (Radio New Zealand, 2016). Instead he spoke of various 'communities of interest' and the material concerns they express. Whether or not he was right, it is highly unlikely that Labour will ever achieve a single-party majority. Progressive-left policies, therefore, would require a coalition between Labour and the Greens. The only other political party with a strong social justice or social movement platform – the Mana Movement – lost its sole MP, Hone Harawira, at the 2014 election due to a poorly judged pre-electoral coalition with the Internet Party.[4] Although entry hurdles for new parties are not as high in New Zealand as in some other countries, it is unlikely that any serious new contender representing the poorer and disadvantaged sectors of society will enter the fray. At the time of writing, moreover, the most recent election results and opinion polls suggest that, under New Zealand's proportional representation system, a Labour–Green coalition would not muster sufficient votes to form a majority coalition government.

Core Green electoral support tends to be urban professional or small business, and hence not all that far apart in some quarters from National supporters. By moving closer to the centre, with pragmatic ideas about sustainable business and fiscal transparency, the Greens quietly signalled that they could think the previously unthinkable and maybe support National for a term in office, given suitable policy concessions, and hence that Labour should not take them for granted. The Labour–Green agreement signed in 2016 made no commitments beyond the 2017 election. NZ First has acted as a coalition or support partner for both National and Labour in office in the past, and it can go either way. Its supporters do include many who are 'Labour-leaning', however. And, prior to the 2017 election, the Labour Party leader Andrew Little stated that his party does 'work well together' and has 'plenty of common ground' with both the Greens and New Zealand First, and that he would look to both of those parties to form a government (Tarrant, 2017).

Individuals

The choice of candidates for safe electorates or high places on the party list is inevitably the outcome of internal contest and compromise. Moreover, the leader matters greatly in elections. Although New Zealanders do not directly elect the prime minister, election campaigns, as played out in the media, give the appearance of being presidential races, primarily between the leaders of National and Labour. For many voters, an election campaign looks like a contest between those two individuals.

New Zealand Labour's history is punctuated by two main periods of progressive social democratic reform, under the first and third Labour governments (1935-49 and 1972-75, respectively). These turning points are indelibly associated with leaders who commanded deep and widespread respect. Michael Joseph Savage (Prime Minister from 1935 until his death in 1940) led Labour into its two most resounding electoral victories and oversaw the passage of the Social Security Act

1938. He was followed by Peter Fraser (Prime Minister, 1940-49). The third Labour government's larger-than-life Norman Kirk also died in office, in 1974. His successor, Bill Rowling, lacked Kirk's gravitas, and was defeated by National's Robert Muldoon the following year.

In the eight-year period from 2008 to 2015, NZ Labour had five leaders, including Helen Clark, three of whom stepped down after election defeats. Phil Goff stepped down after the 2011 defeat; his successor, David Shearer, never really 'cut through' and stepped down after months of white-anting from within the caucus. In 2012, the party adopted new rules for electing a leader, sharing the vote between the caucus (40% weighting), party membership (40%) and affiliated unions (20%). The result of the first such election in 2013 put David Cunliffe first, thanks largely to support from members and unions. Only a third of the caucus voted for him. Cunliffe has a business background, but made a pitch for the traditional left of the party, emphasising core social concerns such as child poverty. He was a controversial leader who divided left-wing opinion, and was defeated in the 2014 election. After Cunliffe's resignation and another internal election campaign, Andrew Little, formerly General-Secretary of the influential Engineers' Union, came out in front after three rounds of preferential vote distribution. It was only due to strong backing from union affiliates that Little beat Grant Robertson who was more favoured by the caucus and party members. Robertson was nonetheless rewarded with the Shadow portfolio of finance.

One of the problems with Labour's democratic process for electing their leader is that the published results leave the party open to attack. Prime Minister John Key attacked Labour over the fact that both Cunliffe and Little appeared to lack majority support from their caucus, despite being leader. NZ Labour does not have the kinds of formalised factions found in the Australian Labor Party. But internal factionalisation reached a height during the controversies over the respective leaderships of Shearer and Cunliffe in the years 2011-14. A symptom of this internal disunity is that Labour MPs campaigned at elections for their local constituencies to some extent at the expense of the crucial party vote. In 2014, Labour won 25.1 per cent of the nation-wide party vote, compared with 34.1 per cent for candidates in the electorates (Johansson and Levine, 2015). In 17 out of the 27 electorates won by Labour candidates, National won the most party votes. Many voters were loyal to their MP, who happened to belong to Labour, but split their vote and did not support Labour. Local candidates and voters did not always back the party and its leader.

There was a marked contrast, then, between Labour and National regarding leadership. Key comes from a modest background, but amassed an estimated net worth of over NZ$50 million from working in foreign exchange for Merrill Lynch. He entered Parliament in 2002 and became leader of the Opposition in 2006, and then Prime Minister in 2008. As his wealth is not inherited, supporters viewed it as something to aspire to, rather than resent. Key also undercut resentment by using a relaxed Kiwi idiom and accent. He connected well with his audience, and was not afraid to use aggressive satirical attacks on his opponents. Naturally, many on the left loathed him. But National stood consistently in the high 40s to low 50s in opinion polls, and Key led the party to three successive election victories, so his leadership was unassailable within the ranks of his party. The main electoral embarrassment for Key was the loss of the Northland by-election to Winston Peters in 2015. Otherwise, Key managed to survive numerous political scandals relatively unscathed. No one had anticipated his sudden resignation in December 2016, nor the rapid installation of his successor, Bill English.

During 2016, Andrew Little lagged behind John Key in 'preferred prime minister' opinion polls, but gained credit for improving caucus unity and bringing Labour's opinion poll ratings back over 30 per cent – only to see them fall again. As we will see in the next section, however, such unity was still vulnerable, as Labour found itself on the sharp end of wedge issues, especially the Trans-Pacific Partnership Agreement. To conclude this section, then, it is argued that exceptional leadership is not to be underestimated for electoral success and for building wider political support for social democratic policies. In the 2008-15 period, Labour suffered from an internal lack of cohesion around leadership selection and, correlatively, lacked the strategic vision that would inspire voters across a broad demographic spectrum. It also faced an unusually popular opponent.

Ideas

A major ideological fissure in contemporary Labour parties has opened up between Third Way modernisers who accept globalisation and those who wish to reinstate an egalitarian social democracy blended with contemporary identity politics. NZ Labour is no exception to this. Added to the tensions in the New Zealand case, however, is the heritage left by the fourth Labour government (1984-90). Pushed by Finance Minister Roger Douglas, that government implemented a radical programme of deregulatory free market reforms – and this continued under the subsequent National government (1990-96). As a result of this ideological switch and the shock it caused to the left, Labour suffered a significant reduction in support, leading to its defeat in 1990. By the time it recovered and won the 1999 election, Labour had fully adopted the Blair–Giddens 'Third Way' notion of a 'modernised' social democracy (Chatterjee, 1999). In New Zealand, this meant recycling the vocabulary of traditional social democracy, and nostalgic references to the first Labour government. But, on closer analysis, traditional social democracy and the Third Way had little in common. The Third Way abandoned any real commitment to full employment, preserved the basic monetarist economic paradigm, and pushed 'work-first' social policies (Duncan, 2007, p 245).

There is no shortage of social and economic battles for the left to fight, however. Growing inequalities of wealth, child poverty, precarious employment, unaffordable housing and student debt, for example, are key issues that affect New Zealand as much as they do the UK or Australia. Māori and Pasifika communities, who are traditional Labour voters, suffer ongoing social and economic disadvantages. Why is it, then, that Labour and the Greens did not succeed in rallying a wider section of New Zealand society around these significant concerns with strong leadership and credible policy?

It would be too easy to blame a cardboard cut-out version of 'neoliberalism', claiming that, vampire-like, it has become 'embedded' in policy-making orthodoxy and in the minds of a post-materialist and individualistic populace (Roper, 2011; Kelsey, 2015). What such an analysis overlooks is that elements of social democracy have become embedded and orthodox too, and that John Key's highly pragmatic politics bowed to this. Legislation introduced by the National-led government banned zero-hour contracts and extended the entitlement to paid parental leave, for instance. A National government is obviously more business-friendly, and there have been some instances of contracting out to private enterprise, for instance, in prisons. But, on the other hand, National quietly shelved its 2011 election pledge to introduce competitive private sector provision of the universal accident compensation scheme. Despite some changes around the edges, such as the introduction of a few 'charter schools', there was no longer any 'neoliberal' talk of 'vouchers' or 'free markets' in public education or healthcare. Moreover, Key pledged not to touch the universal old-age pension. Since taking office in 2008, in the midst of recession, National's Finance Minister, Bill English, restricted spending, but did not adopt an austerity policy, choosing instead to borrow and deficit-spend until 2015 (Duncan, 2014).

The relatively 'Keynesian' Key government, therefore, isolated much left critique by quietly satisfying middle-class voters that the elements of the welfare state that matter most to them would not be significantly undermined. To an extent, then, social democratic political parties may have become victims of the success of social democratic policies, if we regard such progress in terms of long-term achievements and 'embeddedness'. Although the Key government produced no effective response to some critical issues such as child poverty, the right has accepted that, in New Zealand, the state matters, politically and practically. And New Zealand can no longer be held up as 'the poster child' of neoliberalism.

Nothing illustrates Labour's ideological dilemma better than the Trans-Pacific Partnership Agreement, an economic integration and trade deal involving 12 countries including the US.[5] Opposition to it became a significant rallying point for left activism in 2015. It was argued that the negotiation process was secretive and hence undemocratic, that it would bargain away important social and environmental protections, and that the investor–state dispute resolution processes would result in the government being sued by trans-national corporations if regulation should lead to lost profits. Protests focused particularly on the perceived threat to 'sovereignty' that the Agreement posed, and this included a strong Māori voice. As some legislative amendments had to be introduced to the House in order to make New Zealand law comply with some provisions of the Agreement, Labour was forced to vote on it. This was not an easy decision, as it was under Clark's Labour-led government that New Zealand had become one of the first state parties to enter negotiations, and some leading Labour MPs spoke openly in its favour. The party chose to oppose the legislation, on the grounds that it would not properly respect New Zealand's sovereignty. But Labour's internal ideological contradiction was revealed, as a faction in the party believed that New Zealand would, on balance, be better off in the agreement rather than out of it. To illustrate the point, the former mayor of working-class Porirua, Nick Leggett, defected from Labour to National in late 2016, citing Labour's attitude towards the Agreement as one reason. As he saw it, the Labour caucus was dominated by 'utopians' who prefer to be the Opposition, as compared to 'pragmatists' like himself who were serious about government. From that viewpoint, the 2016 agreement with the Greens had pushed Labour too far to the left (Espiner, 2016).

To distinguish itself, on the other hand, Labour announced a policy of eliminating tertiary education fees. This would naturally be welcomed by families on lower incomes, but the majority of beneficiaries would be among the middle class, whose children would be relieved of accumulating fees-related debts. So this policy sought to raise support from a wide socioeconomic constituency. It could also encourage students, as first-time voters, to vote Labour. In general, though, Labour shied away from any boldly redistributive social security policies, as they may have met resistance from centrist middle-class voters if seen to benefit only the poor; furthermore, they would leave Labour vulnerable to the accusation that the party would be fiscally irresponsible in office. On the other hand, the Greens tended to adopt more redistributive policies than Labour; it was more consistent on policies that address tertiary education fees and child poverty, for example. The irony here is that it should have been NZ Labour that held the clearest focus on material inequalities, leaving the Greens to excel at policy to do with ecology and sustainability.

Conclusion

The first Labour government addressed the interests of a wide spectrum of social sectors or classes. It abandoned the socialist policy of nationalisation of land, and hence 'joined up' the interests of the small family farmer, through minimum prices for produce, and the urban worker, through social security and state houses, and the urban middle classes, through free education and subsidised healthcare. By the 1960s and 1970s, the norm for both Labour and National governments – or the ideological centre-ground – was basically social democratic, with commitments to social security and full employment.

Today the population is more urbanised and farms are more corporatised. But, following the radical neoliberal era of 1984–96, the norms for many people became low incomes, precarious employment, student debt, high rents and unaffordable house prices, and hence tougher prospects for achieving basic life goals, especially the formation of stable secure families. As freehold homeownership declines, the effectiveness of the public pension in preventing poverty will also decline, as it relies on most of those eligible having paid off a mortgage. Unequal opportunities, determined by unequal educational achievement and health status, and unequal lifelong asset accumulation, are creating a more divided society with less upward social mobility and opportunity. A progressive social democratic politics needs solutions to these social issues; it must cut through complacency among 'the commentariat' that 'things are going quite well' and that everyone is paid according to 'the value added'. Leaders such as Jeremy Corbyn and Bernie Sanders have at least revealed that there exists a young and diverse audience looking for more progressive politicians who are unafraid of attacking inequalities. But, in the period covered by this chapter, 2008–15, this kind of ideology went under-represented in New Zealand, as the dominant left-wing parties were afraid to mobilise it for fear of losing their support in the centre. The 'centre' had shifted to the right, compared with the 1970s.

Labour's neoliberal turn in the late 1980s shook voter confidence, and the subsequent 'Third Way' approach of the Clark years went only some of the way towards reinvigorating a parliamentary politics of the progressive left. Labour is not formally factionalised, but was internally divided between 'globalists' and 'protectionists'. It had not fully thrown off its neoliberal past (of the 1980s), and it was somewhat uncomfortable in its own identity politics (acquired in the 2000s). It sought to join the international movement that is taking up the fight against material inequalities, but struggled to find an inspiring policy mix that addresses work and productivity in a digitised economy and that will not be branded as old-fashioned 'cloth-cap socialism'. Most of its MPs are university-educated professionals, and yet it must strive to represent and inspire those who do not share in such cultural capital. The MMP electoral system has allowed the Greens and NZ First to flourish on either side of Labour, thus splitting the left vote across the three parties. Having bled support to both, Labour was then unable to contend for office without at least one of them – if not both of them – the latter implying an awkward three-party agreement or coalition. The nightmare long-term scenario for Labour would resemble Germany's social democrats or Spain's socialists, supporting their erstwhile centre-right opponents in office – the alternative being another bruising election. Things have not even approached that dilemma in New Zealand, but a fractured left was beaten in three straight elections by a centre-right party whose success was in no small part attributable to a gradual and pragmatic claiming of the left's social policies. How can the left win when if it presents such a soft target?

The electoral surge for Labour in the 2017 election, under the leadership of Jacinda Ardern, was partly at the expense of the Greens. It resembled the rise of UK Labour under Corbyn earlier that year, however. It showed that the left's fortunes can revive, and that leadership makes the difference.

Notes

1 Since the break-up of the National/NZ First coalition in 1998, this kind of governing arrangement has become the norm in New Zealand, including under National from 2008. For more details on the different kinds of agreements in practice, see Boston (2009).

2 New Zealanders of Māori descent can choose to enrol on either the general or the Māori electoral roll. As of November 2016, the Electoral Commission reported 3,129,839 registered electors, comprising 2,895,293 on the general roll and 234,546 (7.5% of the total) on the Māori roll.

3 For example, in 2013, on a personal vote, 27 National MPs, including John Key, voted in favour of marriage equality for same-sex couples, and 32 against, at its final reading. The Bill passed overall by 77 ayes and 44 noes.

4 However, Harawira indicated that he and the Mana Movement would contest the 2017 election.

5 President Trump withdrew the US from the Agreement soon after taking office in 2017.

References

Boston, J. (2009) 'Innovative political management: Multi-party governance in New Zealand', *Policy Quarterly*, vol 5, no 2, pp 52-9.

Chapman, J. and Duncan, G. (2007) 'Is there now a new "New Zealand model"?', *Public Management Review*, vol 9, no 1, pp 1-25.

Chatterjee, S. (1999) *The new politics: A third way for New Zealand*, Palmerston North: Dunmore Press.

Duncan, G. (2007) *Society and politics: New Zealand social policy*, Auckland: Pearson Education.

Duncan, G. (2014) 'After neo-liberalism, what could be worse?', *New Zealand Sociology*, vol 29, no 1, pp 15-39.

Electoral Commission (2015) *Report of the Electoral Commission on the 2014 General Election*, Wellington: Electoral Commission.

Espiner, G. (2016) 'Wellington politics: The pragmatic Mr Nick Leggett', *The Listener*, 5 October, www.noted.co.nz/currently/politics/wellington-politics-the-pragmatic-mr-nick-leggett/

Esping-Andersen, G. (1990) *The three worlds of welfare capitalism*, Cambridge: Polity Press.

Feinberg-Danieli, G. and Lafferty, G. (2007) 'Unions and union membership in New Zealand: Annual review for 2006', *New Zealand Journal of Employment Relations*, vol 32, no 3, pp 31-9.

Franks, P. and McAloon, J. (2016) *Labour: The New Zealand Labour Party 1916-2016*, Wellington: Victoria University Press.

Johansson, J. and Levine, S. (2015) *Moments of truth: The New Zealand general election of 2014*, Wellington: Victoria University Press.

Kelsey, J. (2002) *At the crossroads: Three essays*, Wellington: Bridget Williams Books.

Kelsey, J. (2015) *The FIRE economy: New Zealand's reckoning*, Wellington: Bridget Williams Books.

Radio New Zealand (2016) '"I don't know what the centre is" – Andrew Little', *Nine to Noon*, 8 December, www.radionz.co.nz/national/programmes/ninetonoon/audio/201826910/i-don't-know-what-the-centre-is-andrew-little

Roper, B. (2011) 'The fifth (key) National Government's neoliberal policy agenda: Description, analysis and critical evaluation', *New Zealand Sociology*, vol 26, no 1, pp 12-40.

Shor, F. (2002) 'Bringing the storm: Syndicalist counterpublics and the industrial workers of the world in New Zealand, 1908-14', in P. Moloney and K. Taylor (eds) *On the Left: Essays on socialism in New Zealand*, Dunedin: Otago University Press, pp 59-72.

Tarrant, A. (2017) 'A Labour-Greens-NZ First coalition would be a "very good government" for NZ, Andrew Little says', interest.co.nz, 4 July, www.interest.co.nz/news/88615/labour-greens-nz-first-coalition-would-be-very-good-government-nz-andrew-little-says

FIVE

Australian social democracy: capitalist constraints and the challenges of equality

Carol Johnson

It will be argued in this chapter that the experience of the Australian Rudd and Gillard governments (2007-13) reflects deeper problems faced by social democratic governments, and that the Australian experience therefore has relevance for social democracy internationally.[1] In particular, an analysis of why the left (so often) loses in Australia needs to look not just at specific national features but also at longer-term problems and dilemmas that social democracy has faced in regard to managing capitalist economies and attempting to mitigate diverse forms of inequality. This chapter therefore focuses on the attempts of the Australian Rudd and Gillard governments to tackle some of these issues. In doing so, it does not aim to give detailed analyses of their legislative programmes, nor the multiple factors that contributed to their electoral difficulties.[2] Rather, given the focus of this collection, it intends to concentrate on identifying some key issues that have a broader relevance.

Institutional factors and democratic constraints

At first sight, Australian political institutions should provide favourable contexts for electing social democratic governments. Indeed, Australia was a pioneer of electoral reforms (Sawer, 2001) that facilitated working-class voting. Australia elected its first state Labor government in 1899 and a (brief) federal Labor government in 1904, thereby arguably forming both the first Labor government anywhere in the world and also the first national one (Murphy, 1971; McMullin, 2006). Nonetheless, the issue of 'why the left loses' is particularly relevant for Australia. Despite such a promising start, as of the 2016 election, Labor had won only 14 of the 45 federal elections held since Australia became a nation in 1901.

Consequently, it is worth noting that Australia's political institutions have also posed some difficulties for Labor nationally. A preferential voting system helped keep Labor out of power in the 1950s and 1960s when the preferences of a conservative, Catholic-influenced, anti-Communist party formed after a split in Labor assisted the Liberal Party (Australia's equivalent of the British Conservatives) in winning office. However, in more recent years the preferential voting system has allowed preferences from left-wing voters, such as Greens supporters, to flow to Labor for key House of Representatives seats, where the government is formed, thereby partly compensating for a major drop in Labor's primary vote, and making Labor's electoral competition with other parties marginally less of an issue than in first-past-the-post systems such as Britain's (see, for example, Bale, 2015, pp 268-9). Nonetheless, Australia's proportional representation system in the Senate has facilitated the election of minor party and independents to the Upper House because of the small proportion of votes required to fill a Senate quota.[3] As we shall see, Labor governments have sometimes faced problems with enacting their legislative agenda when the Greens hold the balance of power in the Senate.

There have also been institutional issues with the internal structure of the Labor Party. The ongoing influence of affiliated unions in the Labor Party, which still accounts for 50 per cent of elected delegates, has been used by right-wing opponents to suggest that Labor is union-dominated, although the extent of union influence has been disputed (see Markey, 2016). Up until 2013, Labor leaders (including prime ministers) could be replaced by a simple vote of Labor politicians (the Federal Parliamentary Labor Party, or FPLP). Factional leaders, often closely associated with influential unions affiliated to the Labor Party, did influence how some politicians voted.[4] As we shall see, this structural issue contributed to significant leadership instability when Labor governments faced difficulties during the Rudd and Gillard period. Under new Constitutional rules, the leader is elected by both Labor politicians and the general party membership, with both having equal weight (ALP, 2015, p 20). Under a 2013 FPLP decision, such an election could only be triggered by a leader resigning, an election loss or 75 per cent of federal Labor politicians petitioning for a leadership change when in government and 60 per cent when in Opposition. However, these latter provisions were not enshrined in the Labor Party's Constitution.

Importantly, the Australian Labor Party (ALP) has also faced more fundamental challenges, common to social democratic parties internationally, that arise from the nature of liberal democratic institutions in capitalist societies – liberal democracy both enables the election of social democratic governments and puts constraints on their power. While liberal democracy provides absolutely crucial freedoms of speech and association and electoral rights, the actual practice of representative democracy is largely confined to the parliamentary sphere and severely limited in the economic sphere. For example, there is a lack of workplace democracy, a lack of control over decisions made by private companies and (especially in English-speaking countries) limits to the degree to which it is seen as desirable for the state to interfere in the private sector, either via regulation or public sector provision.

Consequently, social democracy has always battled with the constraints of managing a capitalist economy. As Adam Przeworski, among others, has pointed out, private enterprise has a privileged and powerful position in capitalist economies (Przeworski, 1985, pp 7-46, 139). Such economies largely depend on private investment in order to employ workers. That investment in turn depends on the profitability of the private sector. So governments need to ensure private profitability, and thereby face structural constraints when it comes to regulating, taxing or replacing the private sector, or ensuring excellent pay and working conditions. Measures that are seen as too adverse by the private sector can result in capital strikes in respect to new investment, threats to move investment offshore to more favourable regimes and well-funded campaigns against proposed reforming legislation. Not only will governments then appear to be poor economic managers, but, more importantly, they also risk losing the support of a significant proportion of voters whose employment depends, directly or indirectly, on the relative prosperity of the private sector.

Overall, private enterprise has a structural position in the economy that provides it with tremendous power that reforming social democratic governments have to negotiate. Arguably, it is these constraints, rather than, as Escalona et al suggest, a particularly benign post-war period of capitalism, that helps explain the lack of fundamental transformation of capitalist political and economic structures (Escalona et al, 2013, pp 15-16). Berman (2006) is correct to identify a belief in the primacy of politics as a key feature of social democracy. However, Berman doesn't adequately address the economic constraints, including economic power relations and opposition from capital, that social democratic parties may encounter when they try to exercise their political will. Furthermore, many of the problems governments are forced to deal with result from economic factors that are often largely out of a national government's control, including the impact of international economic crises on government revenue and private sector employment, competition from industries in countries with lower levels of wages and regulation, and the investment decisions made by footloose international capital.

Ideology, practice and structural constraints

From the mid-20th century on, social democratic governments, particularly in the English-speaking world, have had two main economic strategies for attempting to negotiate those economic structural constraints (both involving a partial denial of the structural power of capital). One is to embrace broadly Keynesian-influenced strategies that argue that state action and the public sector can be highly beneficial to the private sector, particularly in times of economic downturn. The state is therefore justified in going into temporary deficit when required, but also in ensuring that it has sufficient revenue. In this view, the state can assist the private sector by helping to smooth out the cycles of boom and bust that plague capitalist economies, and there is therefore a perceived harmony of interests between the public and private sectors. For example, state intervention can help to keep up levels of consumption of private sector goods in times of economic downturn through providing adequate welfare income for the unemployed, employing people in public works and, if necessary, directly releasing money to consumers. The Curtin and Chifley Labor governments of 1941 to 1949 played a central role in introducing such Keynesian-influenced policies to Australia (see Battin, 1997, pp 33-51). As we shall see, the Rudd and Gillard governments of 2007-13 were also influenced by Keynesianism.

The second way in which social democrats have tried to deal with (and sometimes wish away) the problem of capitalist structural constraints is via the partial embrace of neoliberal arguments that draw on the arguments of Keynes' free market opponents. In this view, which the Hawke and Keating Labor governments (1983-96) played a major role in introducing to Australia, also influencing Blairite conceptions of the Third Way, market mechanisms were not seen as being in fundamental tension with social democracy's egalitarian objectives (Scott, 2000; Johnson and Tonkiss, 2002; Manwaring, 2014, pp 85-102). On the contrary, it was argued that market mechanisms could help constrain the power of capital (by ensuring competition between capitalists) and market delivery mechanisms could be used to provide egalitarian outcomes. Governments should therefore restrict their role and government debt while facilitating markets via deregulation and privatisation (see, for example, Keating, 1993; Johnson, 2011; Latham,

2003; Escalona et al, 2013, p 17). However, as we shall see, endorsing such views on the benefits of markets can then pose policy legitimation problems for subsequent Labor governments.

Labor governments and the economy in practice, 2007-13: Ideas and leadership

The experience of the Rudd and Gillard governments illustrates that such longer-term problems and dilemmas about how to manage a capitalist economy are not abstract ones. Indeed, it will be argued below that they were one of the factors that contributed to the leadership instability that plagued Labor during the Rudd and Gillard years. Admittedly, other factors that contributed to that leadership included party rules that made it relatively easy to remove a Labor prime minister, sometimes legitimate concerns about both Rudd and Gillard's performance, by negative poll results and the relentless campaigning of an often hostile media.[5]

Unfortunately for their successors, a consequence of Hawke and Keating's turn to the market was that it helped to undermine a central argument as to why one needed social democratic governments. The traditional role of social democracy had been to mitigate the effects of markets by humanising capitalism, including by lessening inequality (Marliere, 2014, p 99). Underlying that mission was the belief that markets needed regulating because otherwise they led to injustice, hardship, cycles of boom and recession and market failure. Consequently, suggesting that market mechanisms were allies in the fight for social justice and social inclusion made it much harder to argue that social democratic governments had an important role to play in reforming modern societies, particularly in tackling the forms of structural inequality that arose from capitalist markets, even in times of high economic growth.

Rudd was less enamoured with free market-influenced policies than Hawke and Keating. He had provided significant critiques of extreme neoliberalism before coming into office, arguing that it reduced essential health, education and welfare services and increased inequality (Rudd, 2006a, 2006b). Nonetheless, given the ongoing influence of neoliberal ideas on voters' views, Rudd declared during the 2007 election that he would be a 'fiscal conservative' – although he added the important (Keynesian-influenced) rider that he would balance the budget across the business cycle (ALP, 2007). Soon after coming into office, the Rudd government's resolve to balance budgets was sorely tested by the global financial crisis (GFC). The government resorted to a Keynesian-influenced counter-cyclical policy, which Joseph Stiglitz has described as 'one of the best-designed Keynesian stimulus packages of any country' (Stiglitz, 2010).[6]

However, Labor had great difficulty convincing the Australian electorate that it was necessary to increase debt in order to fund a stimulus package. This was despite the stimulus helping to prevent the Australian economy going into recession; despite the size of the deficit being partly due to major falls in revenue; and despite the government's debt being relatively low internationally (see, for example, Swan, 2012; Rudd, 2013). Labor's task was made all the harder by the previous Hawke and Keating governments' embrace of economic rationalist agendas that had reinforced key aspects of neoliberal arguments against government debt. Labor's 'budget crisis' and perceived poor economic management were to be major election issues in both the 2010 and 2013 elections (Wanna and Simms, 2012; Johnson and Wanna with Lee, 2015).

Meanwhile, Labor's difficulties in addressing government debt issues were exacerbated by the opposition they encountered from business when attempting to increase tax revenue. The mining industry mounted a $22 million public relations campaign against the government's attempts to introduce a mining super profits tax, which contributed to the (multiple) pressures on Prime Minister Kevin Rudd's leadership (Davis, 2011). When Rudd was subsequently replaced by Julia Gillard in June 2010, key Labor ministers tried to neutralise business opposition quickly by negotiating compromise measures, which resulted in a massive drop in revenue (Cleary, 2012, p 188).[7]

The Rudd Labor government had also faced major opposition to its climate change policies when attempting to tackle the market's failure to price carbon, especially given the carbon-intensive nature of Australia's economy. Labor's initial attempt to bring in a carbon price-based emissions trading scheme (which would also have raised revenue) had been carefully negotiated with sympathetic sections of business and the then leader of the Opposition, Malcolm Turnbull. However, it was defeated in the Senate by a combination of left-wing and right-wing opposition. The right-wing opposition included opponents from carbon-intensive industries such as coal mining and climate sceptics in the Liberal Party who opposed increased 'taxes' and government intervention in markets (despite the market mechanisms underlying an emissions trading scheme). The internal Liberal Party opponents succeeded in removing Turnbull as leader and replacing him with a more socially conservative, and climate change sceptic leader, Tony Abbott. The left-wing opposition included politicians from the Greens (elected under the Senate system discussed previously), who argued that Labor had sold out to big business by having overly low carbon reduction targets and providing too much compensation for industries detrimentally impacted by a carbon price (Australian Greens, 2010).

Yet Labor's policy reflected the difficulties in managing a capitalist economy. The temporary compensation packages for business aimed to facilitate workers transitioning to employment elsewhere. Although Labor's carbon reduction targets were modest to begin with, Climate Change Minister Penny Wong was following a social democratic strategy that would enable the government to incrementally increase them, while trying to reduce business opposition and keep up employment levels (Wong, 2009). Nonetheless, Rudd's failure to deliver on climate change policy promises contributed to plummeting opinion poll results (Graetz and Manning, 2012, pp 291-2). Meanwhile Opposition Leader Abbott argued that the ETS (emissions trading scheme) was a great big green tax that would impact detrimentally on ordinary voters, and repeatedly tried to suggest that Labor was selling out its traditional supporters on green issues (Abbott, 2010). Rudd's falling opinion poll results exacerbated internal opposition from Labor politicians who were already concerned by a leadership style that was seen to be erratic, not consultative, indecisive and increasingly lacking in communication skills.

However, Rudd's replacement, Julia Gillard, was unable to win the 2010 election outright (Wanna and Simms, 2012), resulting in a hung Parliament. In order to get Greens' support to form government, Gillard brought in a (relatively high) carbon price in the lead up to an emissions tradition scheme. Despite having pledged that there would be no carbon tax under any government she led, Gillard was unwise enough to state that the carbon price was effectively a tax. Abbott now argued that Labor was not only betraying its working-class voters by bringing in such a tax, but that Gillard was a liar as well. Meanwhile the Greens-influenced carbon price proved high compared with international market prices, thereby deepening business opposition (Lane, 2011).

In a revolving door leadership, Gillard was replaced as leader and prime minister by Rudd in June 2013, after falling opinion poll results and arguments that she was failing to connect with voters. Rudd went on to lose the subsequent 2013 election with the impact of the carbon 'tax' on ordinary voters (despite generous compensation packages) being a key issue, combined with accusations of poor economic management (Johnson and Wanna, with Lee, 2015). Abbott claimed that 'Mr Rudd is prepared to sell the soul of the Labor party to the greens in order to realise his own ambitions' (*Daily Telegraph*, 2013). This is despite the fact that the Rudd Labor government had repealed legislation brought in by the previous Howard Liberal government that had attacked unions, pay and working conditions, and had reinstituted many essential protections – even if it had not gone quite as far as some unions wished (Johnson, 2011, pp 577-8). Environmental issues have continued to be used as 'wedge' issues by the Conservative parties, with suggestions that Labor has deserted its traditional blue-collar base to support inner-city 'trendy' environmental issues. During the 2016 election campaign, which Labor also lost, the Liberal Party released an election video suggesting that the Labor Party had been infiltrated by a secret third force of Greens supporters (Liberal Party of Australia, 2016).

The difficulties of managing capitalist markets, business opposition and forces on the left and right of Labor had been graphically illustrated by the governments' experiences described above, which neither Keynesian nor neoliberal-influenced policies could have resolved. Such problems are only likely to increase in future with the impact of technological disruption on economies and jobs, combined with the challenges that the changing geoeconomics of globalisation, especially in the Asian Century, pose to Western economies. The Rudd and Gillard governments' experiences also highlight Labor's difficulties in crafting a narrative that appealed to traditional Labor voters while facing the challenges of the 21st century that went beyond simple constructions of class issues, to environmental and social justice issues. The discussion now turns to an analysis of these problems and dilemmas.

Labor and inequality

The problems social democratic governments have traditionally had in managing capitalist economies have been described above. However, capitalist class relations are not the only inequitable social power relations that social democracy has had to deal with. There are also relations of gender, sexuality, race and ethnicity, among others. It is sometimes implied that these dilemmas constitute new, late 20th-century 'cultural' ones (see, for example, Cramme and Diamond, 2012, p 253; Painter, 2013, pp 97-128, 225-7). In fact, many of these forms of inequality (for example, gender and race) have economic dimensions. Furthermore, while the rise of 20th-century social movements and the impact of globalisation may be influencing the forms these issues currently take, they are far from new.

Originally social democratic parties largely attempted to deal with these broader social power relations by privileging the white, male, heterosexual, working-class head of household, who was seen as *the* citizen whom social democracy focused on supporting, with benefits and entitlements flowing to their wives and children largely at second hand. In other words, it is important to acknowledge that dominant forms of traditional social democracy played a role in reinforcing crucial forms of inequality, despite long-standing struggles within the social democratic movement to make it more inclusive, for example, struggles by feminists (Liddington and Norris, 1978, pp 231-51; Lake, 1992). Not only is Australia a colonial settler society, but ALP supported the White Australia policy, which quite explicitly excluded non-white immigration in the 20th century, with the last vestiges of the policy being removed by the Whitlam Labor government in the early 1970s (Watson, 1901; Lake and Reynolds, 2008). In short, social democracy has long been a site of contest over both whether the diverse identities of the working class itself will be recognised (for example, in terms of gender, race and sexuality), and whether broader forms of inequality that are additional to, and go beyond, class oppression will be addressed.

Conservative forces have frequently exploited such differences and social power relations. In Australia, during the Howard years (1996-2007), Labor faced particularly explicit attempts to wedge off socially conservative voters. Howard argued that the exploitation of ordinary Australians had been happening not at the level of the market but of the state. He alleged that politically correct special interest groups (such as gender or racial ones) had been ripping off ordinary taxpayers' funds under Labor governments via state largesse (Johnson, 2007, p 180). Up until recently, Labor was so afraid of such Howard-style neoliberal wedges that, despite support for some indigenous, same-sex or gender equality policies while in government, Labor tended to pursue 'small target' election campaigns when it came to progressive social issues.

Labor is still concerned about being 'wedged' on asylum-seeker issues, and remains supportive of policies of boat turn-backs and offshore processing that have been strongly condemned by the United Nations among others. However, with the exception of its asylum-seeker policies, Labor rejected small target strategies for the 2016 election. Rather, a major Labor narrative revolved around the argument that the role of social democratic governments is to tackle multiple forms of inequality. Consequently, Labor leader Bill Shorten made strong statements in support of multiculturalism, indigenous, gender and same-sex equality, including same-sex marriage, during the 2016 election campaign (Shorten, 2016b, 2016c, 2016d; ALP, no date).

Labor has tried to reconcile its support for addressing diverse forms of inequality by arguing that increased equality is better for economic growth, in large part because it ensures adequate consumption levels (ALP, 2016; Shorten 2016c). In other words, the implication is that increased equality benefits everyone, including blue-collar workers, and that economic security will therefore help to prevent social divisiveness, including on issues such as immigration (Shorten, 2016a). Such arguments are a clear attempt to counter the type of neoliberal arguments that Howard and others have promoted.

Nonetheless, given that some social power relations transcend class or economics, social democrats in Australia, as elsewhere, still have the problem of how to reconcile previously powerful social groups (such as white, heterosexual men) to a potential loss of power and privilege (not least when, in the case of some traditional supporters, they may be facing economic uncertainties as well). As votes for Brexit, Trump and Pauline Hanson in Australia have shown, some sections of the working class seem prepared to embrace the exclusionary practices of the past in order to shore up their own position in response to job losses resulting from globalisation and fears of major international people movements. Furthermore, Labor's underestimation of the importance of socially conservative positions on issues such as gender was reflected in the fact that Labor powerbrokers did not adequately anticipate the ways in which her gender would be mobilised against Prime Minister Julia Gillard, particularly after she had overthrown first-term Labor Prime Minister Kevin Rudd in a leadership coup (see Johnson, 2015).

Labor's attempts to use its equality agenda to reconnect with its working-class base in the 2016 election, including by arguing that Liberal Prime Minister Turnbull was too close to the big end of town, also led to accusations that it was anti-business. Turnbull claimed that Labor was 'setting up an anti-business, high-taxing high-spending, big borrowing program that will put our economy backwards. It will put our economy into reverse. It will put the jobs of every Australian at risk' (Turnbull, 2016). Labor's ability to manage a capitalist economy was once again being called into question in a way that potentially scared voters and drew on neoliberal arguments that Labor itself had once partly embraced. Labor was beaten yet again (albeit narrowly).

Conclusion

George Ross has noted the tendency of voters in Europe 'to remove incumbents when they cannot provide convincing answers to today's very real and sometimes intractable problems' (Ross, 2013, p 603).

The removal of Prime Minister Rudd in order to replace him with Julia Gillard and then going back to Rudd was an example of Labor pre-emptively anticipating the voters' tendency to do this. However, this chapter has suggested that some of the problems both Gillard and Rudd faced were related not just to individual leadership flaws on their part, but also to longer-term ideational and structural dilemmas and problems.

In particular, it would be unfortunate to neglect the influence of some deeper and longer-term challenges that social democratic governments face, whether that be managing a capitalist economy or difficulties involved in managing the different forms of inequality and social power relations that exist in contemporary societies. Those challenges also intersect with institutional issues regarding the nature of liberal democracy. They have implications for the articulation of ideas, particularly Labor's ability to develop a simple and coherent narrative. Neoliberal ideology may claim that the market is the solution to all major problems, but social democracy neither can, nor should, offer such simplistic and mono-causal policy prescriptions. Perhaps it is time to have a more serious discussion with the electorate about precisely how difficult Labor's policy task can be, as part of a process of trying to develop better policy prescriptions.

After all, neither Keynesian nor neoliberal-influenced attempts have succeeded in wishing away the difficulties in managing capitalist economies (even if Keynesian policies have generally resulted in more egalitarian outcomes than neoliberal ones). Instead, they have left a legacy of dashed hopes and unrealistic expectations that have impacted negatively on electoral outcomes. Nor has social democracy's transition from traditionally reinforcing the inequalities of gender, race and sexuality to challenging them been an unproblematic one. On the contrary, it remains necessary to not just emphasise the intersectional diversity and interests of the working class itself, but also to make the case afresh as to why a social democratic commitment to building a better society involves challenging multiple forms of inequality. There are no easy solutions. However, it is important to identify the problems if social democratic governments are to hope to address them.

As a former Labor Cabinet minister, who has held both the climate change and finance minister portfolios, as well as being a major advocate for gender, racial and same-sex equality, stated, 'One of the things I have learnt – I think we all have learnt – is just how hard reform ... can be' (Wong, 2011). It is clearly not inevitable that Labor loses, or we would not have had reforming Labor governments. However, it does seem inevitable that the task of social democratic governments will always be a very difficult and complex one.

Notes

1 This chapter incorporates some material produced as part of an Australian Research Council (ARC)-funded project (DP140100168) entitled 'Expanding equality: A historical perspective on developments and dilemmas in contemporary Australian social democracy.'

2 See, for example, Johnson and Wanna, with Lee (2015), for a detailed analysis of the multiple factors leading to the electoral defeat of the final Rudd Labor government.

3 The quota to obtain a Senate seat is normally 14.29 per cent in a half Senate election, although this reduces even further to 7.69 per cent on the rare occasions when the whole of the Senate stands for election. On Australia's voting system, see Ward (2012, pp 171-2, 195-197) and the Australian Electoral Commission (2016) on the latest changes to preferential voting in the Senate.

4 Further information on the role of factions is given in Chapter 6 on state Labor governments.

5 On the important role of leadership in state Labor governments, see Chapter 6.

6 Arguably the Rudd government's strategy was much more Keynesian than that of its British counterpart; see Marliere (2014, p 105).

7 In May 2010, the Resource Super Profits Tax had been projected to generate a total of $3 billion in revenue by 2012-13, but projections were reduced to a mere $200 million by the 2013-14 Budget Papers. See Swoboda (no date).

References

Abbott, T. (2010) 'Address to the 2010 Federal Coalition campaign launch', http://pandora.nla.gov.au/pan/22487/20100812-0044/www.tonyabbott.com.au/LatestNews/Speeches/tabid/88/articleType/ArticleView/articleId/7569/Address-to-the-2010-Federal-Coalition-Campaign-Launch.html

AEC (Australian Electoral Commission) (2016) 'Voting for the Senate', www.aec.gov.au/Voting/How_to_vote/Voting_Senate.htm and 'Counting the votes for the Senate', www.aec.gov.au/voting/counting/senate_count.htm

ALP (Australian Labor Party) (no date) 'Marriage equality: Labor will legislate for marriage equality within the first 100 days of the next parliament', www.100positivepolicies.org.au/marriage_equality

ALP (2007) 'Kevin Rudd: Economic conservative', Election advertisement, Australian Labor Party TV, www.youtube.com/watch?v=lQN_btzkg0U

ALP (2015) National Constitution, adopted on 26 July 2015, https://cdn.australianlabor.com.au/documents/ALP_National_Constitution.pdf

ALP (2016) 'Growing together, Labor's agenda for tackling inequality', www.alp.org.au/growing_together

Australian Greens (2010) 'The Greens and emissions trading – your questions answered', 14 January, http://greensmps.org.au/content/news-stories/greens-and-emissions-trading-%E2%80%93-your-questions-answered#cantsupportCPRS

Bale, T. (2015) *Five year mission: The Labour Party under Ed Miliband*, Oxford: Oxford University Press.

Battin, T. (1997) *Abandoning Keynes: Australia's capital mistake*, Basingstoke: Macmillan.

Berman, S. (2006) *The primacy of politics: Social democracy and the making of Europe's twentieth century*, Cambridge: Cambridge University Press.

Cleary, P. (2012) *Mine-field: The dark side of Australia's resources rush*, Melbourne, VIC: Black Inc.

Cramme, O. and Diamond, P. (2012) 'Afterward: The new social democracy', in O. Cramme and P. Diamond (eds) *After the Third Way: The future of social democracy in Europe*, London: I.B. Tauris & Co, pp 251-4.

Davis, M. (2011) 'A snip at $22m to get rid of PM', *The Sydney Morning Herald*, 2 February, www.smh.com.au/business/a-snip-at-22m-to-get-rid-of-pm-20110201-1acgj.html

Daily Telegraph (2013) 'Tony Abbott banishes the greens from the lower house', 14 August, www.dailytelegraph.com.au/news/nsw/tony-abbott-banishes-the-greens-from-the-lower-house/story-fni0cx12-1226696646808

Escalona, F., Vieira, M. and de Waele, J. (2013) 'The unfinished history of the social democratic family', in J. de Waele, F. Escalona and M. Vieira (eds) *The Palgrave handbook of social democracy in the European Union*, Basingstoke: Palgrave Macmillan, pp 3–32.

Graetz, G. and Manning H. (2012)'Environmental issues and the 2010 Campaign', in J. Wanna and M. Simms (eds) *Julia 2010: The caretaker election*, Canberra, ACT: ANU Press, pp 291-302.

Johnson, C. (2007) *Governing change: From Keating to Howard*, Perth, WA: Network Books.

Johnson, C. (2011) 'Gillard, Rudd and Labor tradition', *Australian Journal of Politics and History*, vol 57, no 4, pp 562-79.

Johnson, C. (2015) 'Playing the gender card: The uses and abuses of gender in Australian Politics', *Politics & Gender*, vol 11, no 2, pp 291-319.

Johnson, C. and Tonkiss, F. (2002) 'The third influence: The Blair government and Australian Labor', *Policy & Politics*, vol 30, no 1, pp 5-18.

Johnson, C., Wanna, J., with Lee, S.-A. (eds) (2015) *Abbott's gambit: The 2013 Australian federal election*, Canberra, ACT: ANU Press.

Keating, P. (1993) 'Election ALP policy speech', http://electionspeeches. moadoph.gov.au/speeches/1993-paul-keating

Lake, M. (1992) 'The independence of women and the brotherhood of man: Debates in the labour movement over equal pay and motherhood endowment in the 1920s', *Labour History*, vol 63, pp 1-24.

Lake, M. and Reynolds, H. (2008) *Drawing the global colour line: White men's countries and the international challenge of racial equality*, Melbourne, VIC: Melbourne University Publishing.

Lane, S. (2011) 'Industry launches anti-carbon tax campaign', 21 July, www.abc.net.au/news/2011-07-21/industry-group-steps-up-carbon-ads/2803794

Latham, M. (2003) 'Competitive capitalism versus crony capitalism: The difference between Labor and Liberal' 19 August, www.smh.com.au/articles/2003/08/19/1061261153599.html

Liberal Party of Australia (2016) 'The greening of Labor', www.youtube.com/watch?v=eA4Me7X5Blw

Liddington, J. and Norris, J. (1978) *One hand tied behind us: The rise of the women's Suffrage Movement*, London: Virago.

Manwaring, R.P. (2014) *The search for democratic renewal: The politics of consultation in Britain and Australia*, Manchester: Manchester University Press.

Markey, R. (2016) 'How the influence of the unions on the Labor Party is overestimated', *The Conversation*, 27 April, https://theconversation.com/how-the-influence-of-trade-unions-on-the-labor-party-is-overestimated-57476

Marliere, P. (2014) 'Coping with TINA: The Labour Party and the new crisis of capitalism', in D. Bailey et al (eds) *European social democracy during the global economic crisis: Renovation or resignation*, Manchester: Manchester University Press, pp 99–118.

McMullin, R. (2006) 'Australia's Watson Labor government', Democratic experiments: Lectures in the Senate, Occasional Lecture Series 2004-2005, www.aph.gov.au/binaries/senate/pubs/pops/pop44/mcmullin.pdf

Murphy, D.J. (1971) 'The Dawson government in Queensland, the first Labour government in the world', *Labour History*, vol 20, pp 1-8.

Painter, A. (2013) *Left without a future? Social justice in anxious times*, London: I.B. Taurus.

Przeworski, A. (1985) *Capitalism and social democracy*, Cambridge: Cambridge University Press.

Ross, G. (2013) 'Social democrats today: Tribe, extended family, or club?', in J. de Waele, F. Escalona and M. Vieira (eds) *The Palgrave handbook of social democracy in the European Union*, Basingstoke: Palgrave Macmillan, pp 593–604.

Rudd, K. (2006a) 'Address to the Centre for Independent Studies', 16 November, http://pandora.nla.gov.au/pan/38035/20061201-0000/www.kevinrudd.com/_dbase_upl/061116%20CIS.pdf

Rudd, K. (2006b) 'Howard's Brutopia: The battle of ideas in Australian politics', *The Monthly*, November, pp 46–50.

Rudd, K. (2013) 'The Australian economy in transition: Building a new national competitiveness agenda', 11 July, http://pandora.nla.gov.au/pan/79983/20130830-1433/www.pm.gov.au/press-office/address-national-press-club.html

Sawer, M. (ed) (2001) *Elections, full, free and fair*, Sydney, NSW: The Federation Press.

Scott, A. (2000) *Running on empty*, Sydney, NSW: Pluto Press.

Shorten, B. (2016a) 'Doorstop – Townsville – Saturday, 25 June 2016', www.billshorten.com.au/doorstop_townsville_saturday_25_june_2016

Shorten, B. (2016b) 'Only Labor will champion the march to gender equality', 11 June, www.billshorten.com.au/only_labor_will_champion_the_march_to_gender_equality

Shorten, B. (2016c) 'Q&A, Penrith', www.abc.net.au/tv/qanda/txt/s4454321.htm

Shorten, B. (2016d) 'Reconciliation Australia Dinner, Address', Melbourne, 27 May, www.billshorten.com.au/address_to_the_reconciliation_australia_dinner_melbourne_friday_27_may_2016

Stiglitz, J. (2010) 'In praise of stimulus', *The Sydney Morning Herald*, 9 August, www.smh.com.au/business/in-praise-of-stimulus-20100808-11q8e.html

Swan, W. (2012) 'The budget and the fair go in the Asian Century', National Press Club Post-Budget Address, 9 May, Parliament House, Canberra, http://ministers.treasury.gov.au/DisplayDocs.aspx?doc=speeches/2012/010.htm&pageID=005&min=wms&Year=&DocType=1

Swoboda, K. (no date) 'Revised revenue projections and associated expenditure for the Minerals Resource Rent Tax (MRRT)', Parliamentary Library, www.aph.gov.au/About_Parliament/Parliamentary_Departments/Parliamentary_Library/pubs/rp/BudgetReview201314/MRRT

Turnbull, M. (2016) 'Doorstop, Sunshine Coast, Qld', 11 June, www.malcolmturnbull.com.au/media/doorstop-sunshine-coast-qld

Wanna, J. and Simms, M. (eds) (2012) *Julia 2010: The caretaker election*, Canberra, ACT: ANU Press.

Ward, A. (2012) *Parliamentary government in Australia*, Melbourne, VIC: Australian Scholarly Publishing,

Watson, J.C. (1901) 'Immigration Restriction Bill', Full day's *Hansard*, Friday 6 September, p 4635.

Wong, P. (2009) '2020 targets are only the first step', 23 February, *The Sydney Morning Herald*, www.smh.com.au/news/opinion/2020-targets-are-only-the-firststep/2009/02/22/1235237449799.html?page=fullpage#contentSwap1

Wong, P. (2011) 'Q&A transcript', 11 April, www.abc.net.au/tv/qanda/txt/s3182043.htm

SIX

Exit left: the case of Australian state Labor

Rob Manwaring

Introduction

The Australian Labor Party (ALP) is a distinctive case of social democracy. As Carol Johnson outlines in her chapter in this volume (Chapter 5), the case of federal Labor offers key insights into the plight of the centre-left more generally. The ALP case is striking because it was one of the earliest centre-left parties to implement neoliberal reforms. However, what is often over-looked in the Australian case is the story of state (Labor) governments.

This chapter is a corrective to this narrative that marginalises the sub-national state Labor story. It outlines four distinctive state Labor governments in Australia in the states of New South Wales (NSW), Victoria (VIC), Queensland (QLD) and Western Australia (WA). In all cases, Labor held office for a relatively sustained period of time, before eventually losing. Indeed, from 2002-07 the ALP was in power in every state and territory in Australia – a striking phenomenon that Geoff Gallop, former WA Premier, described as an era of 'strategic government' (Gallop, 2007). These state Labor governments offered a distinctive approach to governance that reshaped and renewed the trajectory of social democracy, especially in the face of neoliberal economic settings. Yet, in almost all these cases, these Labor governments were ejected from office. However, in contrast to some of the other cases in this volume, Labor has regained power in many of the state jurisdictions. So, while the Labor model of 'strategic government' might have passed, there might be further lessons here about how Labor can regain power.

This chapter offers a critical examination of the phenomenon of the dominance of Labor at state level in the mid-2000s. Underpinning this chapter are two key interrelated questions. First, what was 'Labor' about these governments? Clearly, we would identify them as centre-left governments because they were creatures of the ALP. Yet, more critically, what, if anything, made them social democratic? For a range of reasons explored below, there is no clear answer to this question, and the case of sub-national Labor sheds light on the centre-left's ongoing existential crisis. Second, why did these long-standing Labor governments lose office? Did they lose for reasons specific to the centre-left? Or for more general reasons whereby any government might be ejected from office – incumbency, exhaustion in office, failure to renew leadership, and so on?

The chapter is organised in the following way. First, the political context is set out, focusing on the distinctive features of Australian federalism that shaped these governments. The four cases are then briefly introduced. Then, the chapter is then organised around the three core themes of the book, namely, institutions, individuals and ideas. Here, the institutional and structural issues facing state Labor are examined.

Labor in the states

Australia's federal system is notably asymmetric, with both a fiscal and legal balance that has historically strengthened the Commonwealth government. Indeed, the national government raises about 80 per cent of all taxes raised, and state governments spend nearly 50 per cent of all tax revenues. This places the Commonwealth government at a strong advantage, especially in leveraging policy goals – notably under the trailblazing and short-lived Whitlam government in the 1970s. Despite the imbalance, the state governments have significant powers, especially in the realm of education, health and other social policy areas. The four cases considered here constitute just over 20 million of Australia's 24 million population (NSW 7.2 million, VIC 5.5 million, QLD 4.5 million and WA 2.2 million). To get a sense of the scale of population served by these governments, the combined population of Denmark, Norway and Finland is just over 15 million. Despite lacking the same policy levers as national governments, and with more limited policy scope, they remain a pertinent case for the centre-left for a number of reasons. Social democracy at its most trailblazing was carried out in Australia at state level – notably the government of Don Dunstan in the 1970s (Parkin and Patience, 1981). Moreover, the dominance of Labor at state level reveals key insights into the renewal of the centre-left where the governments do not have the same economic 'tax and spend' policy tools as a national government.

The 2000s were a time of Labor dominance at state level in Australia (see Table 6.1). In each case, some of the most formidable cohort of

Table 6.1: Labour governments in four Australian states (1995–2015)

State	1995	1996	1997	1998	1999	2000	2001	2002	2003	2004	2005	2006	2007	2008	2009	2010	2011	2012	2013	2014	2015
NSW	▓	▓	▓	▓	▓	▓	▓	▓	▓	▓	▓	▓	▓	▓	▓	▓					
VIC					▓	▓	▓	▓	▓	▓	▓	▓	▓	▓	▓					▓	▓
QLD	▓	█	█	▓	▓	▓	▓	▓	▓	▓	▓	▓	▓	▓	▓	▓	▓				▓
WA							▓	▓	▓	▓	▓	▓	▓	▓							

Labor leaders was to emerge, including Peter Beattie in Queensland, Bob Carr in New South Wales, Steve Bracks in Victoria, and before his resignation on health grounds, Geoff Gallop in Western Australia. While this story focuses on the 'big four', there were also notable Labor governments elsewhere, not least in South Australia and Tasmania (Manwaring, 2016).

New South Wales

If any state lays claim to being a de facto Labor stronghold, it is New South Wales. Until its defeat at the 2011 election, Labor had been in office for an impressive 16 years. For the most part, it was under the leadership of Bob Carr, before a succession of leaders led the party to defeat. What is interesting about the New South Wales case is that longevity and incumbency can only partially explain why the party was defeated under the leadership of Kristina Keneally. The 2011 defeat was emphatic, with Labor facing a huge 16.4 per cent swing against it, and it was reduced to 20 seats, the lowest ever total recorded by a government in the state's history.

Victoria

In Victoria, there is a similar tale of dominance by the ALP. Under the steady, if uncharismatic, leadership of Steve Bracks, Labor won successive elections, before being ejected from office in 2010. After three election wins, Bracks handed power over to John Brumby, who, facing a range of pressures, narrowly lost to the Liberals, who secured a one-seat majority. Strikingly, and unexpectedly, this proved to be a one-term Liberal government, with new Labor leader Daniel Andrews winning in 2014. The focus of this chapter is on the record and loss of the Bracks/Brumby governments.

Queensland

Queensland is a very distinctive polity given its geographic size, and has a much more dispersed population compared to the other states. It has a reputation for throwing up conservative and maverick figures, and its politics tends to swing quite dramatically. Yet, the ALP enjoys a formidable record in Queensland, and between 1989-2012 it won eight straight elections (although it was out of office from 1996-98) (Williams, 2011). Under the leadership of Peter Beattie, and then Anna Bligh, the ALP dominated state politics, before losing at the 2012 election to Campbell Newman's Liberal Party. At the 2012 election, the ALP retained just 7 seats in the 89-seat Parliament. Interestingly, Beattie's successor Anna Bligh was one of the few centre-left governments around the world to win shortly after the global financial crisis (GFC). This chapter focuses directly on Bligh's loss to Newman. Notably, like the Victorian case, this proved to be a one-term Liberal government, with the ALP very unexpectedly regaining office in 2015.

Western Australia

Western Australia is arguably the most conservative of all the states considered here, with the ALP suffering some of its poorest electoral performances. Yet, from 2001-08, under Geoff Gallop, and then, briefly, Alan Carpenter, the ALP took an innovative and distinctive approach to governance (van Schoubroeck, 2010). Carpenter, who had been leader of the party for two years, went to the polls in 2008 earlier than expected, and the result was a hung Parliament, which ultimately saw Colin Barnett triumph as Liberal leader (Phillips, 2013). Barnett proved a canny and formidable Liberal premier, winning the 2013 state election with a landslide; remarkably Labor regained office at the 2017 election. This chapter focuses here on the record of the Gallop government, and the factors behind Labor's loss in 2008.

Overall this chapter asks why these state Labor governments lost office, and whether they lost for similar reasons. The cases are now considered in the institutions/individuals/ideas framework that underpins this volume.

Institutions

In this section we consider the role of institutional and wider structural explanations that account for why Labor lost. We might group these into three sub-categories: (1) political systemic factors; (2) external structural pressures; and (3) internally driven institutional problems. The specific systemic factors inherent in each political state system considered here arguably had some, albeit very limited, impact on the election losses. To some extent, they actually favoured Labor, and in this respect, help explain the longevity of Labor's rule. Data from the Australian Election Study (AES) consistently shows that the Australian public tends to believe that the ALP is the best placed party to deliver on education and health policy (McAllister and Pietsch, 2010). Given the importance of these issues at state level, we can see how this might give the ALP some in-built advantage over the Liberal/National opposition. Indeed, some of the achievements of these state Labor governments – such as Bob Carr's education policy reforms – are a key reason why they held office for as long as they did. In most states, Labor is disadvantaged by the malapportionment of rural seats, and in some states such as South Australia, there was a long history of gerrymandering. In Western Australia, under Geoff Gallop's leadership, boundaries were re-drawn, which helped his overall seat count. As Bowe (2008, p 245) notes, the new system, 'whilst more equitable in theory … assisted Labor by locking conservative votes in country districts … Labor's more modest majority across the metropolitan area was distributed with much greater efficiency.'

The issue here is that, ultimately, we should be circumspect in overstating Labor's dominance in all four cases. The 'softness' of the Labor vote was particularly pronounced in Western Australia, and this remains an enduring issue. As Bowe (2008, p 254) notes in the Western Australia case, of the elections held between 1990 and 2008, Labor only secured 40 per cent of the primary vote once – in 2005.

We can also note other factors that contributed to Labor's defeats. Election analyst Antony Green observed that in New South Wales the optional preference system was not helpful to the ALP (Green, 2012, p 287). The majoritarian electoral systems in each of the states also has the effect of masking a deeper structural problem for the ALP – the decline of its primary vote. In the Victorian case, the mandated date of the election arguably did not help John Brumby, but this was a minor factor. Conversely, Alan Carpenter's decision to call an early election in Western Australia backfired. Similarly, in New South Wales, Labor *winning* the 2007 election actually had the impact of amplifying the huge losses sustained in 2010. In all, the timings of elections to some extent explain the strength of the result, but not necessarily the result itself.

Perhaps more substantively we can identify external structural factors – especially economic conditions – as being a key factor in the downturn in Labor's fortunes. Crucially these were governments impacted by the fall-out from the GFC. In some cases, the impact was not immediate, with Anna Bligh winning the 2009 election, albeit with a reduced majority. By the time of the 2012 election, the financial situation was dire for Queensland Labor, forcing drastic, and ultimately unpopular, measures by the Bligh government. In the case of Western Australia, the end of the resources boom reflected the state's dependence on this sector of the economy. In the run-up to the campaign, the state's AAA credit rating was down-graded, which proved to be a useful fillip for the Liberals. Like the European cases, state Labor was unable to capitalise on the GFC for a wider social democratic 'moment' (Bailey et al, 2014). Lacking the economic policy instruments of national counterparts, this is perhaps unsurprising. Even if we note the limited policy tools available to a state government, as explored in 'Ideas' later, the GFC exposed hollowness in the state-level ALP model.

Other institutional factors also played a crucial part in the demise of these Labor governments. Chief among these is the capacity of the Liberal opposition to rebuild and renew. Indeed, in all cases, Labor (finally) faced a credible opposition. For example, in Queensland, the ultimate merger of the Liberals and National Party secured closer cooperation. Overall, the Liberals managed to successfully rebuild and renew in an effective manner, as, indeed, do many Opposition parties.

While these structural factors had a bearing on Labor's losses, there are other institutional factors – much more under the ALP's control – which contributed more significantly to the series of election losses. Two key interrelated institutional factors went hand in hand – the hollowing out of the party's structures, coupled with a series of linked corruption scandals. The standout case here is New South Wales Labor (Cavalier, 2010; Aarons, 2013).

State Labor has been hollowing out for years, and, despite a number of calls for reforms, there has been a conspicuous lack of effort to reinvigorate the parties (Hawke and Wran, 2002; Bracks et al, 2010). At state level, a rise in factional power is directly linked to the parties' dwindling membership and members' activism (Faulkner, 2006, p 75). Numerous party stalwarts have been warning of the problems of the rise of factional bosses for some time. In a key contribution, Jones (2006, p 9) anticipated the seriousness of the issue:

> The ALP runs the risk of becoming a transactional party rather than a commitment party. The ALP has been privatised and factions are majority and minority shareholders, run by processional managers, some now in the third generation. Factions become ends in themselves, engaging in game-playing, tribalism and turf wars. Ideas? Policies? They are of minor significance.

Institutionally, the problem for state-level ALP is that the 'factional warlords essentially operate at the state rather than the national level, because that is where power and patronage lies' (Jones, 2006, p 10). In New South Wales, these problems became acute. The hollowing out of the party meant that it became much more reliant on the private sector, and especially on the development and planning sectors, and was unable to ensure sufficient financial safeguards were in place. Despite some warnings, New South Wales became engulfed in a series of devastating corruption scandals (Cavalier, 2010; Patrick, 2013). While prominent and successful Labor leaders such as Bob Carr, Geoff Gallop and Peter Beattie (the latter in relation to the electoral scandal in 2010) deserve much credit for cleaning up the ALP in their respective states, this reliance on the leader reflects an inherent institutional weakness of the party. Indeed, the success of state Labor during this period rested on dominant leaders to suppress factional battles. In New South Wales, the subsequent shuffle of leaders from Iemma to Rees to Keneally reflects the depth of patronage these leaders relied on the factions for support. In the Western Australia case, a significant factor in Alan Carpenter's unexpected loss was not the calling of an early election, but the folly of lifting Geoff Gallop's hard line on those factional players involved in what is infamously called 'WA Inc' (Bowe, 2008, p 247).

A key related problem is the factional grip over pre-selections, and this had had the net effect of weakening the representative role of the party. Cavalier is adamant that 'the party of the workers has a machine leadership that is wholly disengaged from the world of work' (Cavalier, 2010, p 9). The hollowing out has seen over 138 branches close in New South Wales alone, but crucially, even where the branches still meet, their role and impact is minimal. The net effect of factional growth is a narrower pool of leaders, tighter control, weaker policy-making and a dormant and dying membership. For Cavalier, 'structure is everything' (2010, p ix). However, laying most of the blame for Labor's various defeats on institutional factors obscures the impact of other factors, such as the ideational fabric of the parties.

Individuals

To understand Labor's losses (as well as its victories), it is crucial to note the role of agency, and specifically, the role and model of leadership that characterised state Labor. In a key volume, Wanna and Williams (2005) compare the different styles and models of leadership of this wave of Labor leaders. While some were notably charismatic and dominant, Carr and Beattie, for example, others were less inspirational, but equally effective, for example, Steve Bracks. In part, some of the losses can be attributed to the difficulty in sustaining such leadership models over time, and the difficulty in moving to a new leadership team. This is a common phenomenon, and the shift from Hawke to Keating is a pre-eminent example. In Queensland, the shift from the popular and engaging Peter Beattie to Anna Bligh looked like a successful model for handling a transition. Indeed, in noting the longevity of these Labor governments, MacKerras (2008, p 901) notes two key factors: first, they 'avoid radical changes', and second, 'Labor leaders seem to know when it is time to retire.'

In part, Labor's losses can be attributed to the breakdown of the leadership's stability. Bob Carr was fortunate in keeping Michael Egan as his Treasurer for most of his period in office, and no successor was able to match this partnership. Similarly, the strength of Steve Bracks' Victorian leadership was his quiet, unassuming style – a direct and welcome contrast to the abrasive neoliberal Liberal Premier Jeff Kennett. As important was Bracks' contrast with his treasurer John Brumby, which allowed each to play to their own strengths (Deane, 2015).

At their best, these Labor leaders were able to both inspire and contain their parties. While Bligh only secured one victory before her defeat in Queensland, it is notable that she convincingly displayed a 'transformational' rather than transactional model of leadership (de Bussy and Paterson, 2012, p 2). Bligh is a striking case, because she faced two key leadership dilemmas. Bligh had to both differentiate herself from the charismatic Peter Beattie and also reinvigorate a government that had held office for a long time. In 2011, dramatic floods hit Queensland, and the state was under siege. Bligh is widely credited with handling this crisis well, and the event was described as her 'political remaking' (de Bussy and Paterson, 2012, p 2). Yet the political pay-off was short-lived. Arguably, Bligh was unable to build a new model of governance, even in the face of very tough circumstances.

In Western Australia, the difficulty for Labor was that Geoff Gallop, a smart, strategic leader – credited with developing and initiating a template for the other Labor leaders – stepped down sooner than expected due to mental health issues. Australia, like other countries, has an increasingly leader-centric culture, and there is a creeping 'presidentalism' taking place at state level. In this context, gifted and inspirational leaders become a double-edged sword, especially for Labor parties. On the plus side, they can paper over the institutional cracks outlined above, and contain the factional power. The downside of such a dominant leadership style is that it leads to a hollowed-out party. This is a more pressing issue for the centre-left than centre-right, because the Liberal Party has had a much longer tradition of organising around strong leaders. A leader-centric political culture leaves the centre-left, with its institutional links with the unions, far more exposed than the centre-right (Phillips, 2013, p 118). In Western Australia, this model quickly unravelled with a number of strategic mistakes made by Alan Carpenter, who assembled a 'dream team' of ministers who were mostly hand-picked from the factions. Indeed, all of Carpenter's picks fared poorly, and indeed, he might have actually won an unlikely victory if he had pushed for stronger pre-selection processes outside of the factional powers (van Schoubroeck, 2010).

Again, we find the starkest problems with this this model of leadership in New South Wales Labor. Cavalier is unsparing in his criticism of what he terms the 'Godhead' model of leadership, demonstrated by Bob Carr (Cavalier, 2010, p 1). In this model – 'the purpose of the ALP is to become an instrument of the leader's will as translated by those who operate the party's central machinery'. While the tight control of caucus and factional warlords ensured electoral success, it was a model that had limited durability. Electoralism, driven by factional power, can deliver sound policy outcomes, and indeed, for a time, economic success, but comes with a host of hidden costs. Strikingly, this was a model of strong leadership that detached the party even further from its base, a process that was masked by the electoral results. Undoubtedly, Labor was fortunate to have a generation of leaders, like Geoff Gallop, who sought to reinvent Labor's mission. Yet this model of leadership hid underlying weaknesses.

Ideas

Finally, we turn to the ideational explanations for the loss of these state Labor governments. It is, to some extent, much harder to show either correlation and/or causation between a party's electoral performance and its ideational make-up, rather than the impact of one-off events. Yet, we can make some tentative judgements about the party's ideological agenda and its impact. Here, it is worth noting the ideational contours of the successful model of 'Labor' government as carried out by the likes of Carr, Gallop, Bracks and Beattie, and in South Australia, Mike Rann. Broadly, as outlined elsewhere, there is a good case to see these as New Labor/Third Way-style governments, which shared some common characteristics.

Generally speaking, these governments were economically conservative, mildly socially reformist, committed to a new environmental politics, and also influenced by the triangulation of the 'Third Way' influence on social democratic thinking. On issues such as criminal justice policy Labor often took a populist approach to claim policy space from the centre-right (Jones, 2006, p 17). Indeed, it is evident that the Third Way paradigm (especially the Blair/Brown variant) also inspired these Labor governments.

In his appraisal of New South Wales Labor, Clune offers the contours of the successful Wran and Carr model of governance:

> Key elements were: occupying the electoral middle ground, superior political skills; crisis evasion where possible and skilful crisis management where not; internal unity; strong leadership; administrative competence; financial responsibility; providing services efficiently; delivering tangible benefits to the electorate; and moderate reformism without getting too far ahead of the electorate. Bob Carr added new elements to account for changed times – environmental protection, market liberal ideology and sophisticated media management. (Clune, 2012, p 309)

Ideationally, we see a hybrid form of politics, at worst confused; at best, electorally successful. Economically, these governments have been described as 'conservative', 'neoliberal', and in the New South Wales case, the goal of running budget surpluses was 'typically Keynesian' (Clune and Smith, 2012, p 114). What seems clear is that, in line with 'Third Way' thinking there was a clearer embrace of neoliberal settings. Oddly, this state Labor model of governance also harked back to an earlier era:

> Carr's ideological conservatism and political pragmatism have combined to produced what is in many ways a 1950s style of government, with much emphasis on job creation, development and the provision of basic services…. (Clune, 2005, p 52)

There are three wider issues that arise from these state Labor cases that link to the wider ideational crisis of the centre-left. First, if we accept that there was a shift by state Labor to accommodate neoliberalism, it was for a time electorally successful and popular. The problem for the reinvention of the centre-left is that, like New Labour, neoliberal social democracy offers some economic prescriptions that attract broader cross-class support. Even if, normatively, we might wish to challenge neoliberalism, or at least half-heartedly expect the centre-left to do so, we nevertheless have to face the uncomfortable reality that neoliberal social democracy did prove electorally successful. Wiseman (1996), writing in a different context, called this the 'kinder road to hell'.

Second, this state Labor model remained successful during periods of relative economic growth. The difficulty, and this might apply to all incumbent governments, is to achieve electoral success when there is a downturn. Rather damagingly, this recalls Thatcher's line that the 'problem with socialism is that you run out of other people's money'. Putting aside the barbarity of the Thatcher experiment, with its reliance on economic inequality, it captures another uncomfortable dilemma for the centre-left – which none of these state Labor governments resolved – how to develop an effective economic model in straightened economic times. The problem is exacerbated for the state governments with minimal tax instruments.

Third, there was an underlying hollowness to this state Labor model, which ultimately led to electoral losses. The fragility and hollowness of this model was exposed in the following ways. First, despite the embrace of neoliberal economic policy settings, at least two of these state governments lost office by pushing this agenda too far, especially through the case of privatisation. In New South Wales, the troubled effort to privatise electricity proved fatal. In Queensland, Bligh's popularity was damaged by her desperate bid to turn the state's finances around, by a major attempt to sell off a series of key state assets. Bligh took a stand against the unions, which ultimately undid her government (Quiggin, 2010).

The fragility of this state Labor model also links back to the social policy agendas of these governments. At times, they clearly provided decent community services, and each sought at times to introduce innovative ways of tackling long-standing public policy issues. Carr, for example, is credited with being innovative in the field of education policy, Bracks, with respect to reinvigorating and measuring 'community strength', Gallop, concerning exercises in deliberative democracy, and so on. Yet the Victorian case is instructive here. Some writers note how Bracks flirted with the ideas of the 'social investment' state, rethinking new ideas to tackle poverty and disadvantage. Perkins and colleagues (2004) offer a good critique, noting that despite some clear efforts to link economic growth with social wellbeing, the dominance of neoliberal settings tended to offset the gains made. Moreover, when the economic situation worsens, the weakness of the policy instruments in place offers little substantive protection for the most vulnerable. Wiseman (1996) suggests that despite good intentions and some gains, it is a poor substitute for wider structural redistribution. The fundamental issue is that the model, while deserving credit, has inherent systemic weaknesses. The same might be said of the Queensland 'Smart State' agenda imitated by Beattie (Althaus,

2008). The limitations of state Labor's social policy agenda reflects a wider weakening attachment by Labor to tackling and dismantling structural forms of inequality. Indeed, this model of state Labor reflects a dilution of social democratic thinking and practice. The dilemma is that, despite this, it proved successful. What incentive is there, then, for factional bosses to seek more radical reforms?

These state Labor governments are stark experiments of the struggles of the centre-left to re-assert its core values. Clune is adamant that in the New South Wales case, 'Labor no longer had a clearly defined image, sense of purpose or set of core beliefs' (Clune, 2012, p 312). Smith suggests that, '[a]nother view is that a version of Labor's egalitarian values remains alive, but that the party has become caught between traditional and newer approaches to achieving equality. Electricity privatisation provided an example of this dilemma' (Clune and Smith, 2012, p 307). In part, state Labor lost because it was not able to resolve this ongoing dilemma.

Conclusion

For a brief period, state Labor seemed to herald a new model of governance in Australia, which in part seemed to offer a bulwark against the more overtly neoliberal national government of John Howard's centre-right Liberal coalition. Yet eventually, this state model broke down, and Labor left office. In the four cases considered here we see both specific factors, and also some general patterns that account for the downfall of state Labor. Some factors, such as incumbency, change of leadership, opposition renewal and the inability to resolve ongoing policy problems (such as transport and health), are characteristics of any major party in a liberal democracy. The 'lessons' here can be applied to any significant government seeking political party. Yet we can also see clear factors inherent in centre-left politics. Institutionally, the hollowing out of the parties has left them in a particularly vulnerable position, and, crucially, it risks weakening the ties between the elites and their core constituents and supporters. Yet, over-playing the institutional factors obscures a more complex story of the ideational struggles that captured these Labor cases, and a weakening attachment to tackling structural forms of inequality.

Strikingly, by 2017, Labor proved resurgent at state level in Australia. By early 2017, it had regained office in Western Australia, Victoria, Queensland, the Northern Territory, retained office in South Australia and the Australian Capital Territory. It could well be that this reflects a shift to more 'valence' style politics – Australians at state level rewarding 'competence' rather than a wider renewal of social democracy. Despite the return of Labor at the state level, it remains unclear how far, if at all, these new Labor governments have resolved some of the ongoing institutional and ideational dilemmas about what a modern centre-left party should stand for.

References

Aarons, M. (2013) 'Mate of the Union: How to corrupt a party', *The Monthly*, Melbourne, VIC: Black Inc.

Althaus, C. (2008) *Calculating political risk*, Sydney, NSW: UNSW Press.

Bailey, D., de Waele, J.-M., Escalona, F. and Vieira, M. (eds) (2014) *European social democracy during the global financial crisis: Renovation or resignation?*, Manchester: Manchester University Press.

Bowe, W. (2008) 'The Western Australian election of September 6, 2008: The first chink in Labor's armour', *Australasian Parliamentary Review*, pp 243-55.

Bracks, S., Faulkner, J. and Carr, B. (2010) *2010 national review*, Canberra, ACT: Australian Labor Party.

Cavalier, R. (2010) *Power crisis: The self-destruction of a state Labor Party*, Cambridge: Cambridge University Press.

Clune, D. (2005) 'Bob Carr: The unexpected Colossus', in J. Wanna and P. Williams (eds) *Yes, Premier: Labour leadership in Australia's states and territories*, Sydney, NSW: UNSW Press.

Clune, D. (2012) 'Why Labor lost', in D. Clune and R. Smith (eds) *From Carr to Keneally: Labor in office in NSW 1995-2011*, Crows Nest, NSW: Allen & Unwin.

Clune, D. and Smith, R. (2012) *From Carr to Keneally: Labor in office in NSW 1995-2011*, Crows Nest, NSW: Allen & Unwin.

de Bussy, N.M. and Paterson, A. (2012) 'Crisis leadership styles – Bligh versus Gillard: A content analysis of Twitter posts on the Queensland floods', *Journal of Public Affairs*, vol 12, pp 326-32.

Deane, J. (2015) *Catch and kill: The politics of power*, Sydney, NSW: Penguin.

Faulkner, J. (2006) 'Apathy and anger', in B. Jones (ed) *Coming to the Party: Where to next for Labor?*, Melbourne, VIC: Melbourne University Press.

Gallop, G. (2007) 'Strategic planning: Is it the new model?', *Public Administration Today*, Jan-Mar, pp 28-33.

Green, A. (2012) 'The results', in D Clune and R. Smith (eds) *From Carr to Keneally: Labor in office in NSW 1995-2011*, Crows Nest, NSW: Allen & Unwin.

Hawke, B. and Wran, N. (2002) *National Committee of Review: Report*, Canberra, ACT: Australian Labor Party.

Jones, B. (ed) (2006) *Coming to the party: Where to next for Labor?*, Melbourne, VIC: Melbourne University Press.

MacKerras, M. (2008) 'Australia', *European journal of Political Research*, vol 47, nos 7/8, pp 892-901.

Manwaring, R. (2016) 'The renewal of social democracy? The Rann Labor Government (2002–11)', *Australian Journal of Politics and History*, vol 62, pp 236-50.

McAllister, I. and Pietsch, J. (2010) *Trends in Australian political opinion: Results from the Australian election study, 1987-2010*, Canberra, ACT: Australia National University.

Parkin, A. and Patience, A. (eds) (1981) *The Dunstan decade: Social democracy at the state level*, Melbourne, VIC: Longman Cheshire.

Patrick, A. (2013) *Downfall: How the Labor Party ripped itself apart*, Sydney, NSW: HarperCollins Australia.

Perkins, D., Smyth, P. and Nelms, L. (2004) *Beyond neo-liberalism: The social investment state?*, Melbourne, VIC: Brotherhood of St Laurence.

Phillips, H. (2013) 'The March 2013 Western Australian election: First fixed election date delivers a resounding victory for the Barnett government', *Australasian Parliamentary Review*, vol 28, p 106.

Quiggin, J. (2010) 'Bad politics makes bad policy: The case of Queensland's asset sales programme', *Economic Papers: A Journal of Applied Economics and Policy*, vol 29, pp 13-22.

van Schoubroeck, L. (2010) *The lure of politics: Geoff Gallop's government 2001-2006*, Perth, WA: University of Western Australia Press.

Wanna, J. and Williams, P. (eds) (2005) *Yes, Premier. Labor Leadership in Australia's states and territories*, Sydney, NSW: UNSW Press.

Williams, P. (2011) 'How did they do it? Explaining Queensland Labor's second electoral hegemony', *Queensland Review*, vol 18, pp 112-33.

Wiseman, J. (1996) 'A kinder road to hell? Labor and the politics of progressive competitiveness in Australia', *Socialist Register*, vol 32, no 2, pp 93-117.

Part 2
The centre-left in Western Europe

SEVEN

Germany: little hope in times of crisis

Uwe Jun

Introduction

For many years, the Social Democratic Party (SPD) has performed poorly at the German parliamentary (*Bundestag*) elections (see Table 7.1), and crucially, has been unable to puncture the dominance of the CDU/CSU (Christian Democratic Union/Christian Social Union). From the period when Sigmar Gabriel became party leader in October 2009 until 2017, the SPD has rarely achieved more than 30 per cent at the polls. At the 2013 elections the SPD obtained only 25 per cent of the vote, and there has been no subsequent improvement on that already modest level. The reasons for this poor performance are complex and outlined in this chapter. In line with the other case chapters in this volume, this chapter considers the institutional, ideational/programmatic and individual/agency dimensions of the SPD's plight.

Table 7.1: SPD's parliamentary results (2002, 2005, 2009 and 2013)

Year	2002	2005	2009	2013
SPD share of vote[a]	38.5	34.2	23.0	25.7
Seats won	251/603	222/598	146/598	193/613
Outcome	SPD Red–Green coalition	Grand coalition – SPD junior partner	Opposition	Grand coalition – SPD junior partner

Note: [a] See pp 23-34 of www.bundeswahlleiter.de/en/dam/jcr/397735e3-0585-46f6-a0b5-2c60c5b83de6/btw_ab49_gesamt.pdf

The SPD is facing a range of problems, on numerous fronts. Programmatically, the SPD lacks a vision for society that is sufficiently coherent and forward-looking to attract voters. For some time now, it has become apparent that the SPD lacks a viable, comprehensive, social democratic project capable of securing the support of a sufficiently sizeable proportion of the electorate. Instead, since 1998 (apart from the period between 2009 and 2013), the SPD has adopted a form of electoral pragmatism in government. On the positive side, this has made a major contribution to the stability of the German political system, but also given a social democratic hue to government policy. However, the SPD's input has not increased the party's popularity; on the contrary, the SPD's popularity has continued to decline.

The SPD's credibility has declined over the last two decades largely due to a combination of its failure to implement campaign promises and the difficulties it has experienced while seeking to address its tarnished legacy of office in the periods after 1998 and 2009. The party's organisational structures are also characterised by an ageing, declining membership. Moreover, changes in party competition have restricted the SPD's margin of manoeuvre over recent years. Indeed, the convergence of the SPD and CDU on numerous policies has allowed a left-wing party (Linkspartei) and a Green party (Bündnis '90/ Die Grünen) to occupy the available space on the left. The national Conservative or right-wing populist party, the Alternative for Germany (AfD), founded in 2013, has also attracted voters away from the SPD. The SPD leadership has struggled to address these developments. Additionally, the party's candidates for Chancellor in 2009 and 2013 were relatively unpopular.

Figure 7.1: SPD performance during three legislative terms

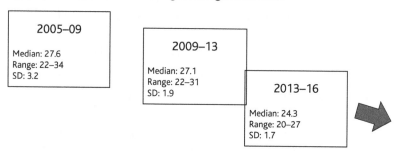

Source: Infratest dimap, ARD-DeutschlandTrend Sonntagsfrage October 2016

Since Martin Schulz's election as party leader in March 2017, the party appears to have taken a turn for the better. The elevation of Schulz had seemingly offered a glimmer of renewal, but any upturn proved ephemeral. The primary focus of this chapter, in line with the other case studies in this volume, is the period from the start of the great financial crisis (GFC) until 2016.

Ideas

Like many other social democratic parties, the SPD has, for many years (or at least since the demise of the so-called 'Third Way'), lacked a social democratic, voter-friendly vision for the future that convincingly addresses the key issues of globalisation, migration and technological change. The SPD has also failed to address in a satisfactory manner the resulting insecurity experienced by many of the wider public in the face of these changes. Instead of re-calibrating a new social democratic form of politics, the SPD has employed a form of executive pragmatism that offers no coherent, centre-left strategic vision.

The SPD is a manifesto-driven party, in that its programme, values and ideas are consolidated in its manifesto statements. The 2007 'Hamburg Principles' were the most recent significant attempt to re-calibrate its core mission and agenda, and they still form the core programme of the SPD (cf Nachtwey, 2009, p 232); they represent the basic ideas of the party with a primary focus on the distribution of justice and retaining democratic socialism. While the 2007 'Hamburg Principles' were categorised as being 'traditional' (Sturm, 2009, p 342), subsequent 'steps on the programmatic terrain were rather tentative … [and] did not follow a clear line' (Butzlaff and Micus, 2011, p 25). An ongoing problem for the SPD is that these underpinning ideas are vague, leaving much room for interpretation; they have consequently had little impact on government policy. The SPD has also failed to address in a convincing manner the fact that members of the middle classes have emerged as the losers of globalisation (cf Mau, 2014) or that fewer members of the working class have attained middle-class status (Niehues, 2014, p 17; see also Köcher, 2007). These failures have led to a palpable increase in feelings of insecurity among voters (cf Burzan, 2014). These groups of people feel insecure in the increasingly globalised economy, and are concerned about the loss of Germany's national identity and the effects of increased migration.

Over the last two decades, the SPD's failure to innovate and advance a more coherent strategy can only be understood by taking into account the wider changes in patterns and types of employment. The SPD identified gainful employment as one of the key means of achieving social integration and economic prosperity. As Huo (2009, p 12) has noted, 'The premise … is on work and better work'. For the SPD, the aim has been to provide everyone with an opportunity to participate in a working life so as to reduce social disadvantage and achieve social solidarity. In accordance with this approach, an individual possesses both rights and duties that serve as the basis of the welfare state. As

Sachs (2008, p 35) has noted: 'Social security systems require a healthy equilibrium between rights and duties in order for tasks to be met.' This model of welfare is based on each citizen's willingness to take part in a working life as far as possible. Each citizen is responsible for taking on this primary duty individually and protecting public services through individual and collective self-help. Furthermore, solidarity enables the community to counter social exclusion by providing the necessary resources and opportunities to enable participation and secure individual livelihoods. Similarly, the state must provide appropriate working conditions for employees, including enforceable rights with respect to employers. At its core, this variant of social democracy seeks to minimise the costs of capitalism to the individual by reducing inequalities of power, achieving economic prosperity and maintaining the rule of law.

Yet, this balancing of individual responsibility and state solidarity has generated major controversies within the SPD, which stem from Gerhard Schröder's *Agenda 2010* social reforms. Initiated in 2005, *Agenda 2010* provoked considerable disagreement within the SPD. Its primary goal was to reduce unemployment (approximately 5 million people were then out of work). To achieve this aim, various actions were implemented that sought to lower non-wage labour costs, strengthen incentives for securing gainful employment and improve Germany's economic competitiveness. The *Agenda 2010* approach was a variant of the 'Third Way' renewal of social democracy, and was designed not to adversely affect employees' interests (cf Hegelich et al, 2011). Rather, it aimed to promote the potential of jobseekers while demanding greater individual responsibility. Within this context, the 'Hartz IV' reforms were particularly controversial as they focused on providing incentives for securing employment by combining unemployment and social benefits for employees via dedicated unemployment and national support programmes. The proposals provoked widespread concern about the loss of social status and the increase in the number of low-paid jobs.

In addition, Franz Müntefering, Minister of Labour and Social Affairs at the time of the grand coalition between 2005 and 2009, was jointly responsible for the decision to defer retirement until the age of 67. This controversial initiative stimulated considerable debate and opposition, both from within the SPD and from the trade unions. The latter viewed *Agenda 2010* with considerable suspicion, leading to a weakening of the traditional trade union–SPD relationship and hastening a subtle, partial separation (cf Neusser, 2013, pp 297ff).

Relations between the trade unions and the SPD have been cool for some time (at least since the SPD's adoption of the 'Third Way'), and there has been a standoff ever since (cf Piazza, 2001; Micus, 2010, pp 16ff). Despite this cooling in relations, the trade unions still view social democracy as their main political party reference in relation to matters of labour market policy, welfare state benefits and socially vested rights. Conversely, social democrats recognise that trade union membership is linked to a disproportionately higher number of votes in favour of centre-left parties in almost all European countries (see Wessels, 2010, p 21). Thus, Sigmar Gabriel had every reason to improve the party's relationship with the trade unions. By partially distancing himself from *Agenda 2010,* and implementing various social reforms, he had some success during his term of office from the 2013 election to 2016.

For the grand coalition, in office from 2013, gainful employment was given a prominent position, as demonstrated by the key legislative pledges for a minimum wage and a retirement age of 63 (after 45 years of paid contributions). While the former promise adheres to *Agenda 2010* in many respects, the latter might rather be viewed as a concession to the trade unions, and runs against the grain of *Agenda 2010.* The net effect of these reforms favours the group of 'traditional employees' (who remain a core constituent of the SPD). By adopting this approach, the SPD leadership has responded to the requests of the trade unions and its own members, each of whom viewed themselves as being relative losers under *Agenda 2010.* However, the policy for retirement at the age of 63 is likely to have electoral implications outside the SPD's own voter base. This is particularly important given that the CDU has simultaneously proposed its own socio-political redistribution measure (that is, the 'mothers' retirement' proposal) that seeks to consider periods of childraising when calculating pension entitlements.

The SPD's left faction and many journalists view *Agenda 2010* as being largely responsible for the SPD's current plight; the reasons for the party's loss of credibility nevertheless run deeper and are more multi-faceted. The 2002 and 2005 election campaigns prepared the ground for the palpable loss of trust that the SPD has experienced. Before this period, the SPD had been able to retain its popularity via a rhetorical appeal to traditional values, coupled with Chancellor Schröder's personal popularity and his adept mastery of the political agenda.

Following the 2002 and 2005 election campaigns, the cohesion and credibility of the SPD declined, along with a wider long-term decline in support for social democracy (cf Jun, 2010; Spier and von Alemann, 2013, p 445; Jun and Berzel, 2015). The SPD lost its credibility by delivering different outcomes and policies to those outlined in their election manifestos. In addition, the SPD's internal disagreements run like a thread through its legislative and election campaign communications. These disagreements included controversies between different factions of the party (that is, modernisers versus traditionalists); disputes over the lack of debate concerning *Agenda 2010* (cf Jun, 2010); increases in value-added taxes that the party had previously campaigned against (for example, the so-called 'Merkel-tax'); and advocating a retirement age of 67, thereby contradicting its own election manifesto. The SPD therefore lost credibility due to the chasm between the party's election pledges and its subsequent actions.

The current party leadership learned from its mistakes, and in 2013, the party only supported measures in the coalition treaty with the CDU/CSU that squared with its election pledges (cf Jun and Jakobs, 2015). However, a long-term loss of credibility can only (if ever) be rectified over the long term. Ultimately, credibility is established by demonstrating a combination of strong problem-solving skills, trustworthiness and a commitment to core ideals (rather than short-term electoralism). Any major party, including the SPD, therefore needs to forge a unity of purpose between those voting for the party and for the leadership. Yet, as we have seen, the SPD has had clear problems in this respect.

The SPD reached its nadir in 2009 when it obtained just 23 per cent of the vote. Following the party's historic defeat at the 2009 national election, internal disputes over policies and strategies seriously weakened the party's capacity to communicate with those outside its ranks. The SPD's dilemma was clear: as an Opposition party, it could not condemn the legislative politics of the previous 11 years outright, as this would have only exacerbated the party's existing credibility gap. However, the party's defining feature (that is, its competence in the field of social policy) had to be revived. At the September 2002 national election, 48 per cent of interviewees had confidence that the SPD was the party most likely to achieve social justice – only 35 per cent had held this view in 2009 (Jun and Berzel, 2014, p 221). Furthermore, at the beginning of its period in Opposition, only one-third of Germans regarded the SPD as competent with respect to its areas of traditional policy strength.

Major political parties seeking to win office also have to be able to demonstrate their ideational and policy competence in domains outside their 'traditional' areas of strength, for example, by effectively combining a pursuit of social justice with a reputation for economic competence (Niedermayer, 2010, p 231). Ultimately, during the period in question, the SPD failed to do this. The approval ratings of the SPD almost halved from 2002 to 2009, from 31 per cent to just 16 per cent. The SPD had failed to develop a credible economic strategy, and by doing so, failed to meet the expectations of the 69 per cent of voters (polled in June 2013) who wanted any future national government to safeguard good basic conditions for the German national economy (Köcher, 2013).

The SPD attempted to burnish its social justice credentials by developing some relevant social reforms (that is, implementing a minimum wage and retirement age of 63, and by occupying related portfolios. Former Secretary-General, Andrea Nahles, took office as Minister of Labour and Social Affairs in the grand coalition following the 2013 election.

To re-build its reputation for economic competence, the SPD pinned its hopes at the 2013 election on Peer Steinbrück (former Finance Minister of the previous grand coalition). Steinbrück had dealt effectively with the financial crisis of 2007/08, and many praised his performance over subsequent years. However, Steinbrück did not prove to be an effective electoral campaigner, and the SPD remained well behind the CDU in the national election. When Steinbrück failed to gain political office, it was hoped that Sigmar Gabriel, Economy and Energy Minister, would restore the SPD's reputation for economic competence, but this did not prove to be the case. While the SPD prioritised the 'labour' area of economic policy, polling data shows that voters expect parties to demonstrate their competent handling of wider national economic conditions.

Institutions

The SPD faces a range of institutional and structural problems. There is a declining proportion of workers who are members of trade unions and who continue to support social democracy. During the last 40 years, most social democratic parties have sought to compensate for the decrease in their traditional support base by increasing their appeal to other social groups. The SPD has also pursued this strategy of trying to build a cross-class coalition of support. Since the 1990s, this has largely been carried out via the implementation of a 'catch-all' strategy. This involves utilising modern forms of party organisation, appealing to the 'centre ground' and adopting a more pragmatic style of politics (cf Jun, 2004). However, modernisation has also caused the SPD to lose support and alienated certain traditional groups of supporters, resulting in the irreversible loss of this group of former core voters. This shift has nevertheless simultaneously attracted new groups of voters and led to electoral success in the era of Chancellor Schröder.

The ability to change is a fundamental characteristic of the social democratic family of parties, a quality that also applies to the SPD's chief competitor in the German party system, the CDU. Research shows that in recent years, both the major parties in the German party system have diverged (cf Niedermayer, 2015). Unlike, the SPD, the CDU/CSU has renewed itself, by partially modifying or revising its programmatic traditions in order to adjust to the electorate. In contrast, the SPD has emphasised its statist tradition (notably in 2005 and 2009) by highlighting its core brand of social justice in its party programmes. Further, the SPD's decision not to fundamentally rescind *Agenda 2010* in full has facilitated coalition building with the CDU/CSU. Sigmar Gabriel managed to close the gap between modernisers and traditionalists in the party. However, although the integration of the different party factions led to intra-party consolidation, it did not significantly increase the party's share of the vote at the 2013 election.

We can also detect shifts in the major parties in other policy areas. In relation to the socioeconomic axis in the two-dimensional space, both parties shifted towards the left (that is, towards state interventionism). This is indicated by the main decisions in the coalition agreement (for example, the retirement age and minimum wage policies). In relation to the socio-cultural axis, the CDU/CSU was formerly the only party that favoured authoritarian values. However, over recent years, it has shown a clear programmatic shift in policy areas such as family policy and migration policy. Notably, in its migration policy, the CDU abandoned the restrictive attitudes and authoritarian values that it held for decades.

During the Merkel era, the CDU has moved towards the political Centre across both dimensions of competition to ensure that it remains capable of winning a majority. Merkel has been able to enforce her programmatic visions within the CDU due to her pragmatism and her recognition of the need to secure a majority at elections, as the decision-making process focuses on the party leader and Chancellor (cf Zolleis and Schmid, 2014, p 29). Merkel recognised that the SPD is her party's main competitor, and has had considerable success in attracting centrist voters who had previously supported the SPD. The renewal of the CDU via a deliberate centrist appeal has accomplished this objective, and cemented Merkel's dominance.

The popularity of Chancellor Merkel, who was clearly driven by a pragmatic problem-solving style, has played a key role in her party's election success. However, this programmatic shift has left room within the political arena for other competitors, such as the national conservative AfD and the liberal-economic FDP. Coalition building with the SPD has not served to address such challenges. To ensure its majority appeal, the SPD will have to prove its competence in social and economic policies while at the same time resisting the challenges posed by Die Linke (The Left) (Raschke, 2010).

Since the Schröder era, the SPD has abandoned its pragmatic approach and dedicated itself to its core interest, that is, overcoming the difficulties suffered by socially disadvantaged groups. However, due to competition from the CDU, this approach has had limited success. The SPD, as a centre-left party, has a relatively limited programmatic margin of manoeuvre due to the CDU's transformation, especially in relation to the socio-cultural dimension of competition and the threat posed by other competitors on the left of the political spectrum. The space to the left is strongly limited by the post-communist Die Linke in the socioeconomic cleavage and by the Green Party in the socio-cultural cleavage.

Die Linke continues to demand that the welfare state be extended, including increases in almost all welfare state benefits, and calls for greater social equality. Die Linke has also been able to articulate the interests of socially disadvantaged groups in a clear fashion, and thus appears to be an exclusive welfare state party that supports the vulnerable. In response, the SPD, as a responsible centre-left party, finds that its hands are tied. For the party to win a majority, it needs to establish that its economic competence extends beyond its core brand (that is, social justice) and that it is capable of attracting the support of the middle-class core of society. Additionally, the right-wing populist AfD has successfully recruited many protest voters among the socially less privileged groups (Niedermayer and Hofrichter, 2016).

The SPD also has to appeal to the interests and values of the middle classes if it wishes to remain capable of winning a majority. If the SPD were to focus exclusively on ideas of welfare state support, which Die Linke is better equipped to do, it would effectively surrender its chances of obtaining a majority. The party has only been successful in national elections when it has also promised to safeguard economic competence (see Gamble, 2012, pp 45-6). For example, the SPD employed the slogan 'Innovation and justice' in 1998 to target the middles classes. The analysis of the SPD carried out by Peter Lösche and Franz Walter (1992) reached the same conclusion in relation to the 1960s and 1970s, as regards increasing the party's appeal to the middle class. In fact, the SPD has been the party of the middle class for some time. However, due to its own self-perception, it remains highly committed to its ideational core of social justice and its historical heritage as the party of employees. This balancing act is currently not particularly convincing, leading to clear electoral consequences. Conversely, in accordance with its concept of being a 'catch-all party', the CDU has successfully occupied the political centre ground. Moreover, the CDU has for some time made in-roads with groups of voters formerly attracted to the SPD (that is, the so-called 'aspirational' voters). The SPD has in turn had scant success in stealing voters from the CDU, as it primarily views itself as a party for disadvantaged groups in society. However, the SPD is competing with other parties for the support of these disadvantaged groups. The SPD's declining share of the vote is due to diverse social factors, and three merit attention here.

First, the feelings of social and political insecurity experienced by the population groups that have been unsettled by the effects of economic changes due to the globalisation of markets have caused a decline in the SPD's share of the vote. These groups, which have socially and culturally tended to lean towards social democracy, have experienced difficulties in the labour market, are often employed on an insecure basis, and feel their standard of living is under threat. Social democracy's shift towards the 'Third Way' did little to address these concerns, and many such voters switched their sympathies to Die Linke, the AfD or have simply refrained from voting. For the SPD, in line with Gingrich and Häusermann's judgement: 'middle-class voters have clearly become the largest share in the left electoral base in all regimes' (2015, p 58).

In addition, the SPD and the bulk of its remaining voters are much more likely to favour pro-migration and pro-integration policies, and ideologically, have libertarian rather than authoritarian values (cf Wessels, 2011, p 16). These values nevertheless do not reflect the attitude of many potential voters in lower socioeconomic groups. Such groups have shown a preference for stronger, authoritarian attitudes, a stance that has electorally benefited the right-wing, populist party, AfD, particularly since the 2015 immigration crisis across Europe (cf Wiesendahl, 2017, pp 50-3).

Furthermore, social democratic voters, culturally and politically tend to categorise themselves as 'left-of-centre'. However, when major parties pursue 'pragmatic' programmes in office, traditional voters tend to be more quickly disillusioned. Research shows that conservative parties are punished less when they pursue pragmatic courses (cf Wessels, 2011). This high probability of failing to meet supporters' expectations has become a real issue, and has also been affected by the SPD's extensive experience in government (notably, its seven years as the CDU's junior partner). The SPD's leadership has only had limited success in developing a strategy to persuade lost, disparate voter groups to support them. Thus, the centre-left party's room for manoeuvre has become even more limited.

The structural crisis of the SPD's organisation is also palpable. The party's loss of members (see Figure 7.2) and difficulties in recruiting younger voters has led to an ageing support base. Regionally, the organisation is in decline (Dose et al, 2016). With only 400,000 members, it has reached a new low in the history of the German Federal Republic (Mielke, 2009). The party's proportion of workers has, for some years, been below 10 per cent (Butzlaff, 2009, p 46). Joachim Raschke (2010, p 96) reported that in addition to the declining membership and the erosion of the organisation's core in some regions, there has been 'intellectual decline, branches which appear to have lost touch ... loss of motivation, organisational strength and campaigning capacity.'

Agenda 2010 has also left its mark on the party's organisation. It led to the demobilisation of the part of the active membership that was supposed to function as recruiters for party support, as these individuals became disillusioned (Hegelich et al, 2010, p 241). The upshot is that the SPD has lost vital ground troops for use in campaigning at the local level (see Figure 7.2).

The attempt to revitalise the inner life of the party through more direct democratic elements has only been partially successful (for example, the vote by members in favour of the coalition treaty in 2013). The party reforms initiated by Sigmar Gabriel to increase internal democracy had little impact (Bukow, 2014, p 148). Increasing the participation of SPD supporters (that is, non-members) has also proved difficult. In this respect, there has been little incentive to become a member of the SPD. Despite these reforms, there has been a strengthening of the committee-based, representation-oriented membership model (Bukow, 2013, p 148).

A related problem for the SPD's membership base concerns members' profiles. These differ considerably from the party's set of values. Indeed, the SPD has many academics among its members and is dominated by the middle classes, especially those who became members of the party during the 1970s. The SPD originally claimed to represent the socially disadvantaged; however, the less well-off have deserted the party to a significant extent. Strong links between the SPD and the socially disadvantaged are difficult to promote due to the party's membership structure, as the groups that feel socially disadvantaged have distanced themselves from political parties in general. The party's internal processes do little to facilitate a direct link with many of the groups that it claims to represent. This issue goes well beyond the SPD, but the party has been particularly affected as its traditional social base has to a great extent distanced itself from the party.

Figure 7.2: SPD party members (1990-2014)

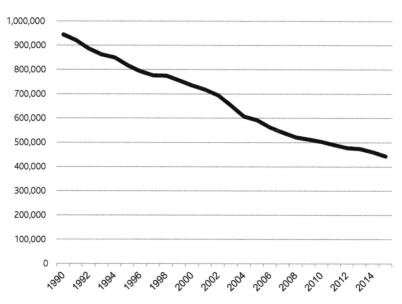

Source: Jun's calculation from Niedermayer (2016)

Individuals

In relation to the role of key individuals and leadership, the SPD has not been able to close the gap with the CDU. In 2009 and 2013, both candidates for Chancellor (Frank-Walter Steinmeier and Peer Steinbrück) attracted far less support than the dominant Angela Merkel (Jun and Pütz, 2010; Jun and Berzel, 2014). During the 2009 campaign, Steinmeier's low personal popularity meant that the party could not build a strategy based on the personalisation of the leader. Generally, voters believed that Chancellor Merkel was more reliable, more assertive, more likeable and a better crisis manager (Murswieck, 2009, p 30). In short: 'the Chancellor's dominance as a candidate was crucial to the CDU's electoral success' (Jung et al, 2009, p 13). Conversely, Steinmeier had little appeal to voters with respect to these factors. More damningly, one in five SPD voters preferred Merkel as

Chancellor to Steinmeier (Jung et al, 2009, p 14). Steinbrück also polled poorly in 2013; he was something of an albatross for the SPD, with the media portraying him as arrogant, clumsy and self-interested.

Merkel's popularity had dipped since 2015, largely due to her immigration policy, but it reached new heights in the summer of 2017. Sigmar Gabriel, the SPD leader from 2009 until March 2017, failed to dent Merkel's dominance (see Figure 7.3). Gabriel was labelled unpredictable, unsteady and erratic, and the party was viewed as being rudderless under his leadership (Schwennicke, 2015). The SPD itself contributed to Gabriel's less than positive image by partially discrediting him at their party conference in December 2015 when he obtained the support of just 74.3 per cent in his re-election as party leader, which constituted one of the worst results in the SPD's history.

Gabriel's standing appeared to improve at the start of the third grand coalition, at the end of 2013. SPD members' vote in favour of the coalition treaty was essentially Gabriel's success (von Alemann and Spier, 2015). Gabriel was strongly in favour of the SPD joining the grand coalition. Despite heated internal party debates on the issue, the membership overwhelmingly endorsed his stance. Gabriel also successfully calmed disputes between the different factions. However, the disappointment of many within the SPD led to further poor polling results for Gabriel, and in 2017 he resigned as party leader. At the same time, Gabriel proposed Martin Schulz, former President of the European Parliament, as new party leader and candidate for chancellor at the 2017 general election. Schulz was elected as party leader and candidate for chancellor with 100 per cent approval for each position at the party convention at the end of March 2017.

New leader, new hope?

Immediately after Schulz became party leader, the so called Schulz–effect appeared to boost the SPD's fortunes (see Figure 7.3), and he reignited hopes that his party might finally regain the chancellorship. In the wake of his election as leader, over 10,000 new members joined the party. A new hype and excitement about Schulz's elevation to the leadership was created and constructed by the media. Schulz became a projection for a wide range of desires, hopes and expectations among voters. In response, Schulz has floated various promises concerning greater social justice: payment of unemployment benefits over a longer period, free education from daycare to university, more money for families, and higher wages for women. Although Gabriel would probably have adopted similar positions, they appear more attractive coming from Schulz.

Figure 7.3: Germany – CDU/CSU and SPD polling data (2013-17)

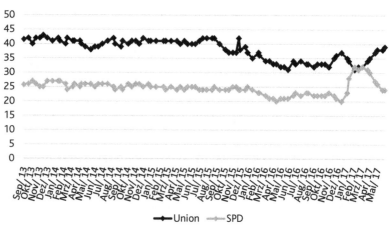

Source: Infratest dimap

If political credibility is forged from trustworthiness, representative appeal and problem-solving skills, then Schulz certainly possesses advantages. Furthermore, he is profiting from the SPD's solid work in government during the last four years, given that it had already partially corrected the *Agenda 2010*, and actually fulfilled the promises made during the election campaign. Schulz frequently, and with a certain passion, defends the balancing of justice and welfare; and his rhetoric is yielding political results, not least as the German economy is currently undergoing an upturn. But recent disappointing federal state election results in the Saarland, Schleswig-Holstein and Northrhein-Westphalia suggest that the Schulz effect lacked substance. The period of hope for the SPD was short-lived as structural disadvantages proved to be insurmountable.

Final overview and outlook

This chapter has considered the SPD's performance in relation to elections and its organisational structure and programme. Neoliberal-economic visions are in retreat; however, due to the lack of a strategy-based approach, German social democracy has failed to achieve greater electoral success. Indeed, it appears that the SPD has experienced a decline. Consequently, the question arises: What are the SPD's prospects at the 2017 national election?

Until recently, the SPD could only have been successful in national elections if it won over both traditional voters (oriented towards the welfare state) and swing voters (with moderately middle-class values and visions that veered towards the centre of the political spectrum in relation to personnel and programmes). Thus, the SPD will only win a majority if it manages to associate itself with a high degree of competence in the areas of labour and the economy while maintaining the core of its brand (that is, social justice).

The SPD has not benefited electorally by having a narrow focus on employment issues. Thus, as recent developments have shown, it needs to develop a broader political agenda to make greater inroads into the CDU's voter base. Such signs do not bode well for the SPD in the upcoming 2017 election campaign, as the SPD is lagging well behind the CDU in the areas of labour and the economy. The party has not managed to reduce the CDU's lead for a long time. The slogan 'Progress and justice' that was propagated by Sigmar Gabriel and the Labour Secretary Andrea Nahles in 2014 has not been backed up with an elaborate overall political approach, and there appears to be no overall strategy. Despite this failing, for a brief period in early 2017 the SPD benefited from its new party leader Martin Schulz as a kind of projection screen for the multifaceted desires, hopes and expectations of a significant number of voters for a better future, as well as gaining from the sense of disappointment felt by many voters as a result of Angela Merkel's refugee policy. But after three defeats in a row for the SPD at regional elections, the so-called 'Schulz-effect' seemed to have disappeared.

With only two months before the national election, the SPD has given no clear response to the differing challenges raised by its competitors on the left of the spectrum (that is, the Greens and Die Linke) and those on the right (that is, the CDU). Further, the CDU has handily positioned itself at the centre in relation to both dimensions of competition. Thus, the party leadership needs to adopt a more convincing communication strategy and ensure that members' concerns are clearly addressed.

Additionally, at present, there are no polarising issues between the SPD and the CDU. Thus, the SPD must do more than target its messages towards a cosmopolitan audience receptive to appeals for social solidarity. Such an approach promises only limited electoral progress. The mobilisation of support at the upcoming national election could also cause difficulties, especially in relation to attitudes towards the SPD's role after the polls have closed.

A continuation of the grand coalition among the parties allied to the CDU is possible, although the prospect is not appealing to many SPD members and supporters. Conversely, a coalition with the Greens and Die Linke is possible, but could only occur under very special circumstances due to the parliamentary arithmetic. However, politically, this 'rainbow' option constellation appears unlikely and is viewed as a 'threat' by many voters (Raschke, 2010, p 73). Sections of Die Linke (the so-called left-wing) and some sections of the SPD (the right-wing 'Seeheimer Kreis') view such coalition building reluctantly and with scepticism. The Greens are in the process of progressively distancing themselves from the SPD when it comes to forming an alliance, and are no longer ruling out a coalition with the CDU and the FDP. Thus, the SPD's chances of success do not appear likely.

References

Bukow, S. (2013) 'Die Wiederentdeckung der mitgliedschaftsbasierten Parteiorganisation Ziele, Prozess und Ergebnisse der SPD-Parteireform 2009-2011', in O. Niedermayer, B. Höhne and U. Jun (eds) *Abkehr von den Parteien?*, Wiesbaden: VS Verlag, pp 231-59.

Bukow, S. (2014) 'Die SPD-Parteiorganisationsreform 2009-2011. Mit Primaries und verstärkter Basisbeteiligung auf dem Weg zur modernsten Partei Europas?', in U. Münch, U. Kranenpohl and H. Gast (eds) *Parteien und Demokratie: Innerparteiliche Demokratie im Wandel*, Baden-Baden: Nomos, pp 133-50.

Burzan, N. (2014) 'Gefühlte Verunsicherung in der Mitte der Gesellschaft?', *Aus Politik und Zeitgeschichte*, vol 64, no 49, pp 17-23.

Butzlaff, F. (2009) 'Verlust des Verlässlichen. Die SPD nach elf Jahren Regierungsverantwortung', in F. Butzlaff, S. Harm and F. Walter (eds) *Patt oder Gezeitenwechsel? Deutschland 2009*, Wiesbaden: VS Verlag, pp 37-66.

Butzlaff, F. and Micus, M. (2011) 'Mao in Berlin? Die SPD auf der Suche nach einem neuen Projekt', in F. Butzlaff, M. Micus and F. Walter (eds) *Genossen in der Krise? Europas Sozialdemokratie auf dem Prüfstand*, Göttingen: Vandenhoeck and Ruprecht, pp 11-30.

Dose, N., Fischer, A.-K. and Golla, N. (2016) *Die Partei im regionalen Fokus. Mitgliederschwund, Alterungsprozesse und Mitgliederpartizipation bei der SPD – Ergebnisse zweier empirischer Studien*, Baden-Baden: Nomos.

Gamble, A. (2012) 'Debt and deficits: the quest for economic competence', in O. Cramme and P. Diamond (eds) *After the third way, the future of social democracy in Europe*, London: I.B. Tauris, pp 45-59.

Gingrich, J. and Häusermann, S. (2015) 'The decline of the working-class vote, the reconfiguration of the welfare support coalition and consequences for the welfare state', *Journal of European Social Policy*, vol 25, no 1, pp 50-75.

Hegelich, S., Knollmann, D. and Kuhlmann, J. (2011) *Agenda 2010. Strategien −Entscheidungen − Konsequenzen*, Wiesbaden: VS Verlag.

Huo, J. (2009) *Third Way reforms: Social democracy after the Golden Age*, Cambridge: Cambridge University Press.

Jun, U. (2004) *Der Wandel von Parteien in der Mediendemokratie, SPD und Labour Party im Vergleich*, Frankfurt/Main: Campus.

Jun, U. (2010) 'Die SPD in der Großen Koalition: Selbstverschuldeter Niedergang oder zwanghafte Anpassung an veränderte Ausgangsbedingungen der Politik?', in S. Bukow and W. Seemann (eds) *Die Große Koalition, Regierung − Politik − Parteien*, Wiesbaden: VS Verlag, pp 299-318.

Jun, U. and Berzel, A. (2014) 'Weshalb verlor die SPD die Wahl? Personal, Organisation, Programmatik, Koalitionsstrategie, Wahlkampf', in E. Jesse and R. Sturm (eds) *Bilanz der Bundestagswahl 2013: Voraussetzungen, Ergebnisse, Folgen*, Wiesbaden: Nomos, pp 205-29.

Jun, U. and Jakobs, S. (2015) 'Programmatic change in the two main parties: CDU and SPD on their way to the Grand Coalition', in G. D'Ottavio and T. Saalfeld (eds) *Germany after the 2013 election: Breaking the mould of post-unification politics*, Aldershot: Ashgate, pp 129-53.

Jun, U. and Pütz, J. (2010) 'Die organisierte Unverantwortlichkeit? Aus dem Innenleben einer Kampagne. Kommunikationsstrukturen und strategien des SPD-Kampagnenmanagements im Bundestagswahlkampf 2009 − Das TV-Duell als Fallbeispiel', *Zeitschrift für Politikberatung*, vol 3, no 2, pp 197-215.

Jung, M., Schroth, Y. and Wolf, A. (2009) 'Regierungswechsel ohne Wechsel-Stimmung', *Aus Politik und Zeitgeschichte* 51/2009, pp 12-19.

Köcher, R. (2007) 'Der selektive Aufschwung', *Frankfurter Allgemeine Zeitung*, 21 February, p 5.

Lösche, P. and Walter, F. (1992) *Die SPD: Klassenpartei, Volkspartei, Quotenpartei*, Darmstadt: Wissenschaftliche Buchgesellschaft.

Mau, S. (2014) 'Die Mittelschicht − das unbekannte Wesen?', *Aus Politik und Zeitgeschichte*, vol 64, no 49, pp 3-10.

Micus, M. (2010) 'Organisationsidentität und-reform sozialdemokratischer Parteien in Europa', in F.E. Stiftung (ed) *Internationale Politikanalyse*, November.

Mielke, G. (2009) 'Endspurt mit schweren Beinen. Zur innerparteilichen Lage der SPD', in M. Machnig and J. Raschke (eds) *Wohin steuert Deutschland? Bundestagswahl 2009 – Ein Blick hinter die Kulissen*, Hamburg: Hoffmann und Campe, pp 229-42.

Murswieck, A. (2009) 'Angela Merkel als Regierungschefin und Kanzlerkandidatin', *Aus Politik und Zeitgeschichte*, vol 51, pp 26-32.

Nachtwey, O. (2009) *Marktsozialdemokratie: Die Transformation von SPD und Labour Party*, Wiesbaden: VS Verlag.

Neusser, C. (2013) *Pluralisierte Partnerschaften: Über den Wandel der Parteien-Gewerkschafts-Beziehungen*, Berlin: Edition Sigma.

Niedermayer, O. (2010) 'Triumph und Desaster: Die SPD im deutschen Parteiensystem nach der Vereinigung', *Gesellschaft – Wirtschaft – Politik*, vol 59, no 2, pp 225-36.

Niedermayer, O. (2015) 'Das deutsche Parteiensystem nach der Bundestagswahl 2013', in O. Niedermayer (ed) *Die Parteien nach der Bundestagswahl 2013*, Wiesbaden: Springer VS, pp 1-23.

Niedermayer, O. and Hofrichter, J. (2016) 'Die Wählerschaft der AfD: Wer ist sie, woher kommt sie und wie weit rechts steht sie?', *Zeitschrift für Parlamebntsfragen*, vol 47, no 2, pp 267-84.

Niehues, J. (2014) 'Die Mittelschicht – stabiler als gedacht', *Aus Politik und Zeitgeschichte*, vol 64, no 49, pp 10-17.

Piazza, J. (2001) 'De-linking Labor: Labor unions and social democratic parties under globalization', *Party Politics*, vol 7, no 4, pp 413-35.

Raschke, J. (2010) 'Zerfallsphase des Schröder-Zyklus: Die SPD 2005-2009', in C. Egle and R. Zohlnhöfer (eds) *Die zweite Große Koalition, Eine Bilanz der Regierung Merkel 2005-2009*, Wiesbaden: VS Verlag, pp 69-98.

Sachs, M. (2011) *Sozialdemokratie im Wandel. Programmatische Neustrukturierungen im europäischen Vergleich*, Wiesbaden: VS Verlag.

Schwennicke, C. (2015) 'Morbus SPD', *Cicero*, vol 9, p 30.

Spier, T. and von Alemann, U. (2013) 'Die Sozialdemokratische Partei Deutschlands (SPD)', in O. Niedermayer (ed) *Handbuch Parteienforschung*, Wiesbaden: Springer VS, pp 439-67.

Sturm, D.F. (2009) *Wohin geht die SPD?*, München: Deutscher Taschenbuch Verlag.

von Alemann, U. and Spier, T. (2015) 'In ruhigerem Fahrwasser, aber ohne Land in Sicht? Die SPD nach der Bundestagswahl 2013', in O. Niedermayer (ed) *Die Parteien nach der Bundestagswahl 2013*, Wiesbaden: Springer VS, pp 49-69.

Wessels, B. (2010) 'Was ist dran an der These vom Ende der Sozialdemokratie? Eine empirische Analyse der Wahlergebnisse und Wählerprofile sozialdemokratischer Parteien in Europa in den letzten zwanzig Jahren', in F.E. Stiftung (ed) *Internationale Politikanalyse*, May.

Wessels, B. (2011) 'Das wählerische Herz schlägt links der Mitte. Regierungszufriedenheit und Einstellungen sozialdemokratischer Wähler im europäischen Vergleich 2002-2008', in F.E. Stiftung (ed) *Internationale Politikanalyse*, December.

Wiesendahl, E. (2017) SPD 2017. *Eine Partei zwischen Zuversicht und ungelöster Standortbestimmung*, Sankt Augustin/Berlin: Konrad-Adenauer-Stiftung.

Zolleis, U. and Schmid, J. (2015) 'Die CDU unter Angela Merkel – der neue Kanzlerwahlverein?', in O. Niedermayer (ed) *Die Parteien nach der Bundestagswahl 2013*, Wiesbaden: Springer VS, pp 25-48.

EIGHT

The Swedish Social Democrats and the 'new Swedish model': playing a losing game

Claes Belfrage and Mikko Kuisma

Introduction

After the 2006 Swedish elections, the Social Democratic Party (SAP), the 'natural party of government' during the construction and heyday of the famous 'Swedish model' in the second half of the 20th century, entered opposition for eight long years. Initially at least, some might have taken this to represent just a regular short-term slump in electoral politics. However, for reasons discussed below, it could also be seen as the beginning of a long decline. In 2014, the former hegemons managed to return to power, but under relatively bittersweet circumstances. The elections resulted in a hung Parliament and a Red–Green coalition, incidentally also one of the weakest minority governments in Swedish history. Under Göran Persson's leadership (1996-2007), while the post-war glory years were already long gone, the SAP was able to secure 35-40 per cent of the national vote. In 2014, the fragile victory of Stefan Löfven's SAP was built on a lowly 31.0 per cent of the vote, up only marginally from the result of the 2010 election (by 0.3 per cent from 30.7 per cent).

Under these new circumstances to which SAP's own actions and policies have contributed significantly, as we will discuss later, the party is dedicating much of its energies to trying to demonstrate economic governance competence (very much defined by these constraints) rather than being visionary, redistributive and fair. The party is playing a losing game and, as we discuss, the only way in which it can reverse its fortunes is by calling the very foundations of the 'new Swedish model', now ironically perhaps associated with the Conservative administration of Fredrik Reinfeldt, into question. This will be a difficult task and will involve some serious soul searching, as the 'new Swedish model' is rooted in social democratic politics, especially the

Third Way approach of the SAP governments in the late 1990s and early 2000s. The party also faces challenges at the individual/agency and ideational levels but, as we argue below, the problems they face are ultimately of a profoundly institutional nature. Nevertheless, strong, visionary leaders with social democratic ideas might be able to find at least some short-term solutions to these challenges.

No more bright ideas?

Ideationally, one of the most significant turning points in post-war Swedish social democracy took place under Göran Persson's leadership in the 1990s. Linked to a wider renewal project of European social democracy, Persson and the SAP bought into the Third Way (Giddens, 1998), associated largely with Tony Blair's New Labour and, to a certain extent, Bill Clinton's New Democrats (Andersson, 2006). Based largely on Anthony Giddens' work, the key Third Way argument was that traditional social democracy was 'incapable of dealing with contemporary "realities" of technological change, globalization, and post-industrial "risk society"' (Kuisma, 2007, p 18). Hence, a new ideational departure was deemed necessary and, taken partly in good faith (Andersson, 2010). This resulted in a significant break with the past, and also at the level of policy and institutional arrangements. Certain core ideas associated with the Nordic model were also recast largely due to the influence of Third Way politics.

Overall, for some, the central role of the British Labour Party spreading the Third Way message across Europe might have been rather surprising since one would not necessarily identify the UK as a specifically strong breeding ground for social democratic politics. Despite this, many European social democratic leaders, including Göran Persson, looked to the UK and the US for inspiration, and, in so doing, managed to return their parties to office in the 1990s (Kuisma and Ryner, 2012). This is where the novelty of the Third Way lies. The Anglo-American connection was not so counterintuitive after all. Indeed, the Third Way of European social democracy was very much constructed on the belief that the US model could be copied (Sapir, 2003). With this approach in mind, European social democratic leaders sought to redefine the political centre and to widen their appeal, away from representing the interests of their traditional working-class electorate towards becoming the advocates of a wider post-industrial knowledge society (Ryner, 2002).

The context within which the ideas were recast or, rather, more centrist and economically liberal ideas took hold, is important. For instance, by the 1990s, the traditional working-class constituencies of the social democrats had shrunk, and those who remained became more and more politically passive. The decline of working-class turnout in national elections in Sweden at the time of the adoption of the Third Way is remarkable: the turnout had gone from just under 90 per cent in the 1970s and around 85 per cent in the 1980s and early 1990s to just 75 per cent in the 1994 election (Hedberg, 2009, Figure 3). As such, it is possible to argue that some of the changes in the direction of social democratic politics were done in good faith since many social democrats genuinely believed that old-style social democracy could not survive in the post-industrial global age.

In terms of central policy ideas, a key departure for the Third Way was to move away from a more traditional needs-based approach in social and health care policy, to a stronger focus on increasing individual activation, conditionality, and longer-term individual investment (attached to welfare in general). These changes are especially important in the Nordic context where the welfare state had been seen as the ultimate achievement of working-class politics. The Third Wayers identified old-fashioned 'unconditional' social rights as promoting a 'moral hazard'. The solution was said to be found in the 'responsibilisation' of social citizenship rights with the principle of 'no rights without responsibilities' (Kuisma and Ryner, 2012, p 330). The very fact that universal social rights would be considered to be 'unconditional' is an interesting discursive departure in its own right. To attach this kind of label to universalist welfare principles surely made it easier to promote a discourse of virtue around conditionalisation. Persson himself was very clear about this. While defending the foundations of the Swedish model of welfare, he emphasised that rights were not a 'free for all'. Indeed, everyone should have now accepted that there were 'no rights without responsibilities' (Persson, 2007).

After the relative electoral success of Persson's Third Way politics, the party struggled to renew itself ideologically. One potential explanation for its demise lies in the party's failures to launch new political and economic ideas. Ironically, the root cause of this failure to find new ideas was linked to the nature of the new ideas of the 1990s, that is, the dominance of the Third Way paradigm. As has been argued in the literature, despite being sold as essentially a renewal project of social democracy, the Third Way incorporated, directly or indirectly, a range of neoliberal ideas, values and policies (Ryner, 2002). These were by no means completely new or alien to the SAP either. Nonetheless, the ideas of the Third Way were translated into concrete policy reforms. For instance, the SAP, under Persson's leadership, abandoned the principle of full employment as a macroeconomic commitment, reduced the social insurance replacement rates, introduced wholesale pension reform and accepted price stability as a key point of reference in wage bargaining. All of these policy departures served to blur the party's social democratic identity and values and, maybe most importantly, confused and frustrated the party's traditional constituency that was becoming more passive.

Under Mona Sahlin's crisis-prone leadership (2007-11), the 2009 European Parliament elections resulted in an all-time low in the history of the SAP. Some recognised that the party was not clear with respect to its core values and had not managed to renew itself after the Persson years. Consequently, the party went into soul-searching mode and released a new 'Programme of Principles' later that year. Perhaps partly as an outcome of the wider problems associated with Sahlin's leadership, it did not generate the desired effect, and the party lost further votes in the 2010 general election. Quite correctly, some commentators explained the defeat due to the SAP being incapable of offering a credible alternative to the centre-right Alliance government (Wennemo, 2010). While failing to do this, a turn 'back to the left' was not conceived as possible either, as it might have been interpreted as retrogressive nostalgia (Kuisma and Ryner, 2012). The party had created an ideological trap for itself.

The irony of the Swedish battle of political and economic ideas was that while SAP was trying to find ways to reinvent itself ideologically, the Moderate Party, leading the new centre-right Alliance government, also shrewdly reinvented itself by celebrating the 'Swedish model' and by adopting Third Way ideas. In the spirit of 'responsible market capitalism', the 'new Moderate' leader Fredrik Reinfeldt adopted Third Way ideas and repackaged them with a distinctly Conservative spin in order to appeal to his core audience. This approach worked very well with the Swedish electorate. Furthermore, the new Moderates and the Alliance government also managed to win the discursive game about being the party most trusted with managing the economy. As Göran Persson himself admitted, some core Third Way ideas, such as 'activation before benefits' ('*verksamhet före bidrag*') were appropriated extremely well by the new Moderates and the Alliance (2007, p 387). In fact, at the 2006 election campaign, they went so far as to use a largely pro-welfare position to their benefit (Agius, 2007). Discursively, they started calling themselves both the 'new workers' party' and the 'only workers' party' of Sweden. So, while SAP was struggling with its Third Way legacy, the new Moderates ironically benefited from adopting Third Way ideas.

Since the 2010 general election, a further challenge in terms of ideas has emerged, this time from the populist-nationalist Sweden Democrats (SD). SD's rapid rise has squeezed SAP's political space even further. SD combine nostalgia for a substantial welfare state with an anti-immigration and nativist platform, blaming immigration for the former's decline. One of the SD's main criticisms is that the mainstream parties betrayed the Swedish welfare state (Bergmann, 2017). Their ideas resonate with segments of the voters of the two largest mainstream parties, taking votes especially from the Moderates and SAP since the 2010 elections. Taking on the challenge from the SD therefore presents a further ideological trap for the SAP. If the SAP were to launch a 'new' defence of the traditional welfare model, it would undermine its attempts at ideological renewal, because it has invested so much energy in refuting this same model since the 1990s (see Andersson, 2009).

Leadership and controversy

Individuals and leadership can also be highlighted as a factor in SAP's decline. After the successful Persson years, the party put a lot of hope in Mona Sahlin as its new leader. However, Sahlin was no stranger to controversy, as already in the 1990s her reputation was tarnished in a rather ugly expenses scandal. The infamous 'Toblerone affair' was later concluded without Sahlin being charged with any wrongdoing, but it did not make her career at the top of Swedish politics any easier. After returning to politics in 1998, she continued her rise to the very top of the party organisation, becoming one of the leading candidates to replace Persson as party leader in 2006. The party was determined to have a female leader and, as her three competitors, Carin Jämtin, Margot Wallström and Ulrica Messing withdrew from the contest and announced their support for Sahlin, she was elected leader in 2007. However, she continued to be a controversial figure and did not gain the full support of the party membership. Indeed, at a time when the party should have been working hard on renewing its approach to politics, the defining feature of its politics was the seemingly uncertain position of its leader.

The Sahlin leadership came to an end in 2011 after two disastrous election defeats, the 2009 European Parliament election and the 2010 general election. After the second defeat, a surprise candidate, Håkan Juholt, replaced Sahlin as the party leader. The process by which he was chosen was already a cause for controversy, as, rather than appealing to a sense of democratic unity through a membership vote, the party resorted to 'party tradition' by appointing a selection committee consisting of 11 representatives who were mainly sitting and former MPs. After a process of nominations, informal interviews and lengthy discussions with different party representatives and branches, their decision to endorse Juholt was unexpected. Also according to party culture, the formal selectorate (the delegates to a special party congress) did not challenge the nomination and voted unanimously for Juholt to become the next SAP leader (Aylott and Bolin, 2016). Juholt was not an obvious choice as party leader and he faced an uphill struggle from the beginning. Like Sahlin, he was also distracted from the task of leading the party. Only months after taking over as leader he was also involved in an expenses scandal and, while he, too, was not convicted of any wrongdoing, the party's poll ratings suffered, resulting in significant internal pressure for him to go. In January 2012, Juholt resigned and was swiftly replaced by Stefan Löfven, leader of the powerful trade union IF Metall. In many ways, Löfven's election signified an important break from the past for the party. The new leader was a newcomer to electoral politics, untarnished by political games and corruption. While his leadership, compared to that of Sahlin and Juholt, has been less crisis-prone, it has not been easy for him to convince swing voters. In fact, the results from the two elections held in 2014, the European Parliament election in June and the general election in September, would suggest that Löfven had failed to succeed in what the party had been hoping to achieve, in other words, a return to the position of the 'natural party of government'.

Certainly the instability created by the leadership of Sahlin and Juholt was something the party could have done without. Equally, the party and its supporters might have expected better electoral outcomes than those produced under Stefan Löfven's leadership. However, in the end, the leaders and the political and economic ideas they promote are not the main sources of SAP failures in the longer term. Rather, as we argue in the next section, it is the changed institutional framework within which politics is conducted that explains why the SAP has 'fallen from grace'. This is also why it is playing a losing game, at least unless it can find broad domestic and international support for changing the rules of that game. While some of the changes in the institutional context of Swedish politics are exogenous, ironically, some of the endogenous factors are of the SAP's own making.

The institutional dimension in SAP's failures

The current social democratic soul-searching largely derives from a shift in the wider global structural, institutional and economic context. For Sweden, in particular, there has been a change in its economic growth model, with a shift in focus from the export sector to the financial sector, a shift from wage-led to profit-led growth, and a shift to a stronger focus on debt-led and asset-based consumption (Belfrage and Kallifatides, 2016a). Neoliberal ideas and financialisation are key drivers in explaining this shift, and these were accelerated, to a large extent, by the emergence of Third Way politics in the 1990s. However, we argue that while the Third Way is an important part of the story, the transformation had already begun much earlier.

Social democracy established its hegemonic position in Sweden under particular historical circumstances. The 'Swedish Model', a contested, perhaps even mythical notion and certainly never implemented in full, became the policy framework of Swedish social democracy during the decades immediately after the Second World War. Designed by key strategists of the labour movement, this growth model focused not only on economic policy-making and the thriving export sector, but also on politics capable of ensuring the support of the working classes as well as significant elements of the middle classes. Under the institutional constraints set by the Bretton Woods system of fixed exchange rates and US hegemony, social democrats also sponsored the development of an advantageous institutional framework for large exporting corporations, and thus secured at least temporary support from capital. This constituted a class compromise (see Alestalo and Kuhnle, 1987), according to which wage-earners received a 'fair wage' and market protection through an ambitious project of welfare state expansion, while capital benefited from monopolistic competition policy, centrally controlled wage expansion and preferential politics of investment. The latter was intimately connected with the organisation of the welfare state, and thus provided the socioeconomic foundations for a comparatively stable social formation. The electoral and parliamentary systems also privileged stability over change (Belfrage, 2015).

The end of the Bretton Woods system by the US Nixon administration in the early 1970s and subsequent recurring oil crises created the exogenous shocks that enabled the emergence of the alternative imaginary of neoliberal financialisation. In Sweden, this was a gradual process, but it was fundamentally facilitated by electoral reform removing an Upper House from the Riksdagen, which undermined SAP's electoral dominance (Immergut and Jochem, 2006).

Swedish neoliberalism involved the reframing of key institutions of the Swedish model as outright obstacles to modernisation, and the use of rhetoric and discourse to justify the reforms to the electorate. These reforms led to a restructuring of the economy, whereby the wage–labour nexus was gradually relegated and the emphasis on competition and finance took centre-stage.

Meanwhile, divisions within the labour movement between moderate and radical elements weakened social democracy, and led to a conflict between trade unions as well as between trade unions and SAP itself. The failed push for economic democracy through the wage-earner fund initiative in the 1970s became not only the watershed in the creation of this division, but also the symbol for an ostensibly backward-looking utopia. Modernising the Swedish Model became a preoccupation of both an aggressive centre-right and a dismembered SAP, now with powerful neoliberal voices in its midst. The class compromise integral to SAP hegemony was falling apart, resulting in wage inflation and uncertainty in the politics of investment. The increased exposure of the economy to globalised market scrutiny also facilitated a neoliberal shift in politics. A weakened SAP was unable to sustain its electoral dominance in the second half of the 1970s and lost, after over four decades in power, its role as the governing party (Belfrage, 2015).

Yet, subsequent centre-right governments failed to operate within the Swedish model. Returned to power in 1982, the SAP partly reverted to the policy routines of the Swedish model, but also set about undertaking wholesale changes to the institutional framework governing the growth model. Accused of going stale by Opposition parties and supporters alike, Swedish social democracy set about implementing a programme of modernisation (cf Ryner, 2002). Financial deregulation (of capital account and credit markets), new financialised savings policies, a central bank sterilisation policy, pension system and tax reform were high on the policy agenda in the 1980s. This first phase of neoliberal financialisation contributed to the creation of the 1992-93 banking crisis, and the bursting of a speculative bubble, as is so often the case, in the housing market, a phenomenon that would reoccur in the 2000s (Belfrage, 2008).

The further institutional and policy reforms implemented by both SAP in the early 1990s and the subsequent centre-right government, partly to finance the costs of resolving the banking crisis, partly to prevent it from recurring, partly to secure EU membership, and partly to modernise the growth model, bore the hallmarks of neoliberalism. The early 1990s saw the floating of the currency, the establishment of an independent central bank, major tax reform, the introduction of restrictive fiscal rules (for both central and local government) and top-down budget processes, comprehensive pension reform, employment and health benefits reform.

SAP governments under the leadership of Göran Persson in the late 1990s and early 2000s undertook what could be understood as 'marketisation' reforms, especially in the area of education (Andersson, 2014). While the Swedish model involved wage moderation through central wage bargaining, the 1990s and 2000s saw wages stagnate further, partly as the result of a weakened labour movement. Moreover, the centre-right Reinfeldt government which came to power in 2006 introduced labour market flexibilisation policies under the rubric of being the new labour party. Altogether, these policy reforms saw public expenditure being cut from about 70 per cent of GDP in the early 1990s to about 50 per cent in 2012. As Buendia and Palazuelos (2014) demonstrate, the redesign of the institutional framework broke the growth dynamics of the Swedish model (see Schnyder, 2012, for the role played by new market-led investment channels in the new growth dynamic).

From the late 1990s, and into the 2000s, there was relatively high productivity growth, and this led observers to celebrate the advent of a 'new', modernised and more 'open' Swedish model (cf Steinmo, 2010; Bergh, 2014). Yet, this literature, as with much of the rest of the literature on Sweden, overlooks the downside of this restructuring. Observers perceived the SAP to appear 'progressive', 'responsible', 'competent' and increasingly distant from the trade unions, and this perception was fuelled by the SAP's failure to introduce economic democracy through the wage-earner fund initiative in the 1970s. However, we argue that understanding the transformation of the Swedish economy along with the crisis tendencies lurking underneath the positive growth narratives requires an analysis of the role played by financialisation in the new Swedish model. This is crucial for grasping the challenges faced by Swedish social democracy today.

Financialisation refers, according to van der Zwan, to 'the web of interrelated processes – economic, political, social, technological, cultural etc – through which finance has extended its influence beyond the marketplace and into other realms of social life' (2014, p 104). This broad definition, like neoliberal policy-making, is useful because financialisation never looks the same across space. The key characteristics of the financialisation process in Sweden commencing in the 1980s relates to how the welfare state has been reformed to engender a profit-led growth dynamic with declining real wages, rising prominence of debt-led and asset-based consumption centred on the financial sector (not least, the four big banks) (Belfrage and Kallifatedes, 2016a). In contrast with the US and the UK, the economies typically associated with financialisation reforms in the area of corporate governance have lagged behind welfare state developments, particularly in the areas of pensions and housing.

In Sweden, reforms of public and private pension provision have, apart from reducing public expenditure and employer contributions, encouraged a financial *zeitgeist*. Reduced pensions have provided further incentives for private saving schemes. In the prevailing low interest rate climate, a common strategy has focused on turning homes into assets to be managed and tapped for consumption through re-mortgaging. The mix of incentivising tax reform, low investment in new residences, privatisation of the housing stock, rapid urbanisation and stagnant wage growth has generated a speculative ethos and a housing bubble in the big cities. Moreover, this institutional mix has caused a dramatic rise in household indebtedness. Pension reform has thus created the ideological and material impulses to propel financialisation forward in Sweden, while housing policy has provided much of the engine for this process (Belfrage and Kallifatedes, 2016a).

Financialisation, largely under the stewardship of social democratic governments, has combined with processes of marketisation and flexibilisation to drive inequality at an alarming rate (OECD, 2011). The rise in inequality can be seen through an intersectional perspective, but it relates closely to uneven processes of sectoral development. There has been a massive shift in wealth from lower and middle class wage-earners (from which SAP gains its electoral support) to the financial sector. The financial sector is less keen on productive investment. This, combined with the competitive forces deriving from neoliberal globalisation, promise to reduce the competitiveness of the historical growth engine of the export sector in the medium term. With profitability on the rise in the financial sector but in decline in the export sector, the rise of a finance-led growth model is based on the creation of an unusual class alliance between mortgage-holding households and the financial sector. As a result, today Swedish social democracy is hamstrung by the fact that a large part of the electorate is in one way or another dependent on efficient debt and asset management, practices regulated by non-democratic state institutions and directly enabled by sustaining a low interest rate climate, the powers of which are largely beyond the control of state institutions in the small and open Swedish economy (Belfrage and Kallifatedes, 2016b).

Since the 2008 global financial crisis (GFC), the role played by these non-democratic institutions has become more significant. Indeed, 'politics' is now taking place in debates revolving around deflation, debt and housing price inflation, and uneven development (both spatially and demographically), within and between non-democratic institutions. When the economy needs investment, macroprudential policy-making is at the top of the public agenda rather than a meaningful politics of investment. Indeed, much in politics and the economy is riding on the success of macroprudential policy-making, given the bubble dynamics created by financialisation in Sweden. The formulation of macroprudential tools involves formulating how and to what extent banks and other credit institutions must 'say no' to the dominant class alliance, calling for further credit expansion. The weak SAP-led government, in its quest to appear as economically competent, is reluctant to upset a very large segment of the electorate, and is consequently caught in a bind. This bind involves having to choose between appearing to act 'ideologically' on behalf of the part of the electorate that urges further financialisation, or acting on behalf of the growing interests that want to constrain neoliberal financialisation. Given the growth model's financialisation and fiscal constraints within a global low interest climate, the SAP has little choice other than to seek to sustain neoliberal financialisation at the expense of growth-inducing investment policies and more substantial redistribution, until a crisis strikes and it is too late (Belfrage and Kallifatedes, 2016b).

Conclusion

Overall, then, this is a losing game for SAP until the growth dynamics in the new Swedish model is called into greater question. Among the winners are the Sweden Democrats, focusing their politics on mobilising voters from the demographics who lose out under neoliberal financialisation in Sweden. In other words, their 'people's home nostalgia' is working, without the SAP currently having the tools to offer its own alternative. As we argue here, the problems are primarily of an institutional nature, but obviously they entwine with the ideational and individual dimensions. Good ideas are also needed, and skilful political discourse is essential in communicating them, in order to recast the new Swedish model, which is necessary if the SAP is going to return to playing a winning game. It is also clear that strong and visionary leadership is needed, especially in playing the discursive game and countering the ideological squeeze from both the moderate and the radical right. However, as is clear from our reading of the situation, the SAP cannot consider itself completely blameless in its own decline and needs to engage in serious soul searching in order to regain its electoral status as the 'natural party of government'. Above all, to change the structural-institutional context setting the rules of the game disadvantageous to SAP, it needs to call for much broader support from a disjointed European labour movement in crisis as well as hoping for, and to the extent that it can itself encourage, the emergence of a different global context.

References

Agius, C. (2007) 'Sweden's 2006 parliamentary election and after: Contesting or consolidating the Swedish model?', *Parliamentary Affairs*, vol 60, no 4, pp 585-600.

Alestalo, M. and Kuhnle, S. (1987) 'The Scandinavian route: Economic, social, and political developments', in R. Erikson, E.J. Hansen, S. Ringen and H. Uusitalo (eds) *The Scandinavian model: Welfare states and welfare research*, Armonk, NY: M.E. Sharpe, pp 3-38.

Andersson, J. (2006) *Between growth and security: Swedish social democracy from a strong society to a Third Way*, Manchester: Manchester University Press.

Andersson, J. (2009) *När framtiden redan hänt: Socialdemokratin och folkhemsnostalgin*, Stockholm: Ordfront.

Andersson, J. (2010) *The library and the workshop: Social democracy and capitalism in the knowledge age*, Stanford, CA: Stanford University Press.

Andersson, J. (2014) 'Losing social democracy: Reflections of the erosion of a paradigmatic case of social democracy', in D.J. Bailey, J.-M. de Waele, F. Escalona and M. Vieira (eds) *European social democracy during the global economic crisis: Renovation or resignation?*, Manchester: Manchester University Press, pp 116-31.

Aylott, N. and Bolin, N. (2016) 'Managed intra-party democracy', *Party Politics*, doi:10.1177/1354068816655569: 1354068816655569.

Belfrage, C. (2008) 'Towards "universal financialisation" in Sweden?', *Contemporary Politics*, vol 14, no 3, pp 277-96.

Belfrage, C. (2015) 'The unintended consequences of financialisation: Social democracy hamstrung? Pensions dilemma', *Economic and Industrial Democracy*, doi: 10.1177/0143831X15586070.

Belfrage, C. and Kallifatedes, M. (2016a) 'Financialization and the crisis-tendencies in the new Swedish model', *CGMS Seminar*, Stockholm School of Economics, 10 October.

Belfrage, C. and Kallifatedes, M. (2016b) 'The impossibility of depoliticized macroprudential regulation: The Swedish case', *32nd EGOS Annual Colloquium*, Naples, 7-9 October.

Bergh, A. (2014) 'What are the policy lessons from Sweden? On the rise, fall and revival of a capitalist welfare state', *New Political Economy*, vol 19, no 5, pp 662-94.

Bergmann, E. (2017) *Nordic nationalism and right-wing populist politics: Imperial relationships and national sentiments*, London: Palgrave Macmillan

Buendia, L. and Palazuelos, E. (2014) 'Economic growth and welfare state: A case study of Sweden', *Cambridge Journal of Economics*, vol 38, no 4, pp 761-77.

Giddens, A. (1998) *The Third Way: The renewal of social democracy*, Cambridge: Polity.

Hedberg, P. (2009) 'Valdeltagande i Sverige', *Statsvetenskapliga Institutionen*, Göteborg: Göteborgs Universitet.

Immergut, E.M. and Jochem, S. (2006) 'The political frame for negotiated capitalism: Electoral reform and the politics of crisis in Japan and Sweden', *Governance*, vol 19, no 1, pp 99-133.

Kuisma, M. (2007) 'Social democratic internationalism and the welfare state after the "golden age"', *Cooperation and Conflict*, vol 42, no 1, pp 9-26.

Kuisma, M. and Ryner, M. (2012) 'Third Way decomposition and the rightward shift in Finnish and Swedish politics', *Contemporary Politics*, vol 18, no 3, pp 325-42.

OECD (Organisation for Economic Co-operation and Development) (2011) *Divided we stand: Why inequality keeps rising*, www.oecd.org/els/social/inequality

Persson, G. (2007) *Min väg, mina val*, Stockholm: Bonniers.

Ryner, J.M. (2002) *Capitalist restructuring, globalisation, and the Third Way: Lessons from the Swedish model*, London: Routledge.

Sapir, A. (2003) *An agenda for a growing Europe: Making the EU economic system deliver. Report of a high-level study group established on the initiative of the President of the European Commission*, Brussels: Commission of the European Communities.

Schnyder, G. (2012) 'Like a phoenix from the ashes? Reassessing the transformation of the Swedish political economy since the 1970s', *Journal of European Public Policy*, vol 19, no 8, pp 1126-45.

Steinmo, S. (2010) *The evolution of modern states: Sweden, Japan and the United States*, Cambridge: Cambridge University Press.

van der Zwan, N. (2014) 'Making sense of financialization', *Socio-Economic Review*, vik 12, no 1, pp 99-129.

Wennemo, I. (2010) 'Så förlorade Sahlin valet', *Aftonbladet*, 21 September.

NINE

Between a rock and a hard place in Spain: the PSOE

Paul Kennedy

Introduction

The Spanish Socialist Workers' Party (PSOE) remains Spain's most electorally successful political party, having been in office between 1982 and 1996 under Felipe González, and between 2004 and 2011 under José Luis Rodríguez Zapatero. An indication of the straitened circumstances in which the party currently finds itself is provided by the following stark fact: when it last won office at the 2008 general election, the PSOE obtained over 11 million votes, more than at any time in its near 130-year existence.[1] By the time that it went down to its third successive general election defeat in June 2016, the party won less than half this amount, a result that constituted a historic low since democracy was re-established following Franco's death. Although the PSOE has avoided the fate of its Greek sister party, PASOK (Panhellenic Socialist Movement) at the hands of the radical-left Syriza, it has struggled to cope with the emergence of Pablo Iglesias's Podemos ('We can') in 2014. Hitherto all-conquering on the left of the political spectrum, the PSOE has good reason to be concerned about the implications of being overtaken by Podemos. While, up until now, the PSOE has been able to avert this much-feared *sorpasso* ('overtaking'), the party leadership is sufficiently realistic to acknowledge that some, perhaps more gradual, form of *Pasokification* awaits it over the coming years unless it can re-establish its credentials as a credible party of government.

The dilemmas faced by the PSOE are hardly unique. The party nevertheless serves as a case study of the challenging situation in which social democratic parties currently find themselves. With a significant proportion of the electorate having lost confidence in both the way it is governed and in the traditional parties of government, the PSOE has struggled to maintain its credibility, regarded as being stale, irrelevant and incapable of responding to the sense of insecurity felt by many at a time of economic uncertainty. The alternative offered by a new, attractive, media-savvy Podemos, capable of appealing to sections of the electorate that have deserted the PSOE, poses a very real threat.[2] At the June 2016 general election, Podemos, in its latest incarnation as Unidos Podemos (UP), which incorporated the Communist-dominated United left (IU), came within 14 seats of the PSOE. The palpable relief felt by the socialists at having withstood this challenge was itself an eloquent indication of how competitive the Spanish political arena has become as the breakthrough of Pablo Iglesias's party – and the centre-right Ciudadanos (Citizens) – further weakened the foundations of Spain's hitherto resilient two-party system. Notwithstanding the PSOE's maintenance of its advantage over Podemos, the party had nevertheless failed to challenge the dominance of the centre-right Popular Party (PP), which lurched from one corruption allegation to the next under the uninspired premiership of Mariano Rajoy, who consistently obtained the lowest popularity rating of all national-level party leaders in opinion polls.

A number of factors served to undermine the PSOE's credibility following its last general election victory on the eve of the international economic crisis in 2008: dissatisfaction with the functioning of democracy, which is at historic levels (Fundación Alternativas, 2016: 29-50); rejection of political elites; a crisis of capitalism that had given rise to a turbo-charged form of globalisation which left many feeling increasingly insecure within the context of staggering levels of inequality, with unemployment affecting one in four of Spain's workforce by 2013 (and half of Spain's under-25s); austerity policies introduced under the Zapatero-led PSOE government in the wake of the downturn and subsequently intensified under the PP, necessitating swingeing cuts to a welfare state largely put in place under the PSOE between 1982 and 1996; allegations of corruption affecting leading PSOE figures in the party's single remaining stronghold, Andalusia; and opportunities for political mobilisation offered by social networks that the new media-savvy Podemos has been adroit at exploiting. The difficulties experienced by the PSOE in meeting the challenge posed by Podemos on the party's left flank have, to some extent, enabled the PP to occupy a section of the centre ground vacated by the PSOE under Pedro Sánchez's leadership; the PP was the only major party capable of increasing its share of the vote at the June 2016 general election. Sánchez's defenestration in October 2016 and the PSOE's decision to endorse the formation of a minority PP government following his departure indicate the level of concern within the PSOE regarding the consequences of abandoning its traditional political terrain. Faced by the challenge of a still-dominant PP to its right and a confident

Podemos to its left, the PSOE finds itself faced with two equally undesirable alternatives.

Although this chapter's focus is on the PSOE since it lost office at the 2011 general election, it does contain sufficient coverage of the party's experience in office to set the current decline in its fortunes within a historical context. In line with the other contributions to this volume, the chapter draws on the synthetic approach suggested by Randall (2013), considering, in turn, three core themes: institutions, ideas and leadership. In doing so, several tentative conclusions are drawn as to whether the PSOE's maintenance of its lead over UP at the 2016 general election might indicate both its underlying resilience and the start of a recovery after almost a decade of decline.

Institutions

This section considers the degree to which structural conditions have served to re-order the Spanish political arena in such a way as to disadvantage the PSOE over recent years, and possibly, over the coming period, starting with a brief overview of the state of the party when it lost office in 2011. By that stage, the PSOE found itself in quite possibly its worst state since democracy was re-established following Franco's death in 1975. During his second term in office (2008-11), Rodríguez Zapatero had only belatedly acknowledged the seriousness of the economic crisis, and despite having indicated that Spain was sufficiently well-placed to avoid the levels of austerity imposed elsewhere in Europe, he felt impelled, at the behest of the EU, not only to impose the cuts that he had previously indicated would not be necessary, but also to intensify austerity across the board against the background of spiralling unemployment levels.[3]

Moreover, one of his last initiatives in government was to work in tandem with the PP to amend the Constitution in such a way as to prioritise payment of the public debt over all other considerations. Implicit was the suggestion that such a drastic step was necessary to avoid having to request the kind of EU bailout visited on Greece, Ireland and Portugal. It is therefore no surprise that there was a transformation in the character of the Leftist vote following the PSOE's defeat at the 2011 general election as the party appeared to be exhausted, untrustworthy and inept. In short, the conditions were provided for the emergence – in 2014 – of a radical populist party capable of recognising how propitious Spain's situation was with respect to seizing the opportunity provided by a multi-faceted crisis – political, social, economic and institutional – to displace the PSOE from its pivotal role within the party system and replace it as the country's leading progressive party.[4] This new party, Podemos, was determined to take full advantage of this window of opportunity.

With the PSOE's electoral strength already largely confined to poorer, less dynamic regions of Spain such as Andalusia, Extremadura and Castilla-La Mancha – although even here there has been a fall in support for the socialists over recent years – the challenge of retaining the backing of voters in former PSOE strongholds, such as Catalonia, has become more difficult within the context of increased support within the region for independence from Spain. Relations between the PSOE and its Catalan sister-party, the PSC (Catalan Socialist Party), have often been strained over recent years as the PSC has struggled to adapt to growing nationalist demands that have been stimulated by the economic crisis since 2008. The refusal of the PSC's seven parliamentary deputies to obey the party whip in Mariano Rajoy's investiture vote in October 2016, voting against, rather than abstaining, was an indication of the tensions between the PSC and the PSOE. Certain regions continued to reject the PSOE's advances, Madrid being a prime example, although, significantly, Podemos established the capital as one of its strongholds, indicating that it was possible for a radical party opposed to the government to thrive there, particularly appealing to young, highly educated, urban voters. The challenge facing the PSOE was that it would have to do better in the more economically advanced regions, such as the Basque Country – where the PSOE obtained its worst ever result in regional elections in September 2016, losing seven of its sixteen seats – in order to boost its credentials as a credible party of government. The task remains considerable: at the June 2016 general election, the PSOE failed to come first in any of Spain's largest cities.

Not only has the PSOE become a party whose support is largely concentrated in the less prosperous, more rural, parts of the country, it is also largely dependent, as is the PP, on older voters: in its survey following the December 2015 general election, Spain's public research institute, the CIS, indicated that the PSOE obtained more support than any other party in the 45-54 and the 55-64 age ranges – 21.4 per cent and 25.7 per cent respectively, closely followed by the PP (18.6 per cent and 20.9 per cent). For those over 65, the PP was comfortably ahead of the PSOE – 37.6 per cent to 27.2 per cent (CIS, 2016a). Given that there are over 11.5 million voters over the age of 60, the electoral significance of older voters is clear. To provide perspective, those between the ages of 18 and 29 account for less than 15 per cent of the population, that is, below half of those over the age of 60

(Bayón, 2016). At the opposite end of the age spectrum, Podemos outstripped all other parties: 18-24 (31.2 per cent), 25-34 (35.7 per cent) and 35-44 (22.9 per cent).

While it is generally accepted that older voters are more likely to go out and vote, it might be thought that the PSOE's strength with respect to this section of the electorate would be an advantage compared to a party such as Podemos, which has a particular appeal to the young. In fact, the PSOE has long experienced difficulties in mobilising its vote. In 2000, mobilisation of left-wing voters was at its lowest since 1986 (Méndez Lago, 2006, pp 3-4). Al-Qaeda terrorist attacks in Madrid in 2004, which led to the death of 191 people just days before that year's general election, are estimated to have mobilised 1,700,000 people voters who would otherwise have stayed at home, impelled to do so due to the emotive aftermath of the bombings. The 4 per cent increase in voter turnout is likely to have favoured the PSOE, which returned to office under Zapatero, with its highest ever number of votes to date (Michavila, 2005, pp 32-3). The volatility of the PSOE vote makes a sharp contrast with that of the PP, which won an average of 10 million votes at the five general elections held between 1996 and 2011.

The above-mentioned CIS poll noted that the largest proportion of those who had not voted at the December 2015 general election (27.5 per cent) *would* have done so for the PSOE. Even more frustratingly for the party, the same survey indicated that whereas around one-third of voters (34.7 per cent) placed themselves in categories 4 and 5 of a scale in which 1 is extreme left and 10 is extreme right, and almost 45 per cent of respondents viewed the PSOE as being within those same two categories, the PSOE was unable to convert that apparent convergence into votes. This means that despite being the party that most closely matched the ideological profile of the average voter, the PSOE has been punished more than any other party at the ballot box (Fundación Alternativas, 2017, p 23). The CIS's survey following the June 2016 general election was equally dispiriting for the PSOE (CIS, 2016b).

Podemos, in contrast, has been particularly successful in mobilising its vote, that is, ensuring that those who express a preference for the party actually go out and vote for it. While young voters have been a key part of Podemos's electorate, the PSOE has struggled to retain their support. With unemployment reaching vertiginous levels during Zapatero's last term in office (2008-11), the PSOE has found it difficult to convince young voters that it is relevant to their needs. For many young people attracted by Podemos, the PSOE is effectively written off as being the party of their parents' generation, and therefore incapable of responding to their demands.

Regarding the PSOE's relationship with the socialist trade union, the General Workers' Union (Unión General de Trabajadores, UGT), it is worth noting that trade union influence on party policy has been negligible since Felipe González made it clear in the 1980s that trade unions could expect few favours as his government simply did not require the support of trade unions to implement policy. Although the economic boom experienced by Spain between the mid-1990s and 2007, allied to a shared interest in opposing José María Aznar's PP government between 1996 and 2004, served to bring about something of a rapprochement between the PSOE and the UGT, the intensification of the economic crisis during Zapatero's second term in office and related policies, including a significant reform of the labour market in 2010, once again soured relations. The extent to which the PSOE's relationship with the UGT offered any practical political advantage was in any case questionable by this stage as the clout enjoyed by trade unions had fallen significantly due to the economic crisis as coverage of collective bargaining agreements declined (the PP government introduced its own, far harsher, labour reform in 2012) in order to provide employers with greater 'flexibility'. It is worth noting in passing that Podemos has been notable for its critical attitude towards the trade unions, which, it claims, have failed to address the needs of entire sectors of Spanish society, such as those on short-term contracts, the unemployed and younger workers, instead concentrating on the labour 'aristocracy' of older workers on open-ended contracts. Consequently, the PSOE has been provided with a further justification for its own re-assessment of its relationship with the UGT in particular, and the trade unions in general.

To conclude this section, when the PSOE left government in 2011, it had lost credibility due to its handling of the international economic and financial crisis from 2008. Moreover, the government had failed to communicate to the public the reasons behind the many difficult decisions it had been forced to take in order for the country to avoid having to request an EU bailout of its economy. The PSOE 'brand' had therefore become toxic in the minds of a significant proportion of the Spanish electorate. With its support confined to a diminishing number of the less prosperous regions and younger, more educated,[5] voters rejecting the party within the context of a far more competitive political environment in which parties such as Podemos and Ciudadanos appeared more responsive to their demands, the PSOE failed to convince, as it struggled to stem the decline in the base of its support. The PSOE's relations with the trade unions have also been of little practical benefit to the party over recent years within the context of an economy in which one in five are still unable to find employment. Both the political wing of the socialist movement, the PSOE, and its trade union ally, the UGT, were facing no less than an existential crisis, struggling to convince the population of their relevance.

Ideas

As has already been made clear, the PSOE is viewed by many as having reacted ineffectively to the economic crisis before it was ejected from office in 2011. Blame was apportioned and the PSOE is paying the price at the ballot box. Moreover, critics on the left accuse the party of having been unwilling to challenge the neoliberalism that has underpinned the global economy over recent decades. Indeed, it would be more accurate to suggest that not only did PSOE governments under Zapatero and Felipe González not challenge the neoliberal paradigm, but rather, they positively embraced it. Pragmatically accepting that, ultimately, there was little that a socialist – or, indeed, any – government could do to tame the power of global finance, the PSOE accepted the situation in the belief that there was no credible alternative. Given that Zapatero inherited a booming economy from the previous PP government, with growth well above the EU average, it was understandable that he was content to leave in place an economic model that appeared to be delivering the goods. Only when boom turned to bust did the consequences of excessive dependence on the construction sector become apparent.[6] This is not to suggest that the PSOE had no interest in implementing classic social democratic policies. Quite the reverse: the Spanish welfare state was largely established and consolidated under González, while Zapatero, during his first term in office (2004-08), passed a Dependency Law that provided social care to elderly people and those suffering from severe disabilities. Well over 1 million people qualified for assistance under the terms of the Law, which is estimated to have led to the creation of 300,000 jobs. In its editorial on 2 December 2006, Spain's most influential newspaper, *El País*, judged the initiative to be the most important piece of legislation passed by Zapatero's government. It described it as 'the greatest advance in the extension of social rights since public healthcare was universalised.' For its part, the socialist government viewed the measure as providing the welfare state with a 'fourth pillar', alongside existing provision in healthcare, education and state pensions. An apparently buoyant economy enabled Zapatero to translate such social democratic aims into reality: from the mid-1990s until 2006, almost 8 million new jobs were created in Spain under the PP and PSOE governments; economic growth remained well above the EU average throughout this period; public debt fell below 40 per cent of GDP; public accounts were in surplus throughout Zapatero's first term in office at a time when most EU member states carried significant deficits; and unemployment fell below the EU average in 2007.

Given the severity of Spain's economic situation after the intensification of the international economic crisis from 2008, it is important to mention the achievements outlined above to explain the sense of disappointment felt by voters when boom turned to bust. On the night he was elected in 2004, Zapatero appeared before supporters at the PSOE's HQ in Madrid who chanted '¡No nos falles!' ('Don't let us down!'). Within weeks, he had withdrawn Spanish troops from Iraq, an action that at the time attracted considerable international opprobrium, but which undoubtedly met with the approval of the bulk of the Spanish electorate. Over a decade later, the withdrawal of troops appears more prudent than rash. As we have seen, the Zapatero-led PSOE attracted more votes at the 2004 and 2008 general elections than at any time in its history.

Yet, for all his party's achievements, Zapatero *did* ultimately let his supporters down in the sense that he implemented an austerity policy that had little in common with traditional social democratic tenets. The severity of this programme in response to the economic crisis effectively rendered the PSOE unelectable as unemployment rose above 20 per cent. The question therefore arises: could the PSOE government have reacted differently, given the constraints under which it was operating? If Pablo Iglesias, rather than Zapatero, had been Prime Minster when Obama and Wen Jiabao telephoned in May 2010, would he have been able to resist their demands for firm action, that is, public spending cuts that amounted to Zapatero's – and the PSOE's – political suicide? Such questions are highly relevant in any study of the ideas that guide a political party's actions. Ultimately, Zapatero argued that his actions, however unpalatable, enabled Spain to avoid having to request a bailout from the EU, which would have imposed even greater levels of austerity: the national interest was placed above the party's interest. The obloquy directed towards Zapatero ever since has been considerable, not least from Podemos, which sought to characterise him as hapless before the demands made by 'the markets'. Curiously, Alexis Tsipras, Greece's radical Syriza Prime Minister, who enjoyed the personal support of Pablo Iglesias in both Greek general election campaigns in 2015, has escaped such criticism, despite having acquiesced to the

Troika's demands. Whether Podemos is populist – detailed policy proposals have to date not been the party's most prominent feature – it retains its attractions for a significant proportion of the electorate, even though it lost 1.3 million votes in the six-month period between the 2015 and 2016 general elections. For its part, the PSOE has been constrained by the apparently conflicting demands of seeking to remain popular while simultaneously having to implement unpopular policies. Openness from political parties about the scale of the challenges they face tends to be punished at the ballot box. Certainly, the experience of the PSOE over the last decade bears this assertion out. Whether the PSOE illustrates Bismarck's line about politics being the art of the possible at a time when many voters are minded to demand more than what can realistically be delivered in the so-called 'post truth' era, it is undeniably difficult for the party to compete. With populism of both the left and the right gaining in popularity, the centre-left has been particularly affected.

Leadership

Since Felipe González stepped down as PSOE leader in 1997 after 23 years in the post, the party has been through several periods in which the issue of leadership has constituted a major weakness. González hand-picked his successor, Joaquín Almunia, who proved to be uninspiring, leading the party to a crushing defeat at the hands of José Maria Aznar's PP, which obtained its first overall majority at the 2000 general election. Acknowledging his shortcomings, Almunia resigned the leadership on election night. His successor was the relatively unknown Zapatero, a parliamentary deputy who had the advantage of not having served in any of Felipe González's governments, thereby avoiding being tainted by the corruption allegations that contributed so greatly to the party's defeat in 1996. Under Zapatero, the PSOE benefited from the errors of a complacent PP that viewed its comfortable majority as being a mandate for heavy-handed implementation of unpopular policies, most notably, support for the US-led invasion and occupation of Iraq. Aznar holds the dubious distinction of having been the only prime minister to go from having an overall majority to losing a general election. Apart from Adolfo Suárez, Prime Minister between 1976 and 1981, Zapatero is the only party leader capable of winning a general election at the first attempt. Although, as we have seen, the PSOE obtained its highest ever number of votes at the 2004 and 2008 general elections, Zapatero never held an overall majority. When he stepped down before the 2011 general election, he was replaced by his former Interior

Minister and first Deputy Prime Minister, Alfredo Pérez Rubalcaba, a highly experienced, effective politician who appeared to personify the 'safe pair of hands' cliché. In choosing Rubalcaba, the party opted for continuity rather than change at a time when confidence within the PSOE was at a low ebb following its departure from office. The choice of Rubalcaba could nevertheless not be viewed as being risk-free given that he had been a prominent member of Zapatero's government, and was considered by opponents to be tainted by its failure to respond effectively to the international economic crisis. He resigned after obtaining a poor set of results at elections to the European Parliament in 2014. It was Podemos's breakthrough – the party obtained five seats – rather than the PSOE's declining fortunes, which attracted most media coverage. Socialist electoral failure was no longer particularly newsworthy.

In July 2014, Pedro Sánchez was elected as PSOE leader. Much like Zapatero before him, Sánchez was relatively unknown. It was no coincidence that the PSOE opted for a relatively young (early-40s), telegenic individual shortly after Podemos's emergence on to the political scene as it sought to weather the serious challenge posed by Pablo Iglesias. Offering a fresh start for a party patently displaying symptoms of exhaustion, Sánchez nevertheless had an uneven experience as leader. As we have seen, one of the few positive aspects of the 2015 and 2016 general elections for the PSOE was that it remained ahead of Podemos. With Rajoy not having the requisite parliamentary support to form a new government following the December 2015 general election, Sánchez sought, despite having 33 fewer seats than the PP, to put together an alternative government with the support of the centre-right Ciudadanos, but was thwarted by Podemos's decision to join with the PP in voting against Sánchez's bid to become prime minister in March 2016. Although the PP won an additional 14 seats at the June 2016 general election (the PSOE lost 5), it still required the abstention of the PSOE in Rajoy's investiture vote in October 2016 to form a minority government. Although Sánchez indicated that his party would vote against Rajoy in the investiture vote, with a view to seeking to form an alternative centre-left minority government under the PSOE, his authority was immediately challenged when half the members of the party's Executive Committee tendered their resignation. They did so in the belief that a party with such a small number of seats – the PSOE won 52 fewer seats than the PP at the 2016 general election – was not in a position to form a government, much less seek to do so with the support of Pablo Iglesias's Podemos, and, conceivably, regionalist parties advocating independence from

Spain. Sánchez's response was, first, to resign as leader in early October, and second, to step down as a PSOE deputy on the eve of Rajoy's successful investiture vote several weeks later.

Despite the party establishment, including the two former PSOE prime ministers, Felipe González and José Luis Rodríguez Zapatero, having backed the President of the Andalusian region, Susana Díaz, in primary elections for the party leadership in May 2017, Pedro Sánchez unexpectedly emerged victorious – he won in every region except for Andalusia and the Basque Country (the home region of the third leadership contender, Patxi López). The party endorsed the result at a congress the following month. The decisive factor was the vote of rank-and-file party members, who resented the party apparatus's efforts to railroad them into voting for Díaz, and backed Sánchez's more forthright opposition to Rajoy's PP government, as well as his more conciliatory approach to Podemos. Sánchez faced the challenging task of imposing his authority on the party (notwithstanding having lost at both the 2015 and 2016 general elections and despite no longer being a parliamentary deputy following his resignation in October 2016) and establishing a credible strategic approach capable of dislodging the PP from office at the next general election, which is due to take place by 2020. Given that one of the PSOE's defining features has been its disunity over recent years, it remains to be seen whether Sánchez's reinstatement marks the start of a resurgence in the PSOE's fortunes, or rather, whether it constitutes the latest staging post in the party's decline.

Conclusion

The PSOE has made little progress since it left office in 2011. Badly defeated at the 2015 and 2016 general elections, it shows scant signs of recovery. Whereas, to date, the PSOE has been able to resist the challenge of Podemos, its descent into disunity during the course of 2016 means that there is no guarantee that it will continue to do so. With its base of support diminishing significantly, the PSOE hardly needs reminding that no political party has a divine right to exist, even one which in 2019 will be 140 years old. Moreover, the PSOE's woes form part of a narrative whereby a lacklustre social democracy appears to have lost its capacity to convince, judging by European electorates' apparent preference for Conservative, or even populist, policy prescriptions almost a decade after the start of the international economic crisis. Social democratic parties have therefore experienced greater difficulties than their rivals on both the right and left. Whereas centre-right parties have been able to appeal to naked self-interest at a time when electorates appear to find more security in politically conservative policy prescriptions, the centre-left has struggled to gain political advantage from its appeal to voters' feelings of solidarity. Since the economic crisis began in 2008, the centre-right has shown itself to be more adept than the centre-left at convincing electorates that it is best-equipped to assuage their feelings of insecurity in uncertain times. Social democracy has a long and rich history that suggests otherwise. The PSOE represents a prime example of this assertion. Shunning what it views as the ideologically equivocal reductionist solutions proposed by its main competitor on the left, the PSOE, like most of its social democratic sister parties, itself offers no convincing response capable of stemming the fall in its electoral support. This is not to say that the PSOE's competitors do not face challenges: both Podemos and Ciudadanos suffered a significant decline in their vote between the 2015 and 2016 general elections, indicating that the role of the undecided voter in the Spanish political arena remains significant (Fundación Alternativas, 2016, p 23). Whether the PSOE can regain the credibility it has lost over the last decade and continue to display the resilience that has historically been its defining feature remains to be seen.

Notes

1 See my *The Spanish Socialist Party and the modernisation of Spain* for details of the PSOE in government under González and Zapatero (Kennedy, 2013).

2 The literature on Podemos is already extensive and growing. Sympathetic and critical texts in both English and Spanish include: Domínguez and Giménez (2014); Timermans (2014); Fernández-Albertos (2015); Iglesias (2015a, 2015b); Mateo Regueiro (2015); Rivera (2015); Tamames (2015); Torreblanca (2015); and Errejón and Mouffe (2016).

3 In his book on the economic crisis, Zapatero reveals that when the situation went from bad to worse in May 2010 due to Greece's travails, he was contacted by both President Obama and the Chinese premier, Wen Jiabao, and told in no uncertain terms that he must take immediate action to prevent contagion within the EU and beyond. Over the following weeks, Zapatero duly introduced the most significant austerity programme in living memory (Rodríguez Zapatero, 2013). An excellent overview of the PSOE's economic policy during its final years in office is provided by Salmon (2010a, 2010b).

4 For an excellent overview of Spain's political and institutional crisis, see Politikon (2014).

5 Whereas Podemos had more voters than any other party in the three most highly educated sectors of the population, that is, those with higher education (24.3%), professional training (25.4) or who studied after the age of 16 (25.2%), PSOE voters constituted the largest proportion of those with no education whatsoever – 33.7% – marginally ahead of the PP (33.2%) (CIS, 2016a).

6   Construction accounted for 10 per cent of GDP by 2007, double the average of Spain's EU partners (O'Kean, 2010, p 19).

References

Bayón, E. (2016) *El CIS postelectoral a fondo*, Debate 21, 3 May, http://debate21.es/2016/05/03/el-cis-postelectoral-a-fondo/

CIS (2016a) *Estudio Postelectoral 3126: Elecciones Generales 2015. Panel (2ª Fase)*, Madrid, www.cis.es/cis/opencm/ES/1_encuestas/estudios/ver.jsp?estudio=14258

CIS (2016b) *Avance de resultados del estudio 3145 Postelectoral elecciones generales 2016*, Madrid, www.cis.es/cis/opencms/ES/NoticiasNovedades/InfoCIS/2016/Documentacion_3145.html

Domínguez, A. and Giménez, L. (2014) *Claro que Podemos*, Barcelona: Los Libros del Lince.

Errejón, I. and Mouffe, C. (2016) *In the name of the people*, London: Lawrence & Wishart.

Fernández-Albertos, J. (2015) *Los votantes de Podemos*, Madrid: Catarata.

Fundación Alternativas (2016) *Informe sobre la democracia en España 2015*, Madrid: Alternativas.

Fundación Alternativas (2017) *Informe sobre la democracia en España 2016*, Madrid: Alternativas.

Iglesias, P. (2015a) *Politics in a time of crisis: Podemos and the future of democracy in Europe*, London: Verso.

Iglesias, P. (2015b) *Una Nueva Transición*, Madrid: Akal.

Kennedy, P. (2013) *The Spanish Socialist Party and the modernisation of Spain*, Manchester: Manchester University Press.

Mateo Regueiro, E. (ed) (2015) *Hasta luego, Pablo*, Madrid: Catarata.

Méndez Lago, M. (2006) 'Turning the page: Crisis and transformation of the Spanish Socialist Party', *South European Society and Politics*, vol 11, nos 3-4, pp 419-37.

Michavila, M. (2005) 'Guerra, terrorismo y elecciones: Incidencia electoral de los atentados islamistas en Madrid', Documento de Trabajo 13/2005, *Real Instituto Elcano de Estudios Internacionales y Estratégicos*, Madrid, pp 32-3.

O'Kean, J.M. (2010) *España competitiva*, Madrid: Ecobook.

Politikon (2014) *La urna rota*, Barcelona: Debate.

Randall, N. (2003) 'Understanding Labour's ideological trajectory', in J. Callaghan, S. Fielding and S. Ludlam (eds) *Interpreting the Labour Party: Approaches to Labour politics and history*, Manchester University Press, pp 23-56.

Rivera, J. (2015) *Podemos. Objetivo: Asaltar los cielos*, Barcelona: Planeta.

Rodríguez Zapatero, J.L. (2013) *El dilema. 600 días de vértigo*, Barcelona: Planeta.

Salmon, K. (2010a) 'Boom to bust – Reconstructing the Spanish economy. Part One: Into recession', *International Journal of Iberian Studies*, vol 23, no 1, pp 39-52.

Salmon, K. (2010b) 'Boom to bust – Reconstructing the Spanish economy. Part Two: Policy responses to the economic crisis', *International Journal of Iberian Studies*, vol 23, no 2, pp 83-91.

Tamames, R. (2015) *¿Podemos? Un viaje de la nada hacia el poder*, Madrid: Kailas.

Timermans, A. (2014) *¿Podemos?*, Madrid: Última Línea.

Torreblanca, J.I. (2015) *Asaltar los cielos: Podemos o la política después de la crisis*, Barcelona: Debate.

TEN

The French Parti socialiste (2010-16): from office to crisis

Sophie Di Francesco-Mayot

France finds itself in a decisive moment of its history. Ten years of Conservative rule have led her to where she is today, that is to say on the verge of a break with herself. (Hollande, 2012, p 8)

Introduction

The French Socialist Party (Parti socialiste, PS) is one of the least successful of the major European social democratic parties. Since the Fifth Republic, it has occupied the presidential office for 14 (1981-95) out of 54 years, and five years of prime ministerial power compromised by *cohabitation*[1] (Bell and Criddle, 2014, pp 290-1). In 2012, the PS reclaimed the Élysée Palace for the first time since 1995. While the French presidency should have heralded a reversal of fortune for the Socialist Party, over the past four years, under the leadership of François Hollande, it has experienced political and ideological turmoil. This general crisis has coincided with domestic and international economic and socio-political challenges. A majority of European countries have experienced a shift in the political dynamic of their party systems. The rise of extreme right-wing parties increasingly presents an important electoral threat to mainstream parties. Their electoral accession has concurred with societal challenges including the Euro crisis and subsequent sovereign debt crisis.

There is no doubt that Hollande's appointment to executive power initially demonstrated that social democracy could indeed provide a viable and feasible alternative socioeconomic and political paradigm to the neoliberal imperatives of the EU. Shortly after having obtained the presidency, however, Hollande received the lowest popularity vote in the history of the French Fifth Republic. This chapter examines the crisis of the French PS, focusing on the period between the 2008 global financial crisis (GFC) until the end of the Hollande presidency in 2017. It argues that the crisis of the PS is twofold: first, a political crisis that is revealed by the divisive nature of the Party's internal *courants* (factions). Whereas the factions initially contributed to the PS's internal democracy, over the past two decades they have significantly affected the PS's cohesiveness and ability to effectively develop and implement necessary policies. And second, an economic crisis that is exemplified by the PS's inability to adapt to its external and internal environments, such as the neoliberal imperatives of the EU, unprecedented high unemployment and increasing insecurity.

Institutions

When attempting to understand the malaise of the French left in general, and of the PS in particular, it is important to analyse the impact of internal factions on the internal workings of the PS. The history of French Socialism was characterised by numerous *courants* (factions), each of which have their distinct identity, vision and policy approach. Factions within French Socialism have been particularly prevalent throughout the French Revolution (1789-99) and the French Third Republic (1870-1940), and reflected deep ideological cleavages among social movements. Throughout the 1970s, the different factions within the PS worked together by providing an ideological and institutional dynamic that was favourable to militant and electoral growth.

Since the 1980s, however, factions have transformed themselves from being instruments of diversity and flexibility into tools of conservatism and paralysis. By increasingly focusing on personal leadership differences in an attempt to further their ambitions and to establish loyalties, Socialist leaders no longer proposed a genuine party policy direction with which partisans could identify (LaPalombara, 2007, pp 143-54). For example, since 1988, competition among the factions increasingly appeared as an unprincipled struggle for control of the party. The electoral defeats of the PS throughout the 1990s have been attributed in part to 'factionalism'. At the Rennes Party Congress in 1990, the party leadership fought itself to a standstill (a pattern repeated in 2008 at the Reims Congress). In Socialist parlance, this was the 'syndrome de Rennes', whereby party leaders put their ambitions ahead of the general interest. A recurrence of factionalist strife took place at the Reims Congress between Ségolène Royal, the 2007 presidential candidate, and Martine Aubry, the mayor of Lille, who fought for the post of First Secretary (Bell and Criddle, 2014, p 832). Nonetheless, factions remain an important exercise in party democracy during party congresses. There are currently six factions that are organised through policy declarations referred to as *motions* that Party members vote on at each congress. The factions have minor differences in their ideological orientation and therefore in policy prioritisation. They include: Royalists (Moderate social democrats), Aubryists (Christian left social democrats), Fabiusians (progressive democratic socialists), Delanoistes (socialist liberals), New Socialist Party (democratic socialists) and Eco-Socialists. This allows party leaders to meet regularly to decide on the policies and strategies that the party can adopt. Party congresses influence and orientate the party's political attitudes and define its identity (Faucher-King and Treille, 2003, pp 62-3).

The negative impact of factions on the party's ideological and programmatic commitments was further illustrated in Lionel Jospin's Plural left government in the first round of the 2002 presidential elections. Although Jospin's Plural left was the second longest serving government in the Fifth Republic, the pertinent disagreements among faction leaders affected the party's image and its ability to persuade the public that it proposed viable policies for France. With 16.18 per cent of the vote, Jospin came behind Jean-Marie Le Pen's Front National (FN), that obtained 16.85 per cent of the vote, and Jacques Chirac, who obtained 19.88 per cent (Parti socialiste, 2016). This was the second time in the history of the Fifth Republic that the French left had been knocked out of the second round in the presidential election.

A unique feature of the French party system has been the development and growth of the FN under the leadership of Jean-Marie Le Pen. Since the mid-1980s, the party system has been experiencing important structural changes. The lasting presence of the FN has resulted in a 'tripolar' pattern of party competition.[2] The FN's electoral breakthrough has been paralleled with a growing concern with questions of French identity, commitment to European integration and social liberalism. This has provided an opportunity for the FN to develop an alternative political platform to mainstream policies. The implementation and eventual institutionalisation of the FN in France's political landscape has posed a direct electoral challenge to the PS.

Over the past two decades, the French Conservative right (Les Républicains) and the PS have experienced a political and economic convergence, making them largely indistinct in the eyes of the French electorate. The perception that mainstream parties offer similar solutions has contributed to the FN's attempt to mobilise more French voters beyond its traditional supporters. For example, the 2012 presidential elections marked a new beginning for the FN. Marine Le Pen, presidential candidate, successfully recovered a part of the traditional *frontiste* electorate, or what some political scientists refer to as the *brebis égarées* (the stray sheep) of the *lepenisme*.[3] The public's disaffection with the PS was clearly illustrated in April 2002 when the Le Pen vote in the first round of the presidential election was driven by concerns relating to insecurity (74 per cent), immigration (60 per cent) and unemployment (31 per cent). The FN's political success has been fed by a rejection of the traditional mainstream parties and their inability to offer a clear alternative vision for French society.

Moreover, Marine Le Pen's charismatic personality and her astute use of radio and television has contributed to projecting an image of the party as united, modernised, 'women-friendly', and responsive to the needs of French citizens. Unlike her father, Marine developed a party programme based on a blend of socialism and nationalism. She made a 'socialising' shift in her economic approach by defending public services and civil servants. This shift is having considerable electoral implications for the PS, particularly among those who feel that PS leaders have become increasingly 'disconnected' from their daily concerns. At her inaugural presidential speech, Le Pen proclaimed that the FN is 'a great Republican political party' and that the party upholds the values of 'liberty, equality, fraternity'. She also articulated the need to reclaim the spirit of the Fifth Republic. In utilising the idea of Republicanism, Marine created an effective vehicle to propel her reactionary message. Frontists are now guardians of *laïcité* (secularism), the separation of the church and state, and defenders of European minorities and victimised groups.

Ideas

At the heart of the PS's current crisis lies an electoral paradox. While it has been largely successful at the local level – having won all local elections since 2004 (municipal, cantonal, regional) – it has consistently been defeated at national level (Bouvet, 2010, pp 118-19). At the 1993 legislative election, the PS experienced its biggest electoral defeat in the history of French Socialism. Party leaders decided to re-evaluate their economic strategy and engage in a process of auto-critique (self-critique). A prominent idea of this self-critique involved challenging the dominant neoliberal orthodoxy (Clift, 2002, p 328). Lionel Jospin, as minister plenipotentiary (diplomat), proposed an *autre politique* (another political perspective) that was clearly articulated in his 1995 presidential manifesto:

> We must learn the lessons of the past, in order to instigate the reorientations of economic policy, which today are

> necessary.... I reject the idea that the state is powerless, and believe that it should deploy all its capacities to aid job creation. (Clift, 2002, p 329)

The PS, under the leadership of Jospin, attempted to adapt its policies to the changing socioeconomic context. For most of the late 1990s and early 2000s, in light of EU pressures for budgetary stability and the deregulation of capital and production in the global economy, the PS, like the German Social Democratic Party (SPD) and the British Labour Party, adopted a more liberal economic programme. In 1996, the Jospin government adopted a new political programme that was characterised by, first, a more 'realist' economic approach, which meant a shift in mindset, acknowledging that the state was no longer a contractor; and second, maintaining a proactive left that included reducing working hours to 35 and the creation of public jobs, particularly for the young. The Socialist government also adopted a modernising programme in institutional matters by reforming French institutions and social family rights.

Jospin's *réalisme de gauche* programme established an alternative stance between the discredited Jacobin *dirigiste* (state-directed) left, which had been articulated by previous Socialist leaders, and the Third Way model typified by Tony Blair's New Labour government (1997-2007) in the UK. According to Hale et al (2004), the PS provided a distinct vision for the future of social democracy in Europe at the 21st Congress of the Socialist Party International in 1999. Unlike other social democratic leaders, Jospin argued that 'if the Third Way involves finding a middle way between social democracy and neo-liberalism … then the approach is not mine' (Clift, 2001, p 2). Jospin instead maintained that the different elements of the PS strategy constituted an ensemble, which prioritised equality and employment. This was one of the first concrete attempts by the PS to address the Party's political *malaise* by adapting its 'ideas' and policies to the contemporary challenges that France and the European Community (EC) were undergoing.

Jospin's slogan, 'Yes to a market economy, no to a market society', reflected the government's socioeconomic shift vis-à-vis the globalised market economy. By regarding globalisation as contested rather than inevitable, the Jospin government argued that 'room for manoeuvre' existed, and therefore a considerable degree of state interventionism remained possible despite constraining forces. The French state, Jospin claimed, 'should operate as a strategic actor, investor and enabler' (Clift, 2002, pp 330-5). Jospin's term in office revealed, to a certain extent, the 'normalisation' of the PS's policies vis-à-vis other social democratic parties in Europe. Importantly, it revealed how France's unique political culture and political system influenced the development and implementation of the Socialist government's policies. Despite these initiatives, Jospin's government was largely unable to make any appreciable impact. His proposals in the 1995 presidential election, for example, were realistic but limited. One of the main challenges that affected Jospin's Plural left government and that continued to affect the Party under the Hollande presidency was the pertinent factions among Socialist leaders. While these factions have been, and continue to be, characterised by ideological differences, the drastic increase in personality conflicts among Socialist elites has had a negative impact on the Party's legitimacy and on its effectiveness in addressing and responding to domestic and European societal issues. The 'no' vote in the 2005 referendum on establishing a Constitution for the EU clearly illustrated the divisive nature of the PS. Socialist leaders were divided on the question of Europe, which in turn divided Socialist members and partisans. As we shall see in the following section, despite the introduction of 'open' Socialist primaries in 2011, which was intended to render the Party more transparent in the selection process and more unified, Hollande's leadership style – or lack thereof – has further plunged the PS into disarray.

Individuals

François Hollande's victory over former Conservative president, Nicolas Sarkozy, in the 2012 presidential election brought an end to the three straight defeats for Socialist candidates in the two-round semi-presidential electoral system. The previous Socialist victory at the executive level was in 1988, when François Mitterrand returned for a second seven-year term (Clift and Kuhn, 2014). While the 2012 presidential election initially appeared to have 'transformative potential' for the PS and the political direction of France, after winning the presidential election, Hollande struggled to develop and implement a clear, consistent and practical political and economic strategy. It has been argued that a number of contextual factors affected Hollande's capacity to implement the policies he promised in his electoral campaign (Kuhn, 2014, pp 435-56). Despite these external constraints, however, it is important to note that Hollande revealed a lack of certain fundamental leadership qualities. During the 2012 presidential campaign, Hollande stated that he was a *président normal*, unlike the incumbent, Sarkozy. At this time, there was a genuine feeling that the

Socialist candidate was more approachable, and more in touch and compassionate than Sarkozy (Grossman and Sauger, 2014).

Despite these initial impressions, the consistently low popularity ratings for Hollande raise important questions regarding his governing competence and party management capacity with respect to winning the 'battle of ideas'. Even though he saw himself as a 'normal president', Hollande largely conformed to the norms of a serious *presidentiable*, that is, he had the necessary qualities required for a president of the French Republic – for example, his education at Sciences Po in Paris, then at the *École nationale d'administration* (ENA), and his long tenure as head of the PS (Kuhn, 2014, pp 437-57). Unlike former presidents of France, however, Hollande's lack of ministerial experience proved telling. As First Secretary of the PS (1997-2008), Hollande acquired the reputation of being a manager who sought to minimise conflict and seek consensus among the different Socialist tendencies rather than being a genuine 'leader' (Kuhn, 2014). This lack of substantive leadership qualities was most evident in his inability to project an image of an effective leader in the public sphere.

In his assessment of US presidents, Greenstein (2009) focuses on a leader's ability to deliver six main functions: public communication, organisational capacity, political skill, vision of public policy, cognitive style and emotional intelligence. In addition, Buller and James (2011, pp 538-43) utilise the term 'statecraft approach' to assess political leadership in the UK. They highlight four statecraft functions: a winning electoral strategy, governing competence, party management and political argument hegemony (that is, winning the battle of ideas). Hollande's reluctance to assert his political authority and organisational capacity was especially evident during the 2005 referendum campaign on the Treaty establishing a constitution for the EU (Hainsworth, 2006, pp 98-117). Similar to Mitterrand, who promised to 'break with capitalism', Hollande promised to tackle the Eurozone crisis and France's rising unemployment by implementing activist fiscal policies and by transforming the Eurozone economic policy architecture. In defiance of his electoral promises, Hollande's lack of efficient party management and political skills meant that he consistently failed to persuade both the public and a number of Socialist deputies that his economic reform package was the best solution to France's socioeconomic woes. Hollande, like his predecessor, Sarkozy, was unable to recognise the scale of fiscal adjustment that was required for France. As a result, his crisis resolution strategy was not developed on realistic or practical foundations, especially given the constraints of other European partners, and the political economic model underpinning EU authorities, such as the European Central Bank (ECB), the Commission and the EU treaties (Clift and Kuhn, 2014, pp 425-34).

Hollande profited considerably from the damaging legacy of the economic and financial crisis on Sarkozy's record of policy achievements (Kuhn and Murray, 2013; Perrineau, 2013). While the Mitterrand presidency had placed more emphasis on his political programme than on the presidential record of his opponent, Hollande's electoral campaign was characterised by a 'spiral of negativity', focusing particularly on the failure of the Sarkozy presidency (Labbé and Monière, 2014). '[This] register of "indignation" represented 42.5 per cent of the emotional repertory in Hollande's campaign, compared with only 28.4 per cent for Mitterrand's in 1981' (Ballet, 2014, p 180). Rather than positively endorsing his own candidacy and proposing a genuine left-wing political programme, Hollande focused on encouraging the French electorate to reject the incumbent president. Nearly one-third of votes for Hollande in the second round of the electoral process were cast primarily to stop Sarkozy from winning a subsequent term (Sineau and Cautrès, 2013, p 230). Beyond Hollande's lack of leadership and management abilities, it has been argued that his unprecedented public unpopularity is also part of a broader French electoral pattern that dates back to the 1980s. Academic research shows how presidential disappointment has been a normal fate for French presidents since the 1980s. This is due in part to the condition of post-dirigisme, whereby processes of globalisation, Europeanisation, liberalisation and deregulation adopted by successive French governments have limited the autonomy and policy capacity of leaders. It has been particularly difficult for French leaders, notably Socialist elites, given their habit of steering the French economy in an interventionist manner (Clift, 2012, pp 565-90).

The initial success of the Hollande presidency fostered a general sentiment of euphoria among French citizens. This sense of enthusiasm, however, rapidly vanished. Kuhn (2014) suggests that Hollande was hampered by a range of international, domestic and personal factors. For example, the Cahuzac affair in March 2013 concerning the tax affairs of a French budget minister discredited the Socialist government and the president, particularly at a time of 'belt tightening' (Chaffanjon, 2013). Moreover, like numerous European countries, France is having to deal with the economic consequences of the global financial crisis (GFC) within the Eurozone. One of the main economic outcomes revealed during the Sarkozy presidency was the extent to which the Franco–German partnership within the EU had become increasingly dominated by Germany. The disjuncture between the structural limits imposed on the exercise of presidential power in France and voter expectations of a powerful executive affected Hollande's ability to effectively devise and implement his policies (Bell and Criddle, 2014). Two main developments have significantly reduced the autonomy of presidential authority. The first is the European integration process. The creation of the single European market in 1992, which was extended with the formation of the Eurozone in 1999, imposed strict limits on the ability of national governments to diverge from EU-dictated norms. For example, 'one of the most notable [limits] is the public deficit of 3% of GDP [which is] imposed as part of the Stability and Growth Pact' (Kuhn, 2014, p 442). Like other members of the Eurozone, France does not have the freedom to devalue its national currency. During the Hollande presidency, French political elites of both the left and the right stated that the Euro was overvalued, consequently contributing to the country's lack of competitiveness and trade deficit.

One of the main questions posed by political analysts has been how the medium-term commitments of the PS to free market global capitalism and to the EU squares with the pressing demand by the French electorate for an economic policy capable of addressing unemployment, raising living standards and preserving the 'French way of life'. His political programme reflects the ideological 'lineage' of the Michel Rocard and Lionel Jospin dominant internal coalition that prevailed throughout the post-Mitterrand era in the PS (Clift, 2013). Hollande's association with Jacques Delors, a French economist and politician, was critical in the assimilation of a moderate 'culture of government' as a key element in the party's core identity. At the start of his tenure, Hollande focused on two main policies: the first was to change the EU's socioeconomic priorities. There was an emphasis on the need to support public growth, which included renegotiating the Stability and Growth Pact. The second policy comprised different sub-policies that Hollande commonly referred to as the 'toolbox' (Vernet, 2015). This included the creation of public banks for investment, job subsidies (public funding) for young people and pensioners, as well as a tax increase for wealthy people and the middle class. Structural reforms were also promoted by developing a consensus among social partners, such as trade unions and business communities.

In the same year, Hollande's economic policy experienced a shift from a principally anti-finance rhetoric to a more progressive stance on taxation. He emphasised a 'strong redistributive dimension with repeated pledges to tax the rich more and make them bear more of the burden of adjustment' (Di Francesco-Mayot, 2012). The 75 per cent rate reflects a strengthening of French Socialist commitments to egalitarianism and redistribution through progressive taxation. As part of France's 2013 budget, the 75 per cent tax rate was imposed on those earning over 1 million Euros per year and affected around 30,000 French citizens (0.46 per cent of the population). The aim was to reduce the annual deficit of the public purse (Di Francesco-Mayot, 2012).

In February 2014, during his trip and state dinner with US president, Barack Obama, Hollande mentioned his conversion to supply-side economics. This approach focuses on investing in capital and lowering barriers on the production of goods and services. He stated that 'we need to produce more, and better' (Staff, 2014). The problem with this approach is that Socialist elites have failed to articulate a 'clear-cut discourse' that justifies this approach to French citizens. The need for economic policy reorientation in response to the Eurozone crisis was one of the programmatic objectives of Hollande's campaign. In his acceptance speech, Hollande stated twice that his commitment was to revamp European integration by focusing crisis resolution efforts on securing growth as a counterpoint to the focus on austerity adopted by Sarkozy, Merkel and the ECB. Hollande's programme suggested a relatively coherent, growth-oriented, activist and interventionist economic policy vision (Clift, 2013). Despite these objectives, however, Hollande only obtained a 'European Growth Plan' of 130 billion Euros at the same June 2013 European Council meeting during which he accepted that he would have to abandon his attempt to renegotiate the European Fiscal Compact[4] (Chrisafis, 2013; Bouillaud, 2014, p 3695).

Conclusion

While Hollande's electoral success in the 2012 presidential elections was seen as a new phase for the French Socialist Party, after only a few months in power Hollande received the lowest popularity vote in the history of the Fifth Republic. This chapter has identified two main crises that serve to explain the reasons underpinning the PS's electoral and political paradox: although Hollande obtained executive power in the 2012 presidential election, once in office, the PS failed to effectively address issues such as high unemployment, increasing insecurity and questions of immigration. The PS's political crisis continues to affect its capacity to agree on and to develop an inclusive and realistic political narrative that responds to the challenges French society and the EU are currently experiencing. This political malaise is illustrated by the endless 'battle of ideas' among Socialist elites. This chapter has shown that while factions were once instruments of diversity and flexibility, they have largely become a 'battle of personalities', resulting in political paralysis. This has affected the PS's internal cohesiveness and its ability to implement the necessary policies and reforms. Its political crisis is also illustrated by the institutionalisation of the FN in the French political arena. Marine Le Pen's 'socialising' shift in her economic approach has posed a direct electoral threat to a section of Socialist supporters, especially civil servants who increasingly feel that the PS is too distant and no longer represents their needs.

Moreover, Hollande's lack of leadership qualities has also contributed to the PS's political and economic crisis. His ineffective party management and indecisiveness has fostered a sense of anger among the French public who continue to feel that the French left is failing to represent them and to address France's societal challenges. Despite his electoral campaign strategy of being a 'normal president' as a way of differentiating his presidency from that of Sarkozy, and to appear more approachable to the French public, polls on popularity rating showed that Hollande was the most unpopular president in the history of the Fifth Republic. In light of national and international constraints such as the Cahuzac controversy, the Eurozone and GFC crises, Hollande was unable to develop and implement a clear social democratic political economy. In addition, the inconsistency between the structural limits imposed on the exercise of presidential power in France and voters' expectations of a powerful executive leader contributed to Hollande's unfavourable ratings. The European integration process continues to impose limits on a government's ability to operate as it wishes. This has particularly been the case with the issue of the public deficit and the imposed Stability and Growth Pact. Divisions, rather than cohesion, continued to characterise the PS despite the looming 2017 presidential elections. François Hollande's official statement in December, stating that he would not seek a second term in office, underlined the acute political weakness of the Hollande presidency and the disarray of his Socialist party five months before the presidential election. It is the first time in decades that an incumbent French president has not sought re-election. One of the main questions was whether Hollande's decision not to seek a second term would increase the left's electoral chances vis-à-vis Marine Le Pen's FN. If the PS failed to project a united front, France risked facing a run-off between the FN, and the Conservative party, Les Républicains, in the second round of the 2017 presidential election.

Afterword

The 2017 French presidential election proved to be one of the most unpredictable and contested elections in recent times. It was the first time since the creation of the Fifth Republic in 1958 that neither of the traditional government parties – the centre-left Parti socialiste (PS) nor the centre-right, Les Républicains – reached the second round of the presidential elections. Political debates are occurring outside the traditional bi-polar party structure of the left and right mainstream parties. Instead, French politics has witnessed an unprecedented increase in popularity for a new centrist political movement, En Marche! (On the Move!), founded in 2016 by the maverick candidate, Emmanuel Macron, and an increase in support for the far-right Front National (FN) led by Marine Le Pen. Underpinning this shift in partisan political allegiances is a general sense of distrust and exasperation among French citizens vis-à-vis the French traditional political establishment, and particularly the 'perceived' ineffectiveness of mainstream parties that claim to represent them (Chrisafis, 2017).

The so-called Macron phenomenon has transformed the political dynamics of France's bi-polar party system. Despite serving briefly as Minister of the Economy under the Hollande presidency, Emmanuel Macron is considered by many as a political novice. As a former investment banker at the Rothschild firm, he was neither a politician nor a member of the PS, and has been widely criticised for his 'lack of experience' in public life.

His appeal rested, to a large extent, on an electoral campaign promising to transcend the classic left–right divide and to revolutionise the way France is being governed. His 'catch-all' party platform of En Marche! was pitched to offer French citizens an alternative to the corrupt, clan-based and inefficient political system of the two mainstream parties. Macron was able to capitalise on the failures of the Hollande presidency to effectively tackle rising unemployment, immigration and insecurity. The Macron phenomenon attests to the fact that the PS is in complete disarray, and is on the point of becoming irrelevant (Rose, 2017). The PS's internal crisis was reinforced when Manuel Valls, a high-profile member of the PS, confirmed that he would back independent front-runner Macron rather than his own PS candidate, Benoît Hamon. While Hamon, a leftist moderniser, appeated to offer a chance to breathe new life into the party, throughout his electoral campaign and Socialist primaries, he struggled to mobilise support over a volatile election campaign that was dominated by Conservative candidate François Fillon's fake-job scandal and the self-styled anti-establishment pitches of both Macron and far-right leader Marine Le Pen (Bock, 2017).

The 2017 Socialist primaries illustrated the extent to which the French left remains deeply divided between two main camps: pro-market modernisers and left-wing traditionalists that maintain that true socialist values have been betrayed. Macron showed strategic acumen in deciding not to participate in the PS primaries to highlight his independence and distance himself from the PS. In contrast, he was able to present himself as a fresh, new candidate whose ideas have not been tried before, capable of mobilising French voters from across the entire political spectrum. Macron was also able to benefit from the support of figures such PS stalwart François Bayrou (Chrisafis, 2017).

On 23 April 2017, French citizens went to the polls to vote in the first round of France's two-round presidential election. The results revealed an electorate that was deeply divided over the future of France and its place in Europe. The two victors, far-right candidate Marine Le Pen (21.7 per cent of the vote) and the independent candidate Emmanuel Macron (23.7 per cent of the vote) proposed polar opposite visions for the future of France. Macron offered a progressive, pro-EU, pro-business and socially liberal agenda in contrast to Le Pen's anti-EU, protectionist, nativist and anti-immigration agenda. The historic first-round results marked the rejection of the status quo of France's establishment politics, with a calamitous result for Hamon's PS – securing a record low of 6.36 per cent of the vote. The fracturing of the left vote was underlined by the surge of support for the hard-left under Jean-Luc Mélenchon, who secured 19.8 per cent of the vote, and was tantalisingly close to making it to the second round.

The second round of the presidential election, on 7 May 2017, represents a political earthquake in the French political landscape with the exclusion of the two major parties. The presence of two political outsiders in the final round revealed a new cleavage between those supporting an 'open society' and those supporting a 'closed society'. The former, in favour of globalisation, multiculturalism and European integration, voted for Macron (66.7 per cent), while the latter, who advocated welfare for welfare chauvinism and a return to the nation-state, voted Le Pen (33.9 per cent). The result indicated both support for his agenda and opposition to that of Le Pen. Despite Macron's clear victory, French society remains geographically and socially divided. There remains a major faultline between the urban, pro-European electorate and, the rural, anti-EU working class, the so-called 'peripheral France' (Guilluy, 2017).

The dismal result for the PS under Benoît Hamon revealed the gravity of the PS's crisis, and poses questions regarding its continued relevance as the main left-wing contender in French politics. Despite his decisive victory during the January primaries, Hamon failed to command support from other Socialist leaders, many of whom, including former Prime Minister Manuel Valls, endorsed Macron instead. This has further discredited the Party, threatening its very relevance. The French PS's current situation reflects a wider crisis within the traditional social democratic parties in Europe (McDaniel, 2017). French politics may begin to experience a reformulation of its left-wing parties and movements, and under these circumstances, the PS may survive in some form; however, the Socialist Party of François Mitterrand has clearly become history.

Notes

1 Cohabitation or power sharing occurs in semi-presidential political systems when the president is from a different political party to that of the majority of the Members of Parliament (LaPalombara, 2007, pp 141-54).
2 The FN has become the third main competitive political actor in French politics, and is increasingly posing an electoral threat to France's mainstream political parties.
3 Supporters of Jean-Marie Le Pen, former leader of the Front National (FN).
4 An intergovernmental treaty introduced as a stricter version of the Stability and Growth Pact. It was signed on 2 March 2012 by all EU member states with the exception of the Czech Republic, the UK and Croatia. The treaty entered into force in January 2013. By 1 April 2014, it had been ratified and introduced by all 25 signatories.

References

Ballet, M. (2014) Émotions et èlèctions. Les campagnes présidentielles françaises (1981-2012), Paris: INA Éditions.

Bell, D.S. and Criddle, B. (2014) *Exceptional Socialist: The case of the French Socialist Party*, Basingstoke: Palgrave Macmillan.

Bock, P. (2017) 'Millennial man: How Emmanuel Macron is charming France's globalized youth', *New Statesman*, 1 April, www.newstatesman.com/world/europe/2017/02/millennial-man-how-emmanuel-macron-charming-frances-globalised-youth

Bouillaud, C. (2014) *La politique économique française sous le mandate de François Hollande: Un bilan á presque mi-mandat*, Paris: l'Harmattan.

Bouvet, L. (2010) *Who loves the PS? The electoral paradox of the French Socialist Party*, Paris: IPG.

Buller, J. and James, T.B. (2011) 'Statecraft and the assessment of national political leaders: The case of New Labour and Tony Blair', *The British Journal of Politics and International Relations*, vol 14, no 4, pp 534-55.

Chaffanjon, C. (2013) *Jérome Cahuzac, les yeux dans les yeux*, Paris: Plon.

Chrisafis, A. (2013) 'François Hollande annus horribilis: French president's first year in office marked by broken promises, soaring joblessness and low ratings', *The Guardian*, 2 May, www.theguardian.com/world/2013/may/02/francois-hollande-french-president

Chrisafis, A. (2017) 'French progressive dare to hope as maverick Macron surges in polls', *The Guardian*, 2 April, www.theguardian.com/world/2017/jan/15/french-progressives-dare-to-hope-as-maverick-macron-surges-in-polls

Clift, B. (2001) 'The Jospin Way', *The Political Quarterly*, vol 72, no 2, pp 170-9.

Clift, B. (2002) 'Social democracy and globalisation: The case of France and the UK', *Government and Opposition*, vol 37, no 4, pp 466-500.

Clift, B. (2012) 'Comparative capitalisms, ideational political economy and French post-dirigiste responses to the global financial crisis', *New Political Economy*, vol 17, no 5, pp 565-90.

Clift, B. (2013) 'Le changement? French Socialism, the 2012 presidential election and the politics of economic credibility amidst the Eurozone crisis', *Parliamentary Affairs*, vol 66, no 2, pp 106-23.

Clift, B. and Kuhn, R. (2014) 'The Hollande presidency, 2012-14', *Modern & Contemporary France*, vol 22, no 4, pp 425-34.

Di Francesco-Mayot, S. (2012) 'There are no easy solutions for France's economic woes', *The Conversation*, 17 October, https://theconversation.com/there-are-no-easy-solutions-for-frances-economic-woes-10181

Faucher-King, F. and Treille, E. (2003) 'Managing intra-party democracy: Comparing the French Socialist and British Labour conferences', *French Politics*, vol 1, no 1, pp 61-82.

Greenstein, F.I. (2009) *Inventing the job of president: Leadership style from George Washington to Andrew Jackson*, Princeton, NJ: Princeton University Press.

Grossman, E. and Sauger, N. (2014) '"Un president normal"? Presidential (in-) action and popularity in the wake of the great recession', *French Politics*, vol 12, no 2, pp 86-103.

Guilluy, C. (2017) 'French polls show populist fever is here to stay as globalisation makes voters pick new sides', *The Guardian*, 23 April, www.theguardian.com/world/2017/apr/23/populism-france-left-right-elections

Hainsworth, P. (2006) 'France says no: The 29 May referendum on the European Constitution', *Parliamentary Affairs*, vol 59, no 1, pp 98-117.

Hale, S., Leggett, W. and Martell, L. (2004) *The Third Way and beyond: Criticisms, futures and alternatives*, Manchester: Manchester University Press.

Hollande, F. (2012) *Changer de destin*, Paris: Robbert Laffont.

Kuhn, R. (2014) 'Mister unpopular: François Hollande and the exercise of President leadership 2012-14', *Modern & Contemporary France*, vol 22, no 4, pp 435-57.

Kuhn, R. and Murray, R. (eds) (2013) 'Special Issue: French presidential and parliamentary elections 2012', *Parliamentary Affairs*, vol 66, pp 1-233.

Labbé, D. and Monière, D. (2014) *Ne votez pas pour l'autre! La spirale de la négativité*, Paris: l'Harmattan.

LaPalombara, J. (2007) 'Reflections on political parties and political development, four decades later', *Party Politics*, vol 13, no 2, pp 141-54.

Perrineau, P. (2013) *Le vote normal*, Paris: Presses de Sciences Po.

Rose, M. (2017) 'Macron momentum threatens French election frontrunners', *Reuters*, 2 April, www.reuters.com/article/us-france-election-macron-idUSKBN15117X

Sineau, M. and Cautrès, B. (2013) 'Les Attentes vis-à-vis du nouveau président', in P. Perrineau (ed) *La décision électorale en 2012*, Paris: Armand Colin, pp 229-42.

Staff, R. (2014) 'France's Hollande says France must produce "more and better"', 14 January, *Reuters*, http://uk.reuters.com/article/uk-france-hollande-charges-idUKBREA0D10520140114

Vernet, D. (2015) *Economic, political and ideological crises: The metamorphosis of French Socialism*, Dublin: The Institute of International and European Affairs, 6 February.

Part 3
Conclusion: Why the left loses

ELEVEN

The end of revisionism?

Chris Pierson

In *The primacy of politics*, Sheri Berman (2006, p 2) insists 'the ideology that triumphed in the 20th century was not liberalism, as the "End of History" story argues, it was "social democracy".' In a similar tone, in their recent contribution to a collection of essays on *The crisis of social democracy in Europe*, Bo Rothstein and Sven Steinmo (2013) evoke the perhaps apocryphal words of James Callaghan, a man who has some claim to have been Britain's last social democrat: 'crisis, what crisis?' For them, *real* social democracy is a purely Scandinavian phenomenon – but here it is safe and fairly well (although struggling with the political challenge of migration). As we explore what is in general a much more pessimistic view of the state of social democracy, it is as well to keep these counter-examples in mind. Whatever has changed in those developed states that are the focus of this book – and there is much that has – they remain 'mixed economies', with substantial welfare states in which the initial outcomes of markets are (more or less) significantly altered by state's action, and in which the state continues to take a measure of responsibility for the income maintenance of the elderly and disabled, provides public healthcare and funds primary and secondary education. If this is, at least in part, what social democracy *is*, then these continue to be, to this extent, social democratic states.

It is also worth recalling that this is not the first time that social democracy has been seen to be in (perhaps terminal) crisis. In fact, there is a morbid history that, in the British case, trails back through John Gray's *After social democracy* to Abrams and Rose's *Must Labour lose* in 1960 (Abrams and Rose, 1960; Gray, 1996). Donald Rawson's *Labor in vain* (1966) is another example, an Australian one, drawn from social democracy's so-called 'Golden Age'. The new spirit of despondency for our own times is well captured by Donald Sassoon, a man who knows a thing or two about the history of the left (Sassoon, 1996). Of social democracy, in the world after 2008, he writes 'in the midst of a new major crisis, it stands idealess, as a remnant of the past facing an uncertain future' (Sassoon, 2013, p 27). Still more apocalyptically, Yanis Varoufakis, who starred briefly in the Greek tragedy precipitated by the

EU reaction to the great crash of 2008, declared that the term 'social democracy' is 'finished', along with the 'very 20th-century' political economy to which it was relevant (Varoufakis, 2016a). On this account, the challenge for social democracy now is not just electoral – must social democratic parties lose? – it is existential: can social democracy survive as anything other than the decorative shell of a politics that is now entirely spent?

Social democracy after 2008

The contributions in this collection focus on the period since 2008. In the immediate aftermath of the dramatic events of that year, we might have expected to see a renaissance of social democratic fortunes. After all, it seemed that the twin lessons of the sub-prime banking crisis were that the 'neoliberal', global market economy had imploded and that, when it did, *only* states – indeed, only states coordinating their responses, committing vast quantities of public money and racking up enormous debts – were capable of clearing up the mess. But it didn't turn out that way. It is perhaps understandable that incumbents found themselves paying the electoral price for doing what had to be done (although, ironically, for some it was arguably their finest hour) but nearly a decade on, not just former incumbents but those social democrats who were lucky enough to be out of office when the roof caved in have shared a similarly lacklustre electoral performance. Andrew Gamble (2011) is probably right to think that, in times of economic distress, publics have a tendency to cleave to right-of-centre parties on the (probably mistaken) grounds that somehow they can be 'trusted' with managing an ailing economy. On this view, social democracy may just be for 'the good times' – which is not good news if we are (perceived to be) living through times of 'permanent austerity'. But is there some other reason why social democratic forces seem to have benefited so little from the ongoing crisis of a neoliberal global political economy?

The case studies collated in this volume concentrate on three components of the social democratic problem: individuals (or leadership), institutions and ideas. It is always tempting to attribute success (and failure) to good (and bad) leadership. In an age when *all* national elections are deemed to be 'presidential' and when the logic of valance politics and 24-hour news coverage directs our attention resolutely towards those at the head of the contending parties, it is understandable that leadership looks so crucial. With the benefit of hindsight, those who lasted long (and were 'winners' in this limited sense) always look like 'good' leaders. Tony Blair and Bob Hawke – to take two serial election winners – certainly had a capacity for savvy statecraft, although famously the man Hawke displaced as leader of the Australian Labor Party (ALP) in a caucus-room coup in 1983 suggested that that particular election could have been won by 'a drover's dog' (Hayden, cited in Carroll, 2004: 263). And, under some circumstances, the choice of leader *may* make a difference. Had Labour in the UK gone for Denis Healey instead of Michael Foot in 1980 or for David instead of Ed Miliband in 2010 – or not chosen to replace the latter with Jeremy Corbyn – the fortunes of that party *might* have looked a little different. But it is hard to know just *how* different they would have been. And it seems clear that, given a bit of bad luck or bad judgement, leaders who look 'convincing' can still fail. Lionel Jospin was a highly experienced former prime minster when he humiliatingly failed to reach the second round of the French presidential elections in 2002 (Clift, 2011). François Hollande secured a famous and exceptional victory for the French left in the election of 2012. But he has gone on to be profoundly unpopular (Clift, 2013; Clift and Kuhn, 2014). And blaming 'the leadership' for 'betraying' its core constituency is a cottage industry on the left that goes all the way back to the first generation of social democrats (see, for example, Lenin versus Kautsky; Pierson, 1986, pp 62-9). It is hard not to conclude that the *real* problems of social democracy, above all and in the last instance, probably lie somewhere else – with institutions and ideas.

Losses without limits?

Perhaps the starkest of the institutional problems facing social democracy now – at least when the latter is the name of a party – is a growing inability to win elections. The parties reviewed in the collection have for the most part fared badly in the past decade (and, in some cases, for much longer). In New Zealand, Helen Clark did secure three terms of Labour government after 1999, taking more than 40 per cent of the vote in both 2002 and 2005. But since then, the party has lost three elections to John Key's National Party, securing just 27.5 per cent of the countrywide vote in 2014 (fully 20 points behind National). In Australia, Labor won in 2007, bringing to an end 10 years of Howard government. They managed to hang on in 2010 but lost in 2013 and 2016 (if only just). In Sweden, the Social Democrats were the single largest party after the last general election (2014). They took a little less than 31 per cent of the available votes, forming a minority coalition government with the Greens. Elsewhere the electoral fate of social democratic parties looks much worse. In Germany, the SPD has not won a national election since 2002 (when it governed in a Red–Green coalition). In 2013, it secured just 26 per cent of the popular vote. In the UK, since the high-water mark of 1997 (when Labour secured 43 per cent of the popular vote), support has consistently declined. The national vote 'recovered' to 30.4 per cent in 2015, but the party was wiped out by the SNP in its Scottish heartland, leaving it as the party of London and post-industrial England and Wales. Still more extreme was the experience of PASOK in Greece. Having attracted nearly 44 per cent of the vote as recently as 2009, the party secured less than 5 per cent in the national elections of January 2015. Its experience even gave rise to a new word – 'Pasokification', 'reducing a country's main social democratic party to the smallest party in parliament as a result of the rise of a more radical left party' (Collins Dictionary, no date).

Added to this was the challenge of a long-term decline in the industrial wing of social democracy. Historically, social democracy has been the politics of the labour movement, and a key component of this movement has always been trade unions and their members. While that relationship was not always as close as it was in the British or Swedish cases – significantly weaker in France, for example, and institutionally distinct in Germany – trade unionism was almost always the 'other half' of social democracy. But the 1980s were a time of loss – on some accounts, 'loss without limits' – for this 'other side' of social democracy. Of course, a great deal was happening. Trade unions were becoming increasingly feminised, more focused in the public sector and drawing in increasing numbers of middle-class public service members (Hyman, 2001). But the crudest measure of union strength – in both numbers and influence – that is, union densities (the proportion of the employed workforce in unions), saw precipitate declines almost everywhere. Across the OECD, the high point for union densities was at 35.6 per cent in 1975. In Germany, densities peaked at 35.5 per cent in 1978 (now 18.1 per cent); in New Zealand, they peaked at 69.1 per cent in 1980 (now 18.7 per cent); and in the UK, they peaked at 51.9 per cent in 1981 (now 25.1 per cent). Generally, numbers peaked higher and later in the Scandinavian countries (OECD, 2016). Union densities across the OCED now stand at barely half the level achieved in the mid-1970s (16.7 per cent in 2014). The causes of that long-term decline are many and contested. Since trade unions have been widely regarded as the industrial wing of the labour movement (of which social democratic or labour parties are the political wing), have had a major part in financing and staffing these parties, and have been critical in mobilising the vote (and determining party policy), it is hardly surprising that this decline has been seen either (1) to make it harder for social democratic parties to get elected and/or/but (2) to 'free up' the parties to make an extra-class or non-class appeal to a wider voting public.

Of course, there is something cyclical about the electoral performance of political parties. And not just those on the centre-left. When the Conservative Party won in the UK 2015 general election it was the party's first outright win for 22 years. Indeed, if 'Pasokification' weren't just for parties of the centre-left, the Canadian Conservatives would have a good claim to have been 'pasokified' in 1993 (when its representation fell from 154 MPs to just 2!). And, of course, in fewer than 15 years they were back in office. Is there anything more than this swinging of the electoral pendulum involved in the recent under-performance of social democratic parties? In 2011, David Miliband contrasted the then current state of European social democratic parties (out of power nearly everywhere outside Southern Europe) with the position little more than a decade earlier (in government in 13 of 15 EU states). But we have been here before. In the 1980s, the argument that social democratic parties were unavoidably the victims of a long-term (and irreversible) class dealignment – stripping them of a potential 'natural' majority in a blue-collar, urban-industrial working class – was commonplace (for a discussion, see Pierson, 1995, 2001). Social democratic parties were shut out of office in the UK, in Germany and in the US, and their hegemony appeared increasingly to be challenged in what many regarded as their Scandinavian heartland. And yet, by the end of the following decade, they had recovered to attain the position now looked back on so fondly by David Miliband. We might learn something from looking at how social democrats saw the challenge back then, how they managed to move their parties from electoral famine to feast – and whether, and how, things are different now.

'The forward march of Labour halted'

In 1978, a year before Margaret Thatcher was elected Prime Minister in the UK, the impeccably Marxist historian Eric Hobsbawm (1978) offered a survey of the preceding 100 years of British working-class history that had ended, as he saw it, with 'the forward march of Labour halted' (although he did politely add a question mark). To simplify greatly, there weren't enough workers and not enough of them were voting for parties of the left. They barely formed a class 'in itself', let alone 'for itself'. The sense that both the radical and the reformist left almost everywhere had shared through most of the 20th century – that despite reverses and disappointments, in the end history was on their side – looked ever less convincing. In fact, *some* social democrats had always been aware of the challenge that the class structure of capitalism posed to their political ambitions. Long before the term 'catch-all' party had been coined or the role of the 'median voter' discovered, they had worried about an over-reliance on working-class votes. This was one of the key issues that drove Eduard Bernstein, the original revisionist, to break with the then-orthodoxy of the German Social Democratic Party (SPD). Bernstein (1909, pp 101-7) insisted that one of the (many) ways in which Marx had been wrong was in supposing that the working class was going to come to constitute the overwhelming majority of the population under a developed capitalism. The SPD therefore had to think about how it could attract the support of other class elements or about the sorts of alliances it might form with other parties and other subaltern interests. A core claim of the party's mainstream (well represented at this point by Karl Kautsky, 1910) was that, in time, workers would come to constitute an overwhelming majority of the population. This was the way in which democracy could be expected to deliver history's verdict in favour of socialism.

In sociological terms, Bernstein was right. The class structure of capitalism did not simplify itself in a way that enabled (parliamentary) democracy to register the arithmetical inevitability of socialism. Of course, this never meant that the numbers were just as inevitably stacked *against* social democratic forces. The more successful social democratic movements – perhaps definitively the Swedish Social Democrats during the period of their ascendancy between the mid-1930s and the mid-1970s – have shown a remarkable capacity for forging stable class alliances behind a centre-left programme (originally with agrarian interests, later with an expanding middle class). But it did pose the challenge of finding a wider electoral base which Bernstein, and following him other social democrats, characteristically sought by reinstating the ethical case for socialism and/or pressing the idea of social citizenship rather than class democracy. On one reading, in the grandest terms, the politics of the social democratic welfare state was the politics of this broadly progressive alliance. It was, in Esping-Andersen's (1985) words, the institutional form of 'politics against markets'.

In 1978, Hobsbawm attributed a fair share of the blame for the halting of Labour's forward march to the Labour Party – a party that had won four out of five previous general elections – but he didn't have much of an idea about how to reverse it. After the humiliating defeat for Labour in 1983 (with its worst electoral performance since the 1920s), it was something like a social democratic reading of Hobsbawm's historical sociology that set the Labour Party off in a very different direction, trudging down the long and winding road of 'renewal' that ended with Blair, New Labour and the victory of 1997. But there was one further and absolutely crucial component in this reformulation of social democratic politics. That was the judgement that the traditional political economy of the social democrats – what Tony Crosland (1956, p 79) had rather clumsily called 'Keynes-plus-modified-capitalism-plus-Welfare-State' – no longer worked. The emblematic moment in abandoning this approach was captured in James Callaghan's address at the 1976 Labour Party Conference:

> We used to think that you could spend your way out of a recession and increase employment by cutting taxes and boosting government spending. I tell you in all candour that that option no longer exists. (Callaghan, 1976)

Of course, there is a real question about whether social democratic parties, including Labour in Britain, ever *really* prosecuted the political economy of Keynes (at least when push turned to shove). Andrew Gamble (1988, p 43) may well have been right to argue of this political Keynesianism, that 'when it was tried it was not needed and when it was needed it was not tried.' But this was certainly the basis on which more thoughtful social democrats had justified their policy stance after 1950 (through to the 1970s). Paradigmatically, this was the case with Tony Crosland (the classic statement is in Crosland, 1956). Down to the 1930s, social democrats had retained their commitment to change the ownership of the economy. Capitalism should be replaced by socialism. It was just that it should be replaced *incrementally* – and in line with the democratically expressed will of a majority of the population. What had changed by the 1950s, on Crosland's account in any case, was that, while not yet quite socialism, *this was no longer capitalism* ('to the question "Is this still Capitalism?", I would answer "no"'; Crosland, 1956, p 42). We could enjoy the many benefits of having an economy with a large private sector – in terms of choice, innovation, micro-efficiency and the absence of bureaucrats – because capital was no longer a *political* power in the way that it had been in the pre-war world. The newer social democracy of Blair and his supporters – definitively, but not exclusively, in the UK – insisted that 'traditional' social democracy had been fixated with 'public ownership' or, to use the really dirty word, 'nationalisation'. But this was quite untrue. The original social democrats had split from Marxism (in a world before the Soviet Union and the Third International) not over the *need* for social ownership but over the *means* of getting there. A later generation abandoned the end of public ownership (in so far as they did) only because they came to see it as *unnecessary*, given the control the state could exercise over the economy and the investment function, indirectly following Keynes' (1973, p 378) mantra:

> It is not the ownership of the instruments of production which it is important for the state to assume. If the state is able to determine the aggregate amount of resources devoted to augmenting the instruments and the basic rate of reward to those who own them, it will have accomplished all that is necessary.

When they came to realise that this didn't work, some of them rowed back a little (see Crosland, 1974). Others opted for a much more radical Alternative Economic Strategy (AES) that put public ownership (and planning) firmly back on the agenda (Holland, 1975; Wickham-Jones, 1996). But it was too late. The advocates of 'progressive renewal' pressed ahead as if this change didn't matter, but it did.

Third Way?

The best-known and most explicit 'reinvention' of social democracy was the idea of a Third Way and the New Labour 'project' in the UK, a reform path that attracted admirers and imitators elsewhere, including the idea of the 'Neue Mitte' in Germany and Helen Clark's reform under a restored Labour government in New Zealand. But a good claim to be *first* down this road belongs to the Lange–Douglas and Hawke–Keating governments in Australia and New Zealand. Although in both countries a concern with the inability of Labour to win elections was a part of the context, it was the need for immediate economic reform and for *this* to heal the reputation of Labo(u)r as a party that could be trusted to manage the economy that drove the political process. The formative experience for politicians of the Hawke–Keating generation was the government of Gough Whitlam – a man with a claim to be Australia's *only* social democrat – and the debacle of the Dismissal. The serial deregulations of the first Hawke government speak to a desire to re-fashion the Australian economy in a global context, rather than a concern with broadening the ALP's electoral appeal. And, perhaps remarkably, much of this process over a 13-year period was carried through in a series of Accords with the Australian Council of Trade Unions (ACTU), in a context in which workplace rights were eroded and union density fell by 16.7 per cent (from 47.9 to 31.2 per cent) between 1983 and 1996. (On all of this, see Kelly, 1994; Pierson 2002; Pierson and Castles, 2002.)

Although it was dressed up with a lot of fancy talk about 'reflexive modernisation', 'positive welfare' and 'the social investment state' – of which Tony Giddens (1998, 2000) was the key exponent – in substance, the Third Way meant a commitment to deregulation of both capital and labour markets, further private sector involvement in the delivery of public services and an unpicking of the traditional fabric of the welfare state. Perhaps above all, in practice, it meant deregulating finance and banking, the consequences of which became clear in 2008 – and with which we are still living and will continue to live for a very considerable time. Some have forgotten just how substantial was the commitment that these sorts of governments made to using the proceeds of economic growth to fund public goods. In the UK, for example, expenditure on education, healthcare and pensions rose very substantially through the first decade of the new millennium (see Hills, 2015). But social mobility ground to a halt, and this coincided with growing wealth and income inequality, a trend that reached back into the last century, but that has accelerated since 2008 (the world-historical source is Piketty, 2013).

'Selling the family silver'?

When an ageing Lord Stockton (Harold Macmillan) likened the Thatcher governments' privatisations (in the mid-1980s) to 'selling off the family silver', at least one of the ideas he must have had in mind was that this is something you can only do once! Similar judgements have been made about the various changes that social democracy underwent in the 1980s and 1990s. The suggestion is that (more or less) desperate social democratic parties made their peace with their erstwhile societal opponents – above all, the representatives of a newly dominant finance capital. This bought them a 'one-off' vote bonanza – and, for a time, an economic increment that they were able to spend on expanding public services – but only at the expense of further long-term decline. For Varoufakis (2016b), this is part of social democracy's 'Faustian pact' with its opponents. As Varoufakis says of the real Faust, his choice was understandable – but catastrophic.

This claim is systematically explored in a recent paper by Karreth, Polk and Allen (2012), who seek to explain both the upturn in social democratic votes in the late 1990s *and* the subsequent downturn after 2000 as part of a *single process*. The core of their argument is this. In a (more or less desperate) quest for votes, social democratic parties shifted their policy platforms rightwards in the 1990s. A long-standing claim about the 'median voter' suggests that parties seeking to maximise their vote will be drawn toward the political centre-ground. The essence of the Karreth argument is that this is what social democratic parties did in the 1990s (although 'the Centre' itself had shifted significantly right-wards over the previous two decades). In the short term, this returned the votes that social democrats were after. But in the longer run, and for a number of reasons, it proved counter-productive. First, they argue, the Centre is 'fuzzy'. Middling voters are by their nature uncommitted and prone to shift support in ways that are unpredictable. Shifting right-wards meant that 'core' social democrat supporters, and party members, became increasingly disengaged from the party and less willing to lend it either their votes or their time, as it ceased to be less distinctively a party of the left (or centre-left). Third, and variably given differences in the way that party systems operate, this opened up a space to the left of the social democrats – a space that was potentially open to Greens or alternative left parties – as well as 'freeing up' of some working-class voters to be drawn towards populist or nationalist parties of the right. As with the Swedish Democrats, parties to the right could come forward as the defenders of 'traditional' welfare state values (for 'traditional' working-class voters), in a context in which social democrats seemed more interested in either 'identity' politics and/or a less supportive welfare system, in which public expenditure was directed more towards 'social investment' (in education or childcare for working parents) rather than 'social insurance' (compensating those marginalised by rapid economic change). Karreth and his collaborators refer to this as the 'electoral postmoderation drought', and argue that it is empirically vindicated by looking at recent experience in the UK, Germany and Sweden.

Financialisation

The changes that social democracy has undergone over the past 30 years have frequently been re-described as driven by the logic of 'globalisation' (see, for example, Kelly, 1994; Gray, 1996). But in some ways, it is more instructive to think about the social democratic challenge in terms of the (again somewhat generic) process of 'financialisation'. At its simplest, financialisation is taken to describe everything that follows from 'the growth of the financial sector, its increased power over the real economy, the explosion in the power of wealth, and the reduction of all of society to the realm of finance'

(Konczal and Abernathy, 2015, p 4). In his state-of-the-art survey, van der Zwan (2014, p 102) identifies financialisation as 'the web of interrelated processes – economic, political, social, technological, cultural etc – through which finance has extended its influence beyond the marketplace and into other realms of social life.' There is disagreement about whether social democrats have encouraged, embraced or resisted these processes. Within this framework, it makes sense to retrace the origins of the current difficulties of social democracy to a familiar period (the early 1970s), but to re-focus our attention on the changing global financial framework that can be dated, epochally, from the end of the Bretton Woods settlement. This is unambiguously the focus of Varoufakis' (2016a) recent history of the problems of the left in Europe, which is written as an account of the failure to find a new financial architecture to replace the coordination that had existed before the Americans decided to pull the plug on Bretton Woods. It is also the focus of Wolfgang Streeck's *Buying time: The delayed crisis of democratic capitalism* (Streeck, 2014). In his extended essay, Streeck seeks to place the crisis of 2008 – and its long aftermath – in the context of a much longer process, a transformation in the relationship between (increasingly financialised) capitalism and democracy (above all, *social* democracy) that dates back to the early 1970s. Evoking the idea of a displaced crisis familiar in the critical literature of the 1970s, Streeck argues that we can understand the trajectory of the state of advanced capitalism in the intervening 40 years in terms of the rubric of 'buying time' (or deferring crisis) – and in the transition from a 'tax state' to a 'debt state'. In shorthand terms, we have seen the transition from 'Keynesian political-economic institutional system of post-war capitalism into a neo-Hayekian economic regime' (Streeck, 2014, p 5). (Democratic) politics is increasingly reduced to a form of 'public entertainment'. His conclusions are stark: 'The future of Europe today is one of a secular implosion of the social contract of capitalist democracy, in the transition to an international consolidation state committed to fiscal discipline' (Streeck, 2014, p 117).

The end?

All of this points us towards a pretty alarming conclusion. The problem of social democracy is not its leaders, or its incapacity to win elections. Its core problem is that it just doesn't have a political economy of its own. Of course, 'political Keynesianism' never quite was the governing logic of post-war social democracy – and it has never entirely gone away (for good reasons, plenty of which have nothing especially to do with social democracy). But it seems clear that social democracy lacks a distinctive politico-economic logic that could, in Streeck's terms, re-connect the economy to a redistributive mass democracy. This perhaps explains why almost every attempt to 're-tool' social democracy for the present hard times – and this from some very different perspectives – ends up endorsing the idea of a basic income (see, for example, Piketty, 2013; Varoufakis, 2016b). It is not that basic income is a bad idea. It isn't. It has a carefully articulated theoretical basis (thanks to van Parijs, 1998) and, in the face of an ever-more coercive welfare regime that demonises the poor, it is a significant step in a more humane direction. But it is not an alternative political economy of the kind Streeck supposes we need. Other models *are* available. Paul Mason's (2015) *PostCapitalism* is one such. In the latest of a long line of thinkers who believe that technology (in this case, information technology) has the power to take us beyond – or, in Mason's case, around the side of – global capitalism. Mason believes that the basis for a post-capitalist alternative already exists. We – and that includes the 99 per cent of us who don't belong to some sort of global financial elite – simply need the confidence to insist that the global emperor has no clothes – and think about the ways in which can move on without him. *PostCapitalism* offers a welcome blast of fresh air. But it's unlikely to meet the challenges that a more mundane social democracy faces.

Let us return finally to the question of social democracy and its electability. It would be quite extraordinary if a party bearing the social democratic label were not ever to win another election. It's worth remembering that democratic publics don't care too much for all the other parties either – which helps explain why 'pop-up' or anti-party parties are doing quite well. But it's hard to see that any social democratic government is going to deliver a distinctively social democratic programme since, at present, such a programme doesn't exist. The party machine will undoubtedly rumble on – providing career opportunities for its increasingly frustrated representatives – but without new ideas, it's going nowhere.

References

Abrams, M. and Rose, R. (1960) *Must Labour lose?*, Harmondsworth: Penguin.

Berman, S. (2006) *The primacy of politics*, Cambridge: Cambridge University Press.

Bernstein, E. (1909) *Evolutionary socialism*, London: ILP.

Callaghan, J. (1976) 'Leader's speech', Blackpool, www.britishpoliticalspeech.org/speech-archive.htm?speech=174

Carroll, B. (2004) *Australia's prime ministers: From Barton to Howard*, Kenthurst, NSW: Rosenberg Publishing.

Clift, B.M. (2011) 'Ideological and organizational travails of French Socialism', *Renewal*, vol 19, no 1, www.renewal.org.uk/articles/the-ideological-organisational-and-electoral-travails-of-french-social/

Clift, B.M. (2013) '*Le changement?* French Socialism, the 2012 presidential election and the politics of economic credibility amidst the Eurozone crisis', *Parliamentary Affairs*, vol 66, no 1, pp 106-23.

Clift, B. and Kuhn, R. (2014) 'The Hollande presidency, 2012-14', *Modern and Contemporary France*, vol 22, no 4, pp 425-34.

Collins Dictionary (no date) 'Pasokification' (www.collinsdictionary.com/submission/16117/pasokification).

Crosland, A. (1956) *The future of socialism*, London: Jonathan Cape.

Crosland, A. (1974) *Socialism now and other essays*, London: Jonathan Cape.

Esping-Andersen, G. (1985) *Politics against markets*, Princeton, NJ: Princeton University Press.

Gamble, A. (1988) *The free economy and the strong state: The politics of Thatcherism*, London: Macmillan.

Gamble, A. (2011) 'Reply to David Miliband', *Political Quarterly*, vol 82, no 2, p 138.

Giddens, A. (1998) *The Third Way*, Cambridge: Polity.

Giddens, A. (2000) *The Third Way and its critics*, Cambridge: Polity.

Gray, J. (1996) *After social democracy: Politics, capitalism and the common life*, London: Demos.

Hills, J. (2015) *Good times, bad times*, Bristol: Policy Press.

Hobsbawm, E. (1978) 'The forward march of Labour halted?', *Marxism Today*, September, pp 279-86.

Holland, S. (1975) *The socialist challenge*, London: Quartet.

Hyman, R. (2001) *Understanding European trade unionism*, London: Sage.

Karreth, J., Polk, J.T. and Allen, C.S. (2012) 'Release? The electoral consequences of social democratic parties' march to the middle in Western Europe', *Comparative Political Studies*, vol 46, no 7, pp 791-822.

Kautsky, K. (1910) *The class struggle*, New York: C.H. Kerr.

Kelly, P. (1994) *The end of certainty*, Sydney, NSW: Allen & Unwin.

Keynes, J.M. (1973) *The general theory of employment, interest and money*, London: Macmillan.

Konczal, M. and Abernathy, N. (2015) 'Defining financialization', Roosevelt Institute, 27 July, http://rooseveltinstitute.org/defining-financialization

Mason, P. (2015) *PostCapitalism: A guide to our future*, London: Penguin.

Miliband, D. (2011) 'Why is the European Left losing elections?', *Political Quarterly*, vol 82, no 2, pp 131-7.

OECD (Organisation for Economic Co-operation and Development) (2016) 'Trade union density', *OECD.Stat*, https://stats.oecd.org/Index.aspx?DataSetCode=UN_DEN

Pierson, C. (1986) *Marxist theory and democratic politics*, Cambridge: Polity.

Pierson, C. (1995) *Socialism after communism: The new market socialism*, Cambridge: Polity Press.

Pierson, C. (2001) *Hard choices: Social democracy in the 21st century*, Cambridge: Polity Press.

Pierson, C. (2002) '"Social democracy on the back foot": The ALP and the "new" Australian model', *New Political Economy*, vol 7, no 2, pp 179-97.

Pierson, C. and Castles, F. (2002) 'Australian antecedents of the Third Way', *Political Studies*, vol 50, no 4, pp 683-701.

Piketty, T. (2013) *Capital for the 21st century*, Harvard, MA: Harvard University Press.

Rawson, D.W. (1966) *Labor in vain: A survey of the Australian Labor Party*, Melbourne, VIC: Longmans.

Rothstein, B. and Steinmo, S. (2013) 'Social democracy in crisis. What crisis?', in M. Keating and D. McCrone (eds) *The crisis of social democracy in Europe*, Edinburgh: Edinburgh University Press, pp 87–106.

Sassoon, D. (1996) *One hundred years of socialism*, London: I.B. Tauris.

Sassoon, D. (2013) 'The Long Depression, the Great Crash and socialism in Western Europe', in M. Keating and D. McCrone (eds) *The crisis of social democracy in Europe*, Edinburgh: Edinburgh University Press, pp 14–27.

Streeck, W. (2014) *Buying time: The delayed crisis of democratic capitalism*, London: Verso.

van der Zwan, N. (2014) 'Making sense of financialization', *Socio-Economic Review*, vol 12, no 1, pp 99-129.

van Parijs, P. (1998) *Real freedom for all*, Oxford: Oxford University Press.

Varoufakis, Y. (2016a) 'Interview with Yanis Varoufakis', *The Economist*, 31 March, www.economist.com/ESDvaroufakis

Varoufakis, Y. (2016b) *And the weak suffer what they must?*, London: Bodley Head.

Wickham-Jones, M. (1996) *Economic strategy and the Labour Party*, London: Macmillan.

TWELVE

Social democracy and the populist challenge

René Cuperus

Introduction

European social democracy is in the danger zone. It threatens to be undermined and overrun by radical left-wing competitors and right-wing populist opponents. Centre-left social democrats have lost their distinct profile and identity within the political arena as they have sought to accommodate themselves to centre-right, neoliberal policy dominance. Regarding issues of cultural identity, such as European integration or migration, social democracy is suffering more than its competitors from the 'globalisation conflict'. Social democracy appears unable as a political vehicle to bridge the differing concerns between the higher educated and the lower educated, to deal with the issue of open borders and free movement, immigration, European integration and free global trade. European social democracy has not achieved a 'core constituency' in its pursuit of 'the European Union Adventure', as the dramatic outcome of the Brexit referendum has once again demonstrated.

The task of rebuilding social democracy is significant and formidable. First of all, social democracy has to restore within national democracies the post-war social contract of welfare state fairness, a restoration of trust in socioeconomic security and cultural continuity. This is a necessary precondition for a renewed European Project, in which social democrats, in partnership and coalition with other left-wing and Green parties and social movements, should formulate an alternative political economy for European cooperation. It has to shift away from the technocratic, governmental, neoliberal mainstream of contemporary politics. It must get back to its roots, basic values and lost electorates. Otherwise, 'Pasokification' threatens to ruin established social democratic parties, accompanied by the chilling rise of anti-pluralist right-wing populism and anti-democratic extremism (Müller, 2016, pp 101-3).

'Pasokification'

A spectre is haunting European social democracy: 'Pasokification'. This refers to the total disappearance of the formerly dominant powerhouse PASOK in Greece, the social democratic sister-party of the UK and Dutch Labour Parties ('the nearest thing to a social-democratic party in that unfortunate country'; see Marquand, 2015), self-immolated as a direct result of the Euro crisis. Under the authority of the Troika of the European Commission, European Central Bank (ECB) and International Monetary Fund (IMF), and under strong pressure from Northern European politicians, PASOK capitulated in the face of a very severe reform programme of austerity politics. Total collapse of the party ensued. In 2009 it still had 43.9 per cent of the vote; by 2015 it retained just 4.7 per cent. The party was overtaken and replaced by the more radical left Syriza, led by Alexis Tsipras, the acting Greek Prime Minister.

UK Labour activist James Doran categorised this total disintegration of a traditional social democratic party under pressure from a dynamic radical-left alternative 'Pasokification'. He coined the term during the UK national elections, referring to the catastrophic wipeout experienced by the Scottish Labour Party: 'Pasokification happened to Scottish Labour'. The party was indeed wiped out and erased by the Scottish National Party (SNP), which characterised Labour as 'Red Tories'.

Greece undoubtedly presented a special case: PASOK was notorious for being a clientelist, corrupt party (Heyer, 2012; Lowen, 2013). It therefore lacked the necessary legitimacy to force austerity on its own population. Greek political and economic elites should be held to account for the dysfunctional operation of the Greek state, both before and after the Euro crisis. Put bluntly, PASOK presented a special case.

A revolt against austerity?

Even though PASOK's fate was extreme, social democracy throughout Europe faces similar pressures. It could also be torn apart by the competing attractions of radical-left and right-wing populist forces. Large, established centre-left parties threaten to become marginalised. According to the British political commentator Jack Ferguson, Pasokification is an existential threat for all established, mainstream social democratic parties: 'If they cannot mount effective opposition to austerity and social crisis, their voting base begins to see them as irrelevant, and not fit for purpose' (Ferguson, 2015).

And indeed, the implementation of austerity politics has a perverse side-effect: parties in the political centre are converging and overlapping. Differences between centre-left and centre-right are fading away (EUROPP, 2015). This has serious consequences: a 'law' in political science states that when the crucial difference and contrast between left and right fades away or disappears, or, to put it another way, when the left/right divide diminishes, a new cleavage takes its place, the so-called populist cleavage, the divide between 'the people' and 'the elite' (on 'post politics', see Mouffe, 2005).

On the one hand, so-called left-populist parties profit from this new cleavage – 'left-populist' is the demonising label that political opponents use to frame these parties outside the established order. One could also speak about radical-left parties or even about pre-Third Way, anti-neoliberal, social democratic parties. This latter term constitutes the self-image of parties such as Die Linke in Germany or the Socialist Party (SP) in the Netherlands.

In Southern Europe, in particular, anti-austerity movements have emerged, such as Podemos in Spain or Syriza in Greece. These new parties started as grass-roots social protest movements, and in terms of programme, electoral charisma and social mobilisation, constitute a serious and fearsome threat to the sometimes corrupt, more often, 'technocratisised', extinguished and burnt-out social democracy (Butzlaff et al, 2011).

Finally, in Western and Eastern Central Europe, we encounter so-called right-wing populist parties that successfully attack the established politics of the mainstream. These include the Front National (FN) in France, the Party for Freedom (PVV) in the Netherlands, the Scandinavian People's Parties, and the German Alternative für Deutschland (AfD), all of whom profile themselves as anti-EU, anti-migration, anti-Islam and anti-Establishment (Mudde, 2007).

The notion of Pasokification is, in the meantime, even relevant to the Swedish social democratic party (SAP) (Marcal, 2015). The SAP, once an iconic beacon as the mother-party of European social democracy, has been politically attacked from two sides. It is gradually losing its working-class constituency to the right-wing populist Sweden Democrats, which, thanks to the refugee crisis, was experiencing its finest hour. In addition, the SAP is losing out in larger cities such as Stockholm to social progressive and feminist parties that are attractive to urban academic professionals. Former social democratic voters have turned to both anti-Establishment, populist parties, and to those parties that encompass identity politics and appeal primarily to professionals. So social democracy is being squeezed between populism and elitism. Becker and Cuperus (2007) have previously categorised this development as the 'splits of social democracy'.

The 'splits' has hammered down dramatically in the last parliamentary elections in the Netherlands (March 2017). The good news from the Netherlands was that the nationalist-populist tsunami against the post-war Establishment – starting with Brexit and the Trump victory, and assumed to be continued by a Wilders victory, a Marine Le Pen triumph in France, and maybe even a game-changing result of the AfD in Germany – was stopped in the Netherlands. Geert Wilders' Party for Freedom was beaten by the current Prime Minister Mark Rutte and his Conservative-Liberal party (VVD, People's Party for Freedom and Democracy): 33 seats versus PVV's 20 seats in a 150-seat Parliament. Yet, this win over right-wing populism was accompanied by a strong shift to the political right and a total collapse of the social democratic labour party PvdA (Social Democratic Workers' Party): from 38 down to 9 seats, down 29 seats, the deepest fall in Dutch political history. The GreenLeft party, under the charismatic leadership of 'Jessias' (Jesse) Klaver, managed to mobilise anti-populist millennials, and profited from the PvdA losses. This was not the case with the radical-left Socialist Party, which surprisingly lost a seat. The pattern was more one of social democracy exploding or disintegrating in its constituent parts/ingredients. Identity politics took over strategic voting. Social democratic votes went in all directions, including support to the Party of the Elderly, 50PLus (anti-pension reform). The Party of the Animals (PvdD), a newly established migrant/Muslim party, DENK, were both very successful in the migrant majority quarters of Amsterdam and Rotterdam. And the academic professionals and millennial students went to their biotope parties: D66 (Social Liberal) and GreenLeft. This election left a totally fragmented and polarised party political spectrum behind.

The post-war social democratic project of embedding a robust welfare state within capitalism is being undermined by the influences of globalisation, individualisation and the shift to the neoliberal knowledge-based economy. Society is characterised by growing social inequality, an increasing imbalance between 'capital' and 'labour', and between the interests of international corporate power and the public domain. We also find massive unemployment (particularly among young people) and labour insecurity, polarisation between those educated to a higher level and the rest, and a decreasing community spirit in complex, fragmented, multicultural societies (Bauman, 2006; Rodrik, 2010; Piketty, 2014; Atkinson, 2015).

Despite this alarming rise in new inequalities and misbalances, we do not see much out-of-the-box policy creativity from social democrats. A meritocratic class society based on educational inequality is developing, but no correction to this almost social-Darwinist trend has emerged. Democracy itself is under threat from authoritarian and anti-democratic tendencies, with the illiberal developments in Central Europe and the Balkans as a case in point. The rule of law is under attack by right-wing populists, who reject pluralism and embrace the dangerous fiction of a 'one and indivisible (ethnic homogeneous) people' (see Müller, 2016, pp 75-99). And social democrats? They stand passively on the sidelines.

And what of *politics against markets*? This was once the self-definition of Scandinavian social democracy, but social democracy seems to have lost touch with the notion. It is losing out against the interests and power of international business. Even worse, it has become a force contributing to the demolition of the social and public domain. Social democracy is no longer a counterforce to, but rather 'collaborates' with the ideology of the market society. Due to this loss of its fixed political identity, the classical social democratic electorate has been split and fragmented. The neoliberal Third Way renewal of social democracy in the 1990s (in itself a panic-driven response to the endless 'desert years of unelectability' during the 1980s under Reagan, Thatcher and Kohl) led to a crisis of trust and representation, even to feelings of 'social betrayal' within the core social democratic electorate, opening up a space for populist entrepreneurs exploiting these resentments of the 'left behind'. As a result, the 'bridge or umbrella function' of the post-war social democratic People's Parties – big tents encompassing both lower and higher middle classes – threatens to break down.

This crisis of trust and representation, which has adversely affected the post-war 'system parties', such as the social democratic and Christian democratic mass parties, is not restricted to the economic dimension of the process of *technoglobalisation* (Gilman, 2016, pp 7-16). The disruptive, cultural dimension of globalisation seems, especially in Western Europe, to have had even more impact. Fareed Zakaria (2016, p 15) has referred to this process:

> Immigration is the final frontier of globalization. It is the most intrusive and disruptive because, as a result of it, people are dealing not with objects or abstractions; instead, they come face-to-face with other human beings, ones who look, sound and feel different. And this can give rise to fear,

racism, and xenophobia. But not all the reaction is noxious. It must be recognised that the pace of change can move too fast for society to digest. The ideas of disruption and creative destruction have been celebrated so much that it is easy to forget that they look very different to the people being disrupted.

Both the economic and cultural dimensions of globalisation placed the system parties under pressure. This malaise goes further than the parties themselves. The alliances on which social democracy was historically built – workers, the intellectual and professional middle class, trade unions and social movements – have been torn apart or disentangled. The post-war People's Parties have become more and more depopulated: mass parties without masses. As Harold James has indicated, this development can be explained by the interplay of globalisation and technological disruption that has led to mass downward socioeconomic mobility, expanding inequalities and resurrecting that forgotten class from European social history, *the déclassé* (James, 2016, pp 17-24).

Because of all this, we see the manifestation of a populist momentum all over the Western world. Populism is an alarm signal. The resurgence of populism is being driven by a range of factors, including:

- an abrupt modernisation process and rapid transformation of social structures (Polanyi, 1944)
- failing management of change and insecurity
- citizens being disconnected between the political system leading to a clash between elites and non-elites
- an explosion of (perceived) social inequalities, and
- fear of social *déclassement* by 'the squeezed middle' (Cuperus, 2007, pp 102-11; Mudde, 2007, pp 201-56).

Core elements of populism can be traced back to four characteristics: (1) populists emphasise the central position of the pure people; (2) populists criticise the (corrupt) elite; (3) populists perceive the people as a homogeneous entity; and (4) populists proclaim a serious crisis (Rooduijn, 2013). This comes together in the often-used definition of populism by the Dutch political scientist, Cas Mudde (2015):

> Populism is a thin-centred ideology that considers society to be ultimately separated into two homogeneous and antagonistic groups, "the pure people" and "the corrupt

elite", and argues that politics should be an expression of the *volonté general* (general will) of the people.

The key question is, why is this populist momentum taking place? Why now? Why all over the Western world? Why, and since when exactly, have formerly widely supported parties been conceived as being 'the corrupt elite' that is betraying the (ordinary) people? What went wrong with established politics? What went wrong with social democratic politics, once the natural representation of the (ordinary) people?

Revolt of 'The left behind'

The comparative political scientist Steven Wolinetz has analysed the electoral results of European social democratic parties in the period 1950-2015. A clear downward turn can be observed. It can be argued that, on the basis of these figures, social democratic parties have gone from obtaining between 30 and 40 per cent share of the vote on average over recent decades to between 10 and 20 per cent over recent years (Wolinetz, 2016). This applies especially to Austria, the Netherlands, Germany, Flanders and the Scandinavian countries. Here we can see both electoral decline and declining participation in governments. The share of the vote scores of 10 or 20 per cent severely damage the self-image and self-identity of social democracy. Post-war social democracy deliberately defined itself as a broad people's party, home for all, joining together and connecting high and low educated, province and big city, highly educated and middle groups around a programme based on the welfare state and public provision. Parties that do not attain the 30 per cent electoral hurdle have actually dropped below the quantitative norm that German political scientists use to define genuine *Volksparteien* (or People's Parties). Quantity is threatening quality.

Part of the explanation for the poor electoral results of social democracy is the rise of populism. At first sight, right-wing populism might be considered a problem that affects just the right. right-wing populist parties often split off from or form branches of right-wing political parties. The FPÖ of Jörg Haider in Austria, the PVV of Geert Wilders in the Netherlands, the People's Party in Denmark – all sprang from conservative-liberal parties on the right.

However, electorally and programmatically, right-wing populism also poses a challenge to social democracy. Such parties are capable of mobilising large parts of the vulnerable in society, as well those of a lower educational level within the middle class. Diachronically, these voters can often be recognised as the children and grandchildren of the old core labour constituencies of social democracy. Some of these right-wing populist parties transformed themselves into the new workers' parties. More voters possessing a lower educational level are opting for the Front National and the FPÖ than for the classical social democratic French and Austrian parties, as has been noted (Houtman et al, 2008; Lazar, 2015, pp 7-19).

The pan-European rise of right-wing populism has had far-reaching consequences. First of all, the political and public agenda has shifted from a socioeconomic perspective to a cultural perspective. right-wing populism is 'culturalising' (mostly 'Islamising') all political issues, and is characterised by a nativist focus on putting its 'own people first'. Second, right-wing populism portrays and demonises social democracy as forming (part of) the elite 'which betrays ordinary people'. It also depicts social democratic parties as being simply parties for migrants (PvdA = Party for the Arabs – according to Geert Wilders). By doing so, right-wing populists deliberately seek to distance traditional social democratic voters from social democratic parties.

Third, the rise of right-wing populism is increasing opportunities for right-wing or Conservative governments. Unless the left can erect a *cordon sanitaire*, its future appears bleak. In this situation, grand coalitions consisting of political left and right antipodes must be formed to out-manoeuvre right-wing populism. However, this stratagem by definition undermines the left/right divide and 'confirms' the populist view that established politics is forming a 'There Is No Alternative' cartel (Crouch, 2005).

In the analysis of the success of the Front National (FN), the concept of *La France périphérique* came to the surface. FN is strong in those regions and cities that feel excluded from the mainstream of the modernising, globalising society. In those regions, people tend to see themselves treated as second-class citizens, with an uncertain future, without social security and cultural continuity. The concept of peripheral France has been developed by the French geographer, Christophe Guilluy, in his (2014) essay *La France périphérique: Comment on a sacrifié les classes populaires*. In other words, how ordinary people in the province have been sacrificed on the altar of modern progress.

Although voting for nasty, xenophobic, or even racist and extreme-right parties should never be justified or explained away by sociological or cultural-psychological determinism – 'angry, marginalised people' still have different moral options and freedom of manoeuvre – many non-angry, non-marginalised people also vote for right-wing populism. In this connection, the failure of the People's Parties is apparent, especially social democratic parties and their failure to address the causes of the pan-European populist revolt. We encounter a narrative of social orphandom, a feeling of being left behind, alone and vulnerable in the new modernity of the global era (Lipset, 1963; Mair, 2013).

The English political theoretician and former Labour politician David Marquand has argued along the same lines (2015), suggesting that:

> The rise of the populist radical right is an epiphenomenon of a profound crisis of the social-democratic left. right-wing populism is successful with voter groups which feel left behind by globalisation, by Europeanisation, by technological change, by the gales of creative destruction which have swept through the global economy, by the associated decay of settled communities and ways of life, by the rise of the super-rich and growth of inequality, and, not least, by the professionalization and remoteness of mainstream politics.

Robert Reich (2016), former US Secretary of Labor under Bill Clinton, has recently analysed how Democrats lost their working-class base:

> The Democratic party once represented the working class. But over the last three decades the party has been taken over by Washington-based fundraisers, bundlers, analysts, and pollsters who have focused instead on raising campaign money from corporate and Wall Street executives and getting votes from upper middle-class households in "swing" suburbs. Democrats have ... failed to reverse the decline in working-class wages and economic security. Both Bill Clinton and Barack Obama ardently pushed for free trade agreements without providing millions of blue-collar workers who thereby lost their jobs means of getting new ones that paid at least as well. They stood by as corporations hammered trade unions, the backbone of the white working class.... Partly as a result, union membership sank from 22% of all workers when Bill Clinton was elected president to less than 12% today, and the working class lost bargaining leverage to get a share of the economy's gains.... The unsurprising result of this combination – more trade, declining unionization and more industry concentration – has been to shift political and economic power to big corporations and the wealthy, and to shaft the working class.

This created an opening for Donald Trump's authoritarian demagoguery, and his presidency.

Recent developments confirm this diagnosis. Everywhere, we see that a growing number of (new) employees fail to secure a fixed job. In a country such as the Netherlands, the *de facto* permanent job has been abolished, especially for the young and old. People and organisations have been submitted to a regime of hyper-flexibilisation. Due to permanent change and reform, many have been denied access to the welfare state. Moreover, there is a dual European crisis of input – lack of democratic representation – and output – the Euro crisis, ill-managed migration and refugee flows.

Restoration of trust

Everything points in the same direction: Western democracies are entering the future in increasingly separate worlds. Divisive, polarising tensions appear to outweigh binding, bridging forces. Brexit and the Trump Revolt in the US are two key outliers. Other examples were the Dutch Ukraine referendum (6 April 2016) or the presidential elections in Austria between far-right candidate Norbert Hofer versus Green candidate Alexander van der Bellen. The political Centre is out of the game. In Austria neither the former powerhouses of Christian democracy nor social democracy played a role in the iconic president's race. In the French presidential elections something similar was happening: in the political battle between political outsider Emmanuel Macron (En Marche!) and Marine le Pen (Front National), the established parties of the Parti socialiste (PS) and *Les Républicains* were absent.

The alarming news about these events is that they all reconfirmed the populist cleavage or conflict line running through contemporary Western societies – the clash between the Establishment and the non-Establishment, splitting one half of society against the other. This *revolt of citizens* (as it has been dubbed in the Netherlands after the breakthrough of Pim Fortuyn in 2001/02), this 'unpredicted' revolution, demonstrated that both the academic world and the media had lost touch with the undercurrents of discontent, especially within the lower and middle strata in society.

The fact that this 50/50 distributive code or formula resurfaces in research, elections and referenda (Brexit, Trump vs Clinton, Hofer vs van der Bellen) suggests that we are confronted with the following fundamental phenomenon: about half of the population may well resist the future direction of our contemporary society. These people distrust neoliberal globalisation, are against EU integration, resist the overall erosion of the post-war welfare state, criticise increasing inequality, and have major concerns about labour migration and refugee migration in general, and Islam, in particular. They fear that their country is losing many of its characteristic traits due to immigration and open borders.

This analysis has recently been empirically demonstrated by a large country comparative research project of the German Bertelsmann Stiftung – *Fear not values. Public opinion and the populist vote in Europe* (de Vries and Hoffman, 2016), concluding that 'globalisation fears weigh heavily on European voters.' Large groups of citizens feel that they are not at home in their own society because of immigration, and that economic globalisation will not benefit them or their children or grandchildren. And they have a strong conviction that 'people like us' can do little or nothing about these changes and developments. Politics and politicians just go their own way. That is why this near-majority of 50 per cent is in favour of referenda, in order to wake up, correct or punish the political class. They have the feeling that it no longer represents them or listens to them.

What is even more problematic is that this 50 per cent is approximately equal to the proportion of lowly educated and average/secondary/medium-educated people in countries such as the Netherlands. These segments feel much less comfortable in the globalising knowledge-based economy, where the world has become a 'global village', but at the same time the traditional village has become the world. The world a village, a village the world. They obtain less from this new global order. This deep cleavage in our post-welfare state societies does not appear socially sustainable. No country can welcome and embrace the future with such a blatant rift between future-optimistic highly educated professionals and future-pessimistic professionals with a lower educational level, between insiders and outsiders in the new 'meritocratic democracy'. The growing tensions between Muslims and non-Muslims as a result of jihadist radicalisation and terrorism is a further factor. All signals point to the polarisation and sharpening of divisions. What is disturbing is that this divergence of opinion is coupled with a growing number of poisonous smears and slurs on social media and displays of mutual contempt between the Establishment and anti-Establishment.

What such divided countries now need above all is a dismantling of stereotypes and group identities. Concepts such as 'people', 'elite', Establishment, populism and Islam must be refuted and invalidated as false entities. Pluralism and pluriformity must unsettle and shake up solidified contradistinctions. The image of politics as an old boys' network for highly educated professionals is destroying traditional political institutions. The 'elite' should leave its post-political bubble, and not be reticent about actually engaging political opponents in debate so as to facilitate left- and right-wing alternative political futures. Muslims who wholeheartedly and deliberately opt for the Western way of life should distance themselves sharply from radical Islam, as right-wing populists should demarcate themselves sharply from the far and extreme right.

This will result in more varieties of the elite, more flavours of Islam, more kinds of populists, and thereby a visible break-up and deconstruction of stereotypes and identity-political group stigmas. How else might future segregated, divisive, unequal societies be fought?

Despite the fascinating Macron triumph – an anti-Establishment revolt out of the political centre – throughout Europe a populist anti-Establishment mood is still alive and active. For more than two decades, since Jörg Haider in Austria, the Established parties have been challenged and provoked by the so-called populist alternative. Mainstream parties and politicians have hitherto failed to come up with an accurate explanation of this phenomenon, much less an actual solution. There can be no doubt that the populist revolt is a dangerous attack on the post-war liberal order.

The traditional mass parties that have ruled the region since at least the end of the Second World War have lost members, voters, élan and a monopoly on ideas. Because they are the pillars of both the party-oriented parliamentary system and the welfare state, their slow but steady decline affects European societies as a whole. Due to changes in labour, family and cultural lifestyles, the Christian democratic (conservative) and social democratic pillars of civil society are wearing away, leaving behind 'People's Parties' with declining electorates. This erosion of political representation is eating away at the foundations of the European welfare states and European party democracies.

The representation problem of the traditional political party system; the anger about growing inequalities and the growing cleavage between higher educated and lower educated; the discontent with ill-managed mass migration; the growing unease with the European integration process (not a shield against globalisation, but instead, the transmitter and 'visible face' of global competition) – these all fuel the political and electoral potential of (right-wing) populist movements, which exploit feelings of anxiety, fear and resentment while constructing a narrative of social and moral decline.

In the process of adaptation to the New Global World Order, there has been a fundamental breakdown of trust and communication between elites and the general population. The pressures of adaptation to the new globalised world are particularly directed at those who do not fit in to the new international knowledge-based economy, the unskilled and the low-skilled. The overall discourse of adaptation and competitive adjustment has a strong bias against the lower middle class and those professionals with a lower educational level. This bias is one of the root causes for populist resentment and revolt. Policy and political elites are selling and producing insecurity and uncertainty, instead of showing security and stable leadership in a world of flux.

Unease and distrust within contemporary European society must go beyond reform of the welfare state. We are experiencing a shift right across the board. The magic of the post-war period seems to have dispelled the post-war ideal of European unification, the post-war welfare state model and the post-Holocaust tolerance for the foreigner: all seem to be eroding and under pressure. The overall process of internationalisation (globalisation, immigration, European integration) is producing a chasm of trust and representation between elites and the population at large around questions of cultural and national identity.

Europe faces a dangerous populist revolt against the good society of both the neoliberal business community and progressive educated professionals. The revolt of populism is, at least partly, 'produced' by the economic and cultural elites (Lasch, 1995). They advocate, without much historical or sociological reflection, their 'brave new world' of the bright, well educated, entrepreneurial and highly mobile. Their TINA project is creating fear and resentment among non-elites. The deterministic image of a future world of globalisation, open borders, free flows of people and lifelong learning in the knowledge-based society is a nightmare world for non-elites, the 'losers of globalisation'.

In the elite narrative, sizable sections of the middle and working class are being confronted with economic and psychological degradation. Theirs is no longer the future. They feel alienated, dispossessed and downgraded, because the society in which they felt comfortable, in which they had their respected place, and which has been part of their social identity, is being pushed aside by new realities. To what extent can the ideology of 'globalism', multiculturalism and world citizenship be reconciled with the heritage of national democracy and welfare state communitarianism? To what extent can a uniform global culture of neoliberal, consumentistic and hedonistic capitalism be reconciled with the rich cultural diversity of the world?

Contrary to the implicit idea of the self-abolition of the nation-state in favour of new regional power centres, unstable and dislocating undercurrents in European society require not only prudence in (the discourse on) modernisation and innovation, but also the rehabilitation of nation-state democracy as a forum for the restoration of trust, as an anchor in uncertain times, as a source of social cohesion between the less and the better educated, between immigrants and the autochthonous population. A restoration of trust between politicians and citizens might first have to take place at the national level – the tested and recognised arena for democracy – as will the creation of a harmonious multi-ethnic society. Support for international solidarity will be hard to achieve, if people feel or perceive that at the national level solidarity is missing, and inequality and unfairness rising. No International or European Solidarity without National Solidarity.

Indeed, a classical social democratic programme focusing on socioeconomic security and cultural continuity could, in theory, neutralise the breeding grounds of populism. Therefore, it is of the utmost importance that the post-war social contract of the welfare state be restored – at the national level first and foremost, where trust and democratic legitimacy and credibility can more easily be obtained then at European or multilateral levels.

The precondition for regaining political trust is also the renewal or even the reinvention of the *Volkspartei*, as a bridge between the winners and losers of the new world trends. This new *Volkspartei* will possibly emerge from coalition building, encompassing other political parties, as well as civil society actors, and should design a new deal between the privileged and the less privileged: a pact of social-economic security and cultural openness, forging a new idea of progress. It should also be based on a sensitivity towards cultural and identity politics, because widespread discontent and unhappiness in affluent welfare democracies are, to a serious extent, about community, social cohesion and security: postmaterialist problems of social psychology (Becker and Cuperus, 2010, pp 100-15; Krouwel and Pereira, 2015, pp 5-13).

It is important to restore the divide between left and right in politics – with alternative scenarios to adapt to the new world trends – in order to fight the dangerous populist cleavage between the Establishment and (a false entity of) the people: social democrats must be tough on populism and tough on the causes of populism. Social democrats cannot fight populism, without also acknowledging the failures of its own established parties in reaching out to those people who feel left behind, and who were once core constituencies of social democracy (Cuperus, 2007; Cuperus, 2015, pp 57-67). At one point during its history, social democracy allowed the extreme right and extreme left to take over as mass parties. The lesson of the dark 20th century, the scars of fascist and communist totalitarian barbarism, was and is to ensure that this never happens again. There must therefore be a return to social democratic values, roots and principles, and a shift away from the neoliberal, elitist, technocratic politics of recent decades.

As German sociologist Wolfgang Streeck has stated: 'Rather than devising "constructive solutions" and acting as capital's loyal opposition where there is no loyal government, we should support trade unions, even if they are often not very farsighted; no longer vote for the public relations specialists that are now impersonating political leaders; refuse to believe their professionally crafted excuses and There Is No Alternative rhetoric' (Streeck and Roos, 2015, p 13). In the end, social democracy has to overcome what political theorist Chantal Mouffe has called the 'post-political condition'. It has to break out of the Establishment, out of the 'consensus at the centre' between the centre-right and centre-left around the idea that there is no alternative to neoliberal globalisation (EUROPP, 2015).

In a similar vein, Fareed Zakaria (2016, pp 15-16) rightly states:

> Western societies will have to focus directly on the dangers of too rapid cultural change. That might involve some limits on the rate of immigration and on the kinds of immigrants who are permitted to enter. It should involve much greater efforts and resources devoted to integration and assimilation, as well as better safety nets.... But in the end, there is no substitute for enlightened leadership, the kind that, instead of pandering to people's worst instincts, appeals to their better angels.

In conclusion

As the chapters in this book clearly and painfully demonstrate, social democracy is in a state of flux. In a negative state of flux, for that matter. Social democracy is on the back foot, struggling to win elections, struggling to win office, struggling to keep its electoral alliances and constituencies together. This story of social democratic blues seems to be part of a far bigger picture, a *pars pro toto* for what is going on in politics in general. Everywhere we see a crisis of trust and representation, a shortcut between electorates and mainstream political elites. Anti-pluralist, anti-democratic, authoritarian tendencies are attacking the established liberal order. The break-down of social democracy represents a break-down of society at large, and a break-down of solidarity.

One of the manifestations of this shortcut is the pan-European rise, or even global rise, of populist movements and parties. Keywords: Brexit, Trump Revolt, West European right-wing populism. Populism is a huge challenge to all established politics, but especially to social democratic institutions, individuals and ideas. Populism tends to frame social democracy as weak or as an anonymous part of the (centre-right, neoliberal-technocratic) Establishment; it tends to demonise social democracy as an anti-patriotic force, as 'elite and migrant parties'. Furthermore, it tends to portray social democracy as a traitor to its own history and its own traditional constituency.

Social democracy is challenged by populist pressures and discourses at the level of institutions (the crisis of representation), individuals (media-driven authentic-authoritarian leadership) and ideas (anti-globalisation, anti-EU, anti-migration, anti-internationalist, anti-solidarity). Populism is putting the vulnerable social democratic alliance of higher educated and lower educated, cosmopolitans and communitarians, workers and migrants, under extreme strain. Populism may be the face of morbid transition at a time when traditional party systems are fragmenting, when democracy in a global era requires reinvention, when an apolitical technocracy of experts and non-governmental organisations (NGOs) is running the neoliberal global world without much democratic interference.

As the Italian Marxist, Antonio Gramsci, famously stated, when referring to periods of transition, 'The political crisis consists precisely in the fact that the old is dying and the new cannot be born; in this interregnum a great variety of morbid symptoms appear' (Gramsci, 1971).

References

Atkinson, A. (2015) *Inequality: What can de done?*, Harvard, MA: Harvard University Press.

Bauman, Z. (2006) *Liquid fear*, London: Wiley & Sons.

Becker, F. and Cuperus, R. (2007) *Verloren slag. De PvdA en de verkiezingen van 2006*, Amsterdam: Mets & Schilt.

Becker, F. and Cuperus, R. (2010) 'Innovating social democracy Houdini-style. A perspective from the Dutch Labour Party (PvdA)', in *The future of social democracy/Die Zukunft der Sozialdemokratie*, IPG 2010/4, pp 100-15.

Butzlaff, F., Micus, M. and Walter, F. (2011) *Genossen in der Krise? Europas Sozialdemokratie auf dem Prüfstand*. München: Vandenhoeck & Ruprecht.

Crouch, C. (2005) *Post-democracy*, Cambridge: Polity Press.

Cuperus, R. (2007) 'Populism against Globalisation. A new European revolt', in Policy Network, *Immigration and integration: A new center-left agenda*, London: Polity Press, pp 1010–120.

Cuperus, R. (2015) 'Comment les partis populaires ont (Presque) perdu le people? Pourquoi devons-nous écouter le réveil du populisme?', *La Revue Socialiste*, November, vol 60, pp 57-67.

de Vries, C. and Hoffmann, I. (2016) *Fear not values. Public opinion and the populist vote in Europe*, Berlin: Bertelsmann Stiftung, www.bertelsmann-stiftung.de/fileadmin/files/user_upload/EZ_eupinions_Fear_Study_2016_ENG.pdf

EUROPP (2015) 'Five minutes with Chantal Mouffe: "Most countries in Europe are in a post-political situation"', EUROPP blogs LSE, 16 September, http://blogs.lse.ac.uk/europpblog/2013/09/16/five-minutes-with-chantal-mouffe-most-countries-in-europe-are-in-a-post-political-situation/

Ferguson, J. (2015) 'Pasokification of British Labour', *Grenzeloos*, 12 May, www.grenzeloos.org/content/pasokification-british-labour

Gilman, N. (2016) 'Technoglobalization and its discontents', *The American Interest (The Roots of Rage)*, November/December, vol 12, no 2, pp 7-16.

Guilluy, C. (2014) *La France périphérique: Comment on a sacrifié les classes populaires*, Paris: Flammarion.

Heyer, J.A. (2012) 'Corruption continues virtually unchecked in Greece', *Spiegel Online*, 16 October.

Houtman, D., Achterberg, P. and Derks, A. (2008) *Farewell to the Leftist working class*, Piscataway, NJ and London: Transaction Publishers.

James, H. (2016) 'Déclassé: Nothing new under the sun', *The American Interest (The Roots of Rage)*, November/December, pp 17-24.

Krouwel, A. and Pereira, N.R. (2015) 'Gesmolten kern', *S&D*, 2015/2, pp 5-13.

Lasch, C. (1995) *The revolt of the elites and the betrayal of democracy*, New York: W.W. Norton.

Lazar, M. (2015) '"Une crise qui n'en finit pas"', Situations du socialisme Européen', *La Revue Socialiste*, November, vol 60, pp 7-19.

Lipset, S. (1963) *Political man: The social bases of politics*. New York: Doubleday.

Lowen, M. (2013) 'How Greece's once-mighty Pasok party fell from grace', *BBC News*, 5 April.

Mair, P. (2013) *Ruling the void. The hollowing of Western democracy*, London: Verso.

Marcal, K. (2015) 'Löfven gets down to governing', *State of the left/ Policy Network*, 21 March.

Marquand, D. (2015) 'Can social democracy rise to the challenge of the far right across Europe?', *New Statesman*, 8 December.

Mouffe, C. (2005) *On the political*, London and New York: Routledge.

Mudde, C. (2007) *Populist radical right parties in Europe*, Cambridge: Cambridge University Press

Mudde, C. (2015) 'Populism in Europe: A primer', *Open Democracy*, 12 May.

Müller, J.W. (2016) *What is populism?*, Philadelphia, PA: University of Pennsylvania Press.

Piketty, T. (2014) *Capital in the twenty-first century*. Cambridge, MA: Belknap Press of Harvard University Press.

Polanyi, K. (1944 [1957]) *The great transformation: The political and economic origins of our times*, Boston, MD: Beacon Press.

Reich, R. (2016) 'Democrats once represented the working class. Not any more', *The Guardian*, 10 November.

Rodrik, D. (2010) *The globalization paradox: Why global markets, states, and democracy can't coexist*, Oxford: Oxford University Press.

Rooduijn, M. (2013) *A populist Zeitgeist? The impact of populism on parties, media and the public in Western Europe*, Amsterdam, https:// pure.uva.nl/ws/files/1808798/119430_thesis.pdf

Streeck, W. and Roos, J. (2015) 'Politics in the interregnum: a Q&A with Wolfgang Streeck', *Roar Magazine*, 23 December, www.roarmag. org/essays/wolfgang-streeck-capitalism-democracy-interview

Wolinetz, S.B. (2016) 'Sociaaldemocratie in tijden van globalisering', in F. Becker and G. Voerman (eds) *Zeventig jaar Partij van de Arbeid*, pp 36-48.

Zakaria, F. (2016) 'Populism on the march. Why the West is in trouble', *Foreign Affairs*, November/December.

THIRTEEN

The dilemmas of social democracy

Paul Kennedy and Rob Manwaring

Introduction

Any serious political movement faces a range of strategic, tactical and ideational dilemmas. These pressures range from electoral concerns to wider issues of existential identity. In these respects, social democracy is no different. Indeed, there is a strong strain throughout the social democracy literature that highlights the range of dilemmas facing the movement. These include Przeworski and Sprague's (1986) seminal work on the dilemma of electoral support – what happens to social democratic parties as they build alliances between the working and middle classes. In the wider sweep of the history of socialism, there was a long-standing dilemma about how to reconcile (or not) with Marxism (for example, Bernstein's revisionism), and how to respond to the social changes and emergence of identity politics in the 1960s (Sassoon, 2013). Perhaps the most recent set of dilemmas was posed by Giddens (1998) in his synthesis of the 'Third Way' (for a critique, see Przeworski, 2001).

In this concluding chapter, we summarise some of the key issues that arise from the case chapters. Rather than offer a static comparison of the individual cases, we reframe the wider issues through a series of ongoing dilemmas for the centre-left, which straddle the ideational, institutional and individual framework set out in this book. Here, we suggest that a renewal of the centre-left might well rely on a more sustained effort to address the following issues:

- re-balancing principles and pragmatism
- responding to the changing electoral sociology
- meeting the populist challenge

- responding to structural changes in the party system, and new forms of participation
- redesigning its political economy.

We don't claim that this is an exhaustive or definitive list of dilemmas, but, on our reading, they remain some of the most pressing for the family of social democratic and labour parties.

Principles vs pragmatism

As we have seen in the preceding pages, no political family suffered more from the global financial crisis (GFC) than social democracy. The economic downturn exacerbated the tension between principles and pragmatism that affects all political parties, but which is of particular resonance for those on the centre-left. Pragmatism, as encapsulated by Tony Blair's line, 'what matters is what works', retained its credibility in the context of the long economic boom that stretched from the mid-1990s to the collapse of Lehman Brothers in 2008. Thereafter, this accommodation with neoliberalism became something of a liability. In an increasingly hostile environment, the principles that lie at the heart of social democratic politics (particularly its commitment to equality, and offer of a robust countervailing force to the capitalist system) became a further encumbrance as electorates appeared to find greater security in the rival attractions of conservative competitors.

Following the GFC, UK Labour lost office in May 2010, followed, 18 months later, by the PSOE in Spain. It was incumbency rather than the social democratic label that proved lethal in the half-decade following the start of the downturn, as the centre-right Nicolas Sarkozy found to his cost when he was defeated at the French presidential elections by François Hollande in May 2012. As Sophie Di Francesco-Mayot outlines in her chapter on France (Chapter 10), Hollande was unable to build a credible social democratic project that addressed rising unemployment, growing inequality and challenged the all-pervasive politics of austerity. Similarly, the efforts of Gordon Brown's successor as Labour Party leader, Ed Miliband, to renew social democracy came to naught (Goes, 2016). The contest to replace Miliband in 2015 indicated the extent to which the 'pragmatic' quasi-Blairite approach to leadership – as personified by former Labour ministers Andy Burnham and Yvette Cooper, and Liz Kendall – had become redundant as Jeremy Corbyn swept home with just under 60 per cent of the vote in September 2015, a clear mandate that a buoyant membership was prepared to increase further nine months later. Despite being 20 per cent behind in the polls when Theresa May called a snap general election, Labour produced one of the greatest upsets of recent political history when the UK went to the polls on 8 May 2017. With a 40 per cent share of the vote, Corbyn led Labour to within 2.4 per cent of the Conservatives as the government lost its overall majority. Although his party had lost its third consecutive general election, Corbyn's leadership appeared unassailable; in contrast, the Prime Minister, Theresa May, was a much-diminished figure, the very antithesis of the 'strong and stable' leader that had played such a key role in her party's campaign. The Labour Party slogan, 'For the many, not the few', struck more of a chord, particularly with younger voters.

It is difficult to be sanguine elsewhere: the French Socialists failed to make it into the final round of the presidential election in the Spring of 2017, although the former Finance Minister in Hollande's Socialist government, Emmanuel Macron, was able to defeat Marine Le Pen with relative ease; the Spanish PSOE was once again under the leadership of Pedro Sánchez after a bitter contest. Whether, having led the party to two consecutive defeats, he is the person best-placed to guide the PSOE to victory. remains to be seen. In Germany, there appeared to be little likelihood of Martin Schulz dislodging Angela Merkel from the Chancellorship at the general election scheduled for September 2017. The results for Dutch PvDA were calamitous at the 2017 elections. The formation of a minority government by Portugal's Socialist Party under António Costa following the general election held in October 2015 provided a rare success at a time when the very survival of social democracy in that country appeared to be in question.

Contemporary social democratic politics continues to be open to the charge – from both the populist right and left – that its enthusiastic implementation of neoliberal economic policies undermines its credibility. Whatever the claims of 'Third Way' proponents such as Anthony Giddens, the fact remained that social democracy had effectively adopted neoliberalism as its own, albeit with a limited amount of redistribution. For, as Giddens argued, 'it is not possible to run a successful market economy without the confidence and commitment of the major wealth-producers' (Giddens, 2002, p 24). For a brief moment, the Third Way project seemed to have the right balance of a recalibrated social democracy, based on a new set of principles, while accommodating a more 'pragmatic' embrace of the prevailing neoliberal orthodoxy. The Third Way was touted as being highly pragmatic. Yet, this 'pragmatism' has proved to be something of a fallacy; the Third Way has been exposed as an inherently *ideological* approach, and ultimately, one that ceded far too much ground to capitalist economics. If neoliberal social democratic governments could not deliver equality, inclusion, or robust protection from markets, why, then, have social democratic governments at all?

The problem for British Labour – and for its sister-parties as the second decade of the 21st century began to draw to a close – was that social democracy had not only lost the confidence of major wealth producers, but also that of its erstwhile supporters, who either sought reassurance in uncertain times from centre-right parties who had generally been more adept at avoiding blame for the GFC, or populist parties of both right and left. Electorates appeared to have a short memory with respect to the many undoubted achievements of social democracy. For example, it would be a caricature to suggest that the PSOE had been the chief perpetrator of the neoliberal shift in Spain, particularly given the party's many progressive achievements in office, most notably its development of the Spanish welfare state and later extension of civil and gender rights. No other Spanish political party has been able to match the 11 million-plus votes obtained by the PSOE at the 2004 and 2008 general elections, indicating that the electorate viewed the party as being something other than the architect of the country's neoliberal shift. Yet Íñigo Errejón, Podemos's Political Secretary, has claimed that 'it was the Socialist Party, the PSOE, who to a large extent oversaw the neoliberal shift' (Errejón and Mouffe, 2016, p 28). Moreover, Podemos's leader, Pablo Iglesias, chose to join the centre-right Popular Party in the voting lobbies to maintain Mariano Rajoy in office and prevent the formation of a PSOE-led government in March 2016. Populism – whether of the left or right – appeared to enjoy the benefit of the doubt from a significant proportion of Europe's electorates, an indulgence increasingly denied to social democratic parties that failed to build the principles of equality, solidarity, inclusions and related centre-left values into a politically convincing programme.

Changing electoral sociology

Demography is ever changing, and this has been an ongoing concern for socialists and social democrats, which can be tracked back to the critical juncture when socialists advocated the parliamentary route to socialism. Notably, Kautsky suggested that the working class provided the centre-left with an in-built numerical advantage for social democratic parties. This rested on a rather instrumental view of the working-class vote. Changing demography and social structures in most advanced industrial societies pose a series of dilemmas for centre-left parties in how to shore up their 'core vote' but also to find other alliances. Again, using the UK as an emblematic example, we can see the electoral dilemmas facing centre-left parties. The wider patterns and trends are relatively clear – major parties face declining party membership, declining union density and declining party identification.[1]

Kautskian social democracy rested on a majoritarian working-class support, yet the working-class vote has never been homogenous or consistent. In the UK in the 1980s and 1990s, a significant portion of the working class was quite content to vote for the Conservative Party. More recently, debates have centred on the decline of influence of the 'class' voter (see, for example, Franklin, 1982; Andersen and Heath, 1992). By this, a range of writers have noted how class is a much weaker predictor of voting intentions than it used to be. Some see this as a decline, others as a greater flux in class identity, but especially in the UK, there seems to be some consensus on the dominance of 'valence' politics (Green, 2007). In essence, the argument runs that as the major parties have converged in terms of policy, voters have increasingly based their choices on issues such as leadership and economic competence.

The seeming decline of class identity has been borne out by various studies, and Figure 13.1 shows this through the voting behaviour of employees and employers.[2] In sum, the Conservative Party historically drew its support from the middles classes (and employers) and Labour from the working classes (and employees). By 1997, and the advent of Tony Blair, there was an acceleration of class de-alignment and voting behaviour. For British Labour, this cross-class coalition proved an electorally winning formula in the 1990s, although it has bequeathed a complex electoral sociology in the UK.

Figure 13.1: Voting Conservative/Labour by employer/employees (1964-2015)

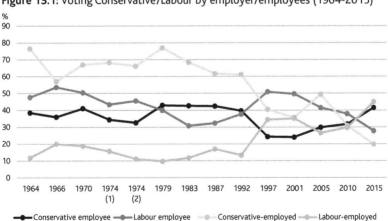

Source: BES

What is clear is that by the 2015 UK general election, the demography and sociology of the electorate was more fluid, fragmented and complex. According to Ipsos MORI survey data, Labour does still draw more heavily from the 'DE' lowest grade occupation group (41% compared to 27% for the Conservatives), while the Conservatives draw from the 'AB' highest occupation group (45% compared to 26% for Labour; see Table 13.1). Among 'C1s' and 'C2s' it is a more complex story, and neither of the major parties has a lead over the other in terms of support from skilled manual workers.[3] Class, then, might be a declining predictor of voting behaviour, but it is still a key part of understanding the fracturing of the vote in many countries.

Evans and Tilley (2011, 2012) offer a key intervention in the debate about the impact of class in the changing electoral sociology. Understanding the impact of class often leads to a focus on either 'demand' or 'supply' approaches. Briefly, the demand approach suggests that class identity is weakening due to changes in wider society. In contrast, Evans and Tilley argue that the class vote has not disappeared; rather, it has been shaped by 'supply'-side factors – particularly the role of political parties in shaping electoral choices. In their reading, it was New Labour's shift to the centre that accelerated ideological convergence, and ultimately, a desertion of many working-class supporters. Part of the story of the 2015 election defeat was the inability of the party under Ed Miliband to win back these voters. In addition, these changes are being shaped by wider changes in the party system, as explored below.

What is also proving particularly troubling for the UK Labour Party is the growing fragmentation of the electorate. The 2015 general

Table 13.1: Class voting at the 2015 UK general election

Occupation group	Conservative	Labour	Liberal Democrats	UKIP	Green	Other	Conservative lead over Labour	Turnout (%)	Conservative–Labour swing (2010–15)
AB	45	26	12	8	4	5	19	75	−3
C1	41	29	9	11	4	7	12	69	−0.5
C2	32	32	6	19	4	7	0	62	4
DE	27	41	5	17	3	7	−14	57	2.5

Source: Ipsos MORI (2015)

election produced a highly regionalised result, with Scotland spurning Labour; inner London remained heavily committed to the party; and there was a backlash in the regions. Regional identity seems to have been unleashed across the UK, arguably – and ironically – fuelled by New Labour's devolution agenda. Moreover, it was the desertion of older voters that hollowed out Labour's vote (Beckett, 2015). Labour is not the only centre-left political party to face these sociological changes, but its problems are particularly acute. In a timely report by the Fabian Society, the verdict was frank – Labour was 'stuck' – too weak to win, and too strong to die (Harrop, 2017). Despite the surge in party membership under Jeremy Corbyn, it remains far from clear how it can deal with the fracturing of the British electorate, although the June 2017 general election indicated that the Labour Party was more resilient than many had predicted.

The populist challenge

The late Peter Mair famously began his final work, *Ruling the void: The hollowing of Western democracy*, with the stark observation: 'The age of party democracy has passed. Although the parties themselves remain, they have become so disconnected from the wider society, and pursue a form of competition that is so lacking in meaning that they no longer seem capable of sustaining democracy in its present form' (Mair, 2013, p 1). There has been no better insight into the conditions that have given rise to an emboldened populism since the start of the GFC. The populist challenge is both a symptom and driver of the structural and ideational problems afflicting the centre-left. With the decline in respect for the political elites, opportunities have arisen for populist parties of both right and left. Both represent a challenge for social democracy, seemingly more attuned to the hopes and fears of a significant proportion of the electorate. It might be argued that the election of Jeremy Corbyn as Labour Party leader fits this 'populist' paradigm, as he attracted the support of Labour sympathisers who were no longer willing to give their backing to their party's elite. In Mair's terms, Corbyn won the party leadership because the party elite, as represented by those who unsuccessfully stood against him in the leadership election, had become disconnected from the party's support base, becoming discredited in the process. The results of the 2017 general election have very uncertain implications for Corbyn-led Labour. Positively, Labour's performance exceeded expectations, and some on the left are hopeful that Corbyn Labour can herald a new form of anti-neoliberal and anti-austerity politics. Yet, the extent to which Labour can bridge what Manwaring and Beech in this volume call the 'values gap' remains to be seen. British politics, especially in the context of Brexit, is more fragmented than ever, and it is far from clear that Corbyn is shaping a new coherent brand of social democracy that addresses such structural changes.

At a time when party elites are viewed as being unresponsive to voters' concerns, the issue of immigration has become even more prominent and problematic. Social democratic parties have lost support to centre-left and right-populist parties due to the perception that they are less likely to take practical steps to control immigration. A striking case is the very public U-turn taken by the Rudd Labor government in Australia to unwind, and then re-wind a new 'Pacific solution' to tackle asylum-seekers arriving by boat. In Sweden, the SAP has struggled to deal with the notable rise of the Swedish Democrats, fuelled by concerns over immigration. In Germany, the populist, Eurosceptic and anti-Islam Alternative for Germany (AfD) only just fell short of securing the minimum 5 per cent threshold at the 2013 federal election, a considerable result given that it was only formed that year. The centre-left's approach to immigration, which at best might be described as ambivalent or confused, signifies the lack of a clear principled approach to dealing with the free(r) movement of labour and people. At times, the centre-left is asked to choose between a false binary – defending the jobs and economic conditions of its 'traditional' white, working-class support, and balancing the claims of new migrants and other communities. In effect, it becomes electorally constrained by the populists, who argue that the centre-left has abandoned the former in favour of the latter. Yet both sets of groups require representation and protection from the contradictions and instabilities of global capital.

In the UK, faced with the prospect of a haemorrhaging of support in its northern heartlands, the Labour Party had good reason to be concerned about UKIP's strategy of targeting traditional Labour seats in the wake of the Brexit vote, although UKIP's failure to obtain a single seat at the 2017 general election indicated the party faced its own set of challenges. Put bluntly, it has become harder for those on the left to compete with populist politicians who have fewer reservations about resorting to 'dog whistle' appeals to voters' concerns. Nevertheless it is incumbent on social democrats to have the confidence to go beyond the populist tactic of feeding voters' sense of resentment; ultimately, populist support can only be contained by offering a credible means of genuinely improving lives. The American journalist H.L. Mencken once quipped that for every complex problem there was an answer that was clear, simple and wrong. The task of social democracy is not to seek to copy populist proposals, but rather, to highlight why the clear, simple, and superficially attractive solutions proposed by populist competitors *are* wrong. Moreover, although the left-populist Podemos has undoubtedly posed a significant challenge to the PSOE in Spain, Pablo Iglesias's party bears out Jan-Werner Müller's contention that 'populist parties are almost always internally monolithic, with the rank-and-file clearly subordinated to a single leader (or, less often, a group of leaders).… [P]opulist parties are particularly prone to internal authoritarianism' (Müller, 2016, p 36).

Podemos illustrated the consequences of this concentration of power around the leader when Iglesias was challenged by his lieutenant, Íñigo Errejón, at the party's second Citizens' Assembly in February 2017. Significantly, Errejón suffered a humiliating defeat. In short, populist parties have their own weaknesses, and their depiction of any opponent as being simply part of a corrupt, exhausted elite or *casta* deserves to be challenged by their competitors on the left, even though Podemos persists in refusing to define itself as a party of the left.[4] As Müller argues, 'Populists do not just criticise elites; they also claim that they and only they represent the true people' (Müller, 2016, p 40).[5] The rise of populism 'should force defenders of liberal democracy to think harder about what current failures of representation might be' (Müller, 2016, p 103). This advice should be particularly relevant to social democratic parties if they have any hope of regaining their former prominence.

Changing party systems and new forms of participation

Politics, clearly, no longer operates in the same structural and institutional context that it used to. Over the past few decades, many advanced industrial societies have experienced changes to their party systems. To take three examples, the UK, Australia and France have all undergone such transformations. In these cases, there were two broad political groupings of left and right. Today, we see a much more complex picture. The advent of UKIP is just one outlier of a wider trend in British politics, a push to a multi-party polity, trapped in a majoritarian, two-party electoral system. As outlined earlier, the old political geography is changing. The Labour Party faces significant competition from the Greens, UKIP, the Liberal Democrats and the Scottish National Party (SNP).

In Australia, a striking phenomenon is the growth of minor parties and independents, in what was traditionally a party system broadly categorised by the Labor/anti-Labor axis. A core problem for Australian Labor is the erosion of its primary vote, especially in the Lower House, where it achieved just 34.9 per cent in 2016 – its second lowest total since 1949. At the 2016 election, just over 23 per cent of voters preferenced a minor party first, a trend that has grown since the 1950s where this figure was about 5 per cent. This growing complexity poses fresh strategic and tactical dilemmas for the traditional major parties – especially the centre-left. In France, the situation is equally complex. Since 2002, the Front National has established itself as a key player in the French party system. At the 2017 Presidential election, it was striking that neither of the traditional major parties made it through the second round – a first in French politics. In sum, the centre-left faces critical decisions, especially in relation to Green and other left parties in its current existential crisis.

The situation is complicated in that the core vote of the centre-left is seemingly going through a period of decline (see Table 13.2). In the countries surveyed over the past two decades, the primary vote for the centre-left has declined in 8 of the 11 countries listed. The centre-left has sometimes governed in coalition, but this is a new reality in many places.

This links to a wider dilemma for the centre-left that is exogenous to the changes with the party system, namely, the changing patterns of political participation. In recent decades, there are some wider trends, including declining turnout in many countries, and seeming evidence of a greater dislike of politicians (Stoker, 2006; Hay, 2007; Mair, 2013). Some of these trends are documented elsewhere, but it is notable that participation remains highly stratified, especially on class lines. More critically, citizens, when they do participate, are doing so in new and different ways. In a well-cited paper, Bennett and Segerberg (2012) have catalogued what they term 'connective action'. Whereas citizens traditionally engaged either individually (signing a petition), or collectively (strikes, group/union membership), the advent of 'connective' action appears to be changing democratic practice. This technological change seems to dovetail with what Giddens called the 'new individualisation'. Connectivity refers to the new, looser, non-geographically based forms of online action, often morphing with and transforming more 'traditional' forms of political action.

The challenge for the centre-left, then, is to respond and address the changing face of political participation. This, to some extent, requires a re-thinking of what constitutes a political party and how it engages and performs its representative function. In places like the UK, there have been attempts to reconfigure the meaning of membership, and a wider push for the party to become more embedded in community activity – ironically revisiting the pre-internet ideals of Alinsky (1972).

Table 13.2: Centre-left parties' share of the vote (1997–2016)

Country	1997	1998	1999	2000	2001	2002	2003	2004	2005	2006	2007	2008	2009	2010	2011	2012	2013	2014	2015	2016
Australia		40.1			37.84			37.63			43.38			37.99			33.38			34.7
UK	43.2				40.7				35.2					29					30.4	
New Zealand			38.74			41.26			41.1			34			27			25		
France (legislative elections)	23.49					24.11					24.73					29.35				
France (presidential – first round)						16.18					25.87					28.63				
Germany (federal election)		40.9				38.5			34.2				34.2				23			
Sweden		36.4				39.85			35					30.7				31		
Spain				34.2				42.6				43.9			28.8			22	22.6	
Canada (NDP)	11.05			8.51				15.68		17.48		18.18			30.63				19.71	
Netherlands		29				15.1	27.2			20.2				19.6		24.8				
Norway	35				24.3				32.7				35.4				30.8			
Greece[a]				43.79				40.5			38.1		43.9			12.3			6.3	
Ireland	10.4					10.8					10.1				19.4					12.8
Austria (legislative elections)			33.15			36.51				35.34		29.26					26.82			

Note: [a] Greece held two elections in both 2012 and 2015. Results are shown for September 2012 and June 2015.
Source: Election Commissions in each country

The central dilemma for the centre-left is both to make sense of these changes, and reshape its transformative and egalitarian agenda in new, more complex settings. Yet, the parties are caught in a bind of two pathologies – the old and the new. Despite some efforts to reinvent or reorient the parties (for example, Ségolène Royal's push for a participatory agenda as part of her ill-fated presidential bid in 2007, or the Milibands' fascination with Blue Labour), the parties remain challenged by some very old problems, such as, at times, the debilitating factional powers that underpin their internal party structures. The professionalised, poll-driven, and often highly centralised parties have also hollowed out working-class participation (Chakelian, 2016). A resurgent centre-left must then navigate this fluid picture with a more pluralistic party system, and find ways to meet the new (and old) forms of engagement. Again, to return to the UK, it is not clear that the Corbyn-supporting Momentum group is either capable of, or seeking to, re-imagine the institutional and representative structures of the party. It remains unclear whether any of the parties covered in this volume have met this challenge head on.

Political economy

The focus of policy-makers in the immediate aftermath of the GFC was to prevent an already cataclysmic crisis turning into a full-blown depression. Western governments, following the lead provided by Gordon Brown in the UK, adopted stimulus fiscal policies that enabled the banking system to survive. There would consequently be no European equivalent of Lehman Brothers, although Brown received little thanks for his efforts. Similarly, in Australia, the Rudd Labor government with Treasurer Wayne Swan's guidance, while achieving some global recognition for shielding Australia from the worst of the GFC, obtained little gratitude from the Australian public for the fiscal stimulus and related measures undertaken.

In the UK, early-2010 fiscal policy was already tightening before austerity was intensified from May that year, following the first Greek bailout. Austerity has been the defining feature of global economic policy ever since. The resilience of the neoliberal economic paradigm in the face of its evident failures has been subject to some examination.[6] Nevertheless, such political upheavals as Brexit in the UK and, in particular, Donald Trump's victory at the 2016 US presidential election indicate the degree of powerlessness and anger felt by many in the face of neoliberalism and globalisation. As Wolfgang Streeck has argued (2014, p 159):

In the early twenty-first century, capital is confident of being able to organise itself as it pleases in a deregulated finance industry. The only thing it expects of politics is its capitulation to the market by eliminating social democracy as an economic force.

It would be foolhardy to view the election of a billionaire to the office of President of the United States and the implementation of the UK's withdrawal from the EU by the Conservative government as constituting a break with the traditional economic policy order. However, these developments do appear to reinforce Streeck's view that the strength of the apparently monolithic neoliberal/globalised hegemony has been over-stated.[7]

Conclusion

The focus on institutions, individuals and ideas adopted by contributors to this volume has sought to identify the factors behind the centre-left's relative failure over the last decade. Although individual authors have placed greater or lesser emphasis on each of the three elements as they illustrate their national case studies, their conclusion is ultimately a shared one: the left has lost the habit of winning. If there is to be a reversal of this volume's title, *Why the left loses*, social democracy must learn from its political opponents. Like it or not, its opponents have been more adroit in at least *appearing* to connect at the basic level with a sizeable proportion of the electorate. Certainly, Brexit and the US election appear to indicate that that is indeed the case. If the extraordinary year 2016 taught us anything, it is that political success can more easily be achieved by mobilising support on the basis of an identification of and opposition to an 'other' that poses a threat to general wellbeing. The reality or otherwise of such an enemy is not the key issue: the approach is a means by which to attract votes. Podemos's concept of a *casta*, or corrupt establishment, which has served that party well, provides a prominent example. The gross inequalities that increasingly scar contemporary society have been exploited by populists of both left and right. Social democrats must aggressively lay claim to what is their own natural political terrain; their economic programmes need to address the genuine concerns of the electorate; and they have to exploit the threat that is currently being posed to such cherished social democratic symbols as state-provided healthcare and social provision. If they fail to do this, the left will not only go on losing; it will deserve to do so.

Notes

1 Obviously, these trends are not uniform, and intriguingly, party membership has increased – especially under Jeremy Corbyn. Other parties across advanced industrial societies have also seen a surge in membership.

2 There is a deep and contested literature on the decline of class voting which, for the sake of brevity, this chapter can only allude to. The emergence of the 'valence' thesis was a challenge to Anthony Down's economic approach and a perceived shift to the 'catch-all' party, with ideological convergence between the two main party groupings.

3 The Office for National Statistics devised a standard coding scheme for occupational status. AB includes higher and intermediate managerial, administrative and professional occupations. C1 includes supervisory, clerical and junior managerial, administrative and professional roles, while C2 includes skilled manual occupations. DE encompasses semi-skilled, unskilled manual occupations, along with the unemployed and lowest grade roles.

4 As Errejón has commented, 'to aspire to subvert or cut across the metaphors of right and left is not a renunciation of ideologies…. There is nothing essential, nothing necessary, in the terms right and left as metaphors around which to structure the political arena' (Errejón and Mouffe, 2016, pp 122-3).

5 Müller advises left-populist parties to 'talk about building new majorities instead of gesturing at the "construction of a people"' (Müller, 2016, pp 98-9).

6 A prominent example being Colin Crouch's *The strange non-death of neoliberalism* (2011).

7 Although, to be fair to Streeck, the title of his most recent book, *How will capitalism end?* (2016), hardly indicates that he has great faith in the resilience of the current economic system.

References

Alinsky, S. (1972) *Rules for radicals: A primer for realistic radicals*, New York: Vintage.

Andersen, R and Heath, A. (2002) 'Class matters: The persisting effects of social class on individual voting in Britain 1964-1997', *European Sociological Review*, vol 18, no 2, pp 125-38.

Beckett, M. (2016) *Learning the lessons from defeat taskforce*, London: The Labour Party.

Bennett, W.L. and Segerberg, A. (2012) 'The logic of connective action: Digital media and the personalization of contentious politics', *Information, Communication & Society*, vol 15, no 5, pp 739-68.

Chakelian, A. (2016) 'How middle class are Labour's new members?', *New Statesman,* 25 January, www.newstatesman.com/politics/staggers/2016/01/how-middle-class-are-labour-s-new-members

Crouch, C. (2011) *The strange non-death of neoliberalism*, Cambridge: Polity Press.

Errejón, I. and Mouffe, C. (2016) *Podemos: In the name of the people*, London: Lawrence & Wishart.

Evans, G. and Tilley, J. (2011) 'How parties shape class politics: Explaining the decline of the class basis of party support', *British Journal of Political Science*, vol 42, no 1, pp 137-61.

Evans, G. and Tilley, J. (2012) 'The depoliticization of inequality and redistribution: Explaining the decline of class voting', *The Journal of Politics*, vol 74, no 4, pp 963-76.

Franklin, M. (1982) 'Demographic and political components in the decline of British class voting 1964-1979', *Electoral Studies*, vol 1, pp 195-220.

Giddens, A. (1998) *The Third Way: The renewal of social democracy*, Cambridge: Polity Press.

Giddens, A. (2002) *What now for New Labour?*, Cambridge: Polity Press.

Goes, E. (2016) *The Labour Party under Ed Miliband. Trying but failing to renew social democracy*, Manchester: Manchester University Press.

Green, J. (2007) 'When voters and parties agree: Valence issues and party competition'. *Political Studies*, vol 55, pp 629-55.

Harrop, A. (2017) 'Stuck: How Labour is too weak to win and too strong to die', 3 January, London: Fabian Society, www.fabians.org. uk/wp-content/uploads/2016/12/Stuck-Fabian-Society-analysis-paper.pdf

Hay, C. (2007) *Why we hate politics*, Cambridge: Polity Press.

Ipsos MORI (2015) *How Britain voted in 2015: The 2015 election – Who voted for whom?*, London: Ipsos MORI, www.ipsos-mori.com/ researchpublications/researcharchive/3575/How-Britain-voted-in-2015.aspx?view=print

Mair, P. (2013) *Ruling the void: The hollowing of Western democracy*, London: Verso.

Müller, J.-W. (2016) *What is populism?*, Philadelphia, PA: University of Pennsylvania Press.

Przeworski, A. (2001) 'How many ways can be Third?', in A. Glyn (ed) *Social democracy in neoliberal times: The Left and economic policy since 1980*, Oxford: Oxford University Press, pp 312–33.

Przeworski, A. and Sprague, J. (1986) *Paper stones: A history of electoral socialism*, Chicago, IL: University of Chicago Press.

Sassoon, D. (2013) *One hundred years of socialism: The West European Left in the twenty-first century* (2nd edn), London: I.B. Taurus.

Stoker, G. (2006) *Why politics matters: Making democracy work*, Basingstoke: Palgrave Macmillan.

Streeck, W. (2014) *Buying time*, London: Verso.

Streeck, W. (2016) *How will capitalism end?*, London: Verso.

Index

Entries for notes are indicated by n

CPSIA information can be obtained
at www.ICGtesting.com
Printed in the USA
BVHW04s2355280618
520388BV00007B/46/P